Donald Capps, PhD

Young Clergy
A Biographical-Developmental Study

Pre-publication
REVIEWS,
COMMENTARIES,
EVALUATIONS . . .

"Writing in the spirit of Eriksonian psychobiography, Capps forges new insights by applying Levinson's stage theory to the lives of five religious figures. His conceptualization of five models of professional formation represents a significant contribution to contemporary understandings of religious growth. This is an important book."

C. Kevin Gillespie, SJ, PhD
Associate Professor
of Pastoral Counseling,
Loyola College in Maryland

"As usual, Donald Capps has managed to take science and its data and creatively and meaningfully relate them to dynamically complex human phenomena, at the same time offering a fascinating and rewarding read. In this instance, he finds in Daniel J. Levinson's developmental theory *(The Seasons of a Man's Life)* the psychosocial materials to help us understand the many nuances in the development of the ministerial career. Presenting five models of professional formation, built around five of America's famous preachers, he illustrates Levinson's life structure of an alternating pattern of stability and transition by drawing upon specific periods in the clergymen's lives. This is not only a good read for those who yearn for intelligent application of the human sciences to religious topics, it also offers a helpful hermeneutic for those who wish to reflect on their choice of a religious vocation, those who may be contemplating such a ministerial career in the twenty-first century, and those who simply enjoy reading the biographies of exciting and interesting persons."

Orlo C. Strunk Jr., PhD
Professor Emeritus of the Psychology
of Religion and Pastoral Psychology,
Boston University; Editor,
*The Journal of Pastoral Care
and Counseling*

More pre-publication
REVIEWS, COMMENTARIES, EVALUATIONS . . .

"**D**onald Capps makes a compelling argument for using Daniel Levinson's developmental theory as a conceptual model for interpreting the lives of contemporary ministers through a biographical study of five prominent historical figures in ministry. It is his hope that in studying the lives of ministers from history, the lives of contemporary ministers will be enhanced. I suggest he has more than succeeded in achieving this goal as I was challenged to reflect on the stages of development in my own career in ministry as well as the trajectories of the seminary students I teach. In Chapter 1, Capps sets forth his proposal for five models of professional formation based on the five sequences identified by Levinson in the 'settling-down' period of a man's life.

Capps argues in an engaging manner that the time which is the most determinative in a minister's life and profession is the middle through late thirties. Why? Precisely because this is the time for 'settling down,' when a solid foundation or life structure is formed for the next twenty-five years in ministry. He notes that this work does not address the developmental issues of second-career men nor does it speak directly to the developmental issues of women but it may be interesting for women to read about their male colleagues in ministry. As a woman in ministry and seminary professor myself, I found his argument convincing and the reading captivating. Indeed, the third conceptual model may explain *why* men and women seek a second or even third career. In Chapter 7, Capps revisits the lives of all five ministers and identifies characteristics that are typical of each conceptual model by highlighting details of their ministries. A young minister today, male or female, would do well to take note of these characteristics, as much heartache resulting from early mistakes could be avoided. How does this theory propose universality? Capps answers the question in his epilogue, which is much more than an afterthought. Here he illustrates the importance of the 'vacillating rhythm between the life and death instincts' for men and women by relating it to the pattern of stability and transition identified by Levinson."

Rev. Carol L. Schnabl Schweitzer, PhD
Assistant Professor
of Pastoral Care, Union-PSCE,
Richmond, Virginia

"**M**inisters whose career paths, willingly or unwillingly, get redirected probably feel, as I have often felt, that any professional redirection is a kind of failure—the fate of ministerial oddballs, eccentrics, and misfits. This book is a strong word of encouragement for them.

Professional formation is an often neglected task, and no clear consensus currently exists. This book provides the cornerstone for a consensus on what it takes to develop competent ministers. In the meantime, it can be a source of encouragement and wisdom to those struggling with their ministerial roles, especially those in the midst of periods of disorganization."

Raymond J. Lawrence, DMin
Director of Pastoral Care,
New York Presbyterian Hospital;
General Secretary, College
of Pastoral Supervision
and Psychotherapy

"This is a fascinating book. In analyzing five biographies of well-known clergymen, Capps convincingly illustrates his thesis that the late thirties are the most decisive phase in any clergyman's professional career. It is a season in life in which one should become one's own man. Life structure finds its foundation and culmination at the brink of middle adulthood when the developmental tasks of finding one's medium (professional capabilities), mission (life's dream), marriage (and friendships), and the support of a mentor are in some way fulfilled. The way in which Donald Capps paints the portraits of Jonathan Edwards, John Wesley, Orestes Brownson, John Henry Newman, and Phillips Brooks brings them to life as if they were our brothers or friends. We experience their conflicts and dreams, their strengths and weaknesses, as if we ourselves were involved in those struggles for change and stability while doubting any advancement because of sure disappointments and certain frustration. This is an excellent book for any member of the clergy, and of many other professions, to reflect upon the strengths and structure of their own personal development and professional formation. In doing so, they may realize that apparently trivial events at the time of their occurrence can have long-lasting effects on their clerical career and social standing."

Reinard Nauta, PhD
Professor of Pastoral Psychology
and Psychology of Religion,
Tilburg University,
The Netherlands

"This unique and fascinating book draws on Daniel J. Levinson's developmental model of adulthood to examine and predict the trajectory of one's ministerial vocation. Peering through Levinsonian lenses and viewing biographies of five ministers who lived in the eighteenth and nineteenth centuries—Phillips Brooks, Jonathan Edwards, John Henry Newman, John Wesley, and Orestes Brownson—Capps argues persuasively that what happens in one's ministry between ages thirty and forty powerfully affects how one's subsequent experience will unfold. Though most think of this period as being marked by less status and influence and fewer resources when compared with later years, it actually has the greatest effect on whether one will experience longer-term success or failure with respect to goals, sense of achievement, and endurance. Paying particular attention to the concept of the 'life structure,' which necessarily includes an alternating pattern of stability and transition, Capps illustrates how what may seem precarious, painful, or meaningless in the young clergyperson's ministry may in fact be the impetus for thriving longer and stronger in the subsequent journey.

Yet another masterpiece by pastoral psychology's supreme artist, this is a splendid resource for young clergy and for all who want to help them flourish."

Allan Hugh Cole Jr., PhD
Assistant Professor of Pastoral Care,
Austin Presbyterian
Theological Seminary,
Austin, Texas

More pre-publication
REVIEWS, COMMENTARIES, EVALUATIONS . . .

"This study of the career development of young clergy is a good read that not only sheds light on the twists and turns of five fascinating lives but also provides a framework by which all clergy careers may be analyzed. Adapting Daniel Levinson's criteria for male adult development, Donald Capps has provided rich psychobiographical illustration of five models of professional formation. He finds the 'settling-down' years of ages thirty-three to forty within each of the models as crucial for the entire career of clergy.

This is an important book for all who work with or mentor young clergy; moreover it is an essential guide for clergy themselves making their way through the complexities of adult development and career. This study gave me insight into my career and I will use it with my trainees in clinical pastoral education."

Rev. John R. deVelder, DMin
Director, Pastoral Care Department,
Robert Wood Johnson
University Hospital,
New Brunswick, New Jersey

"Donald Capps succeeds in raising from the dead five well-known ministers of centuries past as he demonstrates the enduring relevance of their own early vocational perplexities for young ministers today. The developmental psychology of Daniel Levinson serves here to hone in specifically on the thirtysomething years of Phillips Brooks, Jonathan Edwards, John Henry Newman, John Wesley, and Orestes Brownson. With gentle elegance and characteristic psychological insight, Capps discusses the ways in which the decade of one's thirties becomes pivotal for shaping the whole trajectory of a life of ministry. This riveting page-turner is sure to enlighten and encourage a whole new generation of seminarians."

Robert C. Dykstra
Associate Professor
of Pastoral Theology,
Princeton Theological Seminary,
Princeton New Jersey

The Haworth Pastoral Press®
An Imprint of The Haworth Press, Inc.
New York • London • Oxford

Young Clergy
A Biographical-Developmental Study

THE HAWORTH PASTORAL PRESS®
Haworth Series in Chaplaincy
Andrew J. Weaver, MTh, PhD
Editor

Living Faithfully with Disappointment in the Church by J. LeBron McBride

Young Clergy: A Biographical-Developmental Study by Donald Capps

Grief, Loss, and Death: The Shadow Side of Ministry by Halbert Weidner

Prison Ministry: Hope Behind the Wall by Dennis W. Pierce

A Pastor's Guide to Interpersonal Communication: The Other Six Days by Blake J. Neff

Pastoral Care of Depression: Helping Clients Heal Their Relationship with God by Glendon Moriarty

Pastoral Care with Younger Adults in Long-Term Care by Reverend Jacqueline Sullivan

The Spirituality of Community Life: When We Come 'Round Right by Ronald P. McDonald

Pastoral Care from the Pulpit: Meditations of Hope and Encouragement by J. LeBron McBride

Young Clergy
A Biographical-Developmental Study

Donald Capps, PhD

The Haworth Pastoral Press®
An Imprint of The Haworth Press, Inc.
New York • London • Oxford

Published by

The Haworth Pastoral Press®, an imprint of The Haworth Press, Inc., 10 Alice Street, Binghamton, NY 13904-1580.

PUBLISHER'S NOTE
The development, preparation, and publication of this work has been undertaken with great care. However, the Publisher, employees, editors, and agents of The Haworth Press are not responsible for any errors contained herein or for consequences that may ensue from use of materials or information contained in this work. The Haworth Press is committed to the dissemination of ideas and information according to the highest standards of intellectual freedom and the free exchange of ideas. Statements made and opinions expressed in this publication do not necessarily reflect the views of the Publisher, Directors, management, or staff of The Haworth Press, Inc., or an endorsement by them.

Excerpts from *ORESTES BROWNSON* by Theodore Maynard, Macmillan © 1943, Macmillan. Reprinted by permission of The Gale Group.

"Bi-Focal" copyright 1954, 1998 by the Estate of William Stafford. Reprinted from *The Way It Is: New & Selected Poems* with the permission of Graywolf Press, Saint Paul, Minnesota.

Excerpts reprinted from THE SEASONS OF A MAN'S LIFE by Daniel Levinson, copyright © 1978 by Daniel J. Levinson. Used by permission of Alfred A. Knopf, a division of Random House, Inc. Non-exclusive UK English publication: Reprinted by permission of S11/sterling Lord Literistic, Inc. Copyright 1975 by Daniel Levinson.

Excerpts reprinted with the permission of Scribner, an imprint of Simon & Schuster Adult Publishing Group, from JONATHAN EDWARDS 1703-1758 by Ola Elisabeth Winslow. Copyright © 1940 by The Macmillan Company; copyright renewed © 1968 by Ola Elisabeth Winslow.

Excerpts reprinted with the permission of Scribner, an imprint of Simon & Schuster Adult Publishing Group, from FOCUS ON INFINITY: A LIFE OF PHILLIPS BROOKS by Raymond W. Albright. Copyright © 1961 by Raymond W. Albright; copyright renewed © 1989 by Caroline Ayer Albright.

Cover design by Jennifer M. Gaska.

Library of Congress Cataloging-in-Publication Data

Capps, Donald.
  Young clergy : a biographical-developmental study / Donald Capps.
    p. cm.
  Includes bibliographical references and index.
  ISBN-13: 978-0-7890-2669-9 (hc. : alk. paper)
  ISBN-10: 0-7890-2669-4 (hc. : alk. paper)
  ISBN-13: 978-0-7890-2670-5 (pbk. : alk. paper)
  ISBN-10: 0-7890-2670-8 (pbk. : alk. paper)
    1. Clergy—Psychology—Case studies. 2. Protestant churches—Clergy—Psychology—Case studies. 3. Brooks, Phillips, 1835-1893. 4. Edwards, Jonathan, 1703-1785. 5. Wesley, John, 1703-1791. 6. Catholic converts—Psychology—Case studies. I. Title.

BV660.3.C37 2005
253'.2—dc22

                                                                              2005003034

CONTENTS

114790

Acknowledgments

An individual can write a manuscript, but professionals are required to transform the manuscript into a book. I have been extremely fortunate to have been the beneficiary of the highly skilled professionals at The Haworth Press. Andrew Weaver, Bill Palmer, Amy Rentner, Tracy Sayles, Patricia Brown, Jillian Mason-Possemato, Dawn Krisko, and numerous others have been involved in the production of this book. I am grateful to all of them, and appreciate their teamwork. I especially thank the copy editor, Peg Marr, who edited the manuscript with consummate care. I also thank Joan Blyth, faculty secretary at Princeton Theological Seminary, who typed the original manuscript. As a faculty secretary, she has many demands on her time, yet she was able to type this manuscript in a surprisingly short time and with her customary attention to accuracy and detail. I appreciate, too, that several colleagues in the pastoral care field have taken the time to read the manuscript and write endorsements on its behalf. To one and all, my heartfelt thanks.

The author of a book who makes a case for the critical importance of the mid through late thirties age period in one's professional life cannot help but wonder if this case also applies to himself. Because I believe that it does, I would also like to express my appreciation to students and faculty colleagues at Phillips Graduate Seminary, where I taught in this period of my life, for their support, acceptance, and collegiality. My most loyal companions, however, were my wife, Karen, and son, John, who took to Enid, Oklahoma, like ducks to water. A more loving adaptability is difficult to imagine. As the psalmist says so beautifully: "The lines have fallen for me in pleasant places" (Ps. 16: 6, RSV).

ABOUT THE AUTHOR

Donald Capps, BD, STM, PhD, is the William Harte Felmeth Professor of Pastoral Psychology at Princeton Theological Seminary, where he has taught since 1981. He was awarded an honorary ThD degree from the University of Uppsala in Sweden for his writings and professional leadership in the psychology of religion. He has served as Editor of the Journal for the Scientific Study of Religion and as President of the Society for the Scientific Study of Religion. He has written several books on pastoral care and on the psychology of religion, with particular emphasis on developmental issues and the psychobiographical study of religious leaders. His more recent writings have centered on men and their religious interests. He is author of the books *Men, Religion, and Melancholia: James, Otto, Jung, and Erikson; Jesus: A Psychological Biography;* and *Men and Their Religion: Honor, Hope, and Humor.* Dr. Capps' interest focuses on the use of developmental theories and psychobiographical methods to illumine the lives and careers of religious men.

Introduction

At seminary graduation exercises, it is customary for invited speakers to offer words of wisdom to graduating seniors. Many turn to the Bible to buttress their points. I recall a speaker who suggested to the graduating students that, like Jonah, they are likely to discover that they have been sent to modern versions of Ninevah and they, also like Jonah, are likely to experience dejection, frustration, and even anger. He proposed, however, that the most faithful among the graduates would return to their Ninevahs (as Jonah apparently did not) and would have effective and successful ministries in the very locus of their earlier defeats. Having listened to many such homilies over the years, I found myself wanting to endorse his "take" on the Jonah story while acknowledging that if I had been Jonah, returning to Ninevah would be the last thing that I would do.

Another speaker based his words of wisdom on Paul's first letter to the church in Corinth, Chapter 16, verses 5-9,

> I will visit you after passing through Macedonia, for I intend to pass through Macedonia, and perhaps I will stay with you or even spend the winter, so that you may speed me on my journey, wherever I go. For I do not want to see you now just in passing; I hope to spend some time with you, if the Lord permits. But I will stay in Ephesus until Pentecost, for a wide door for effective work has opened to me, and there are many adversaries. (RSV)

In the course of his homily, he noted that Paul appears to have extended his stay in Ephesus beyond his original intentions because "a wide door for effective work has opened to me." Relating this to the graduating seniors, he cautioned them against trying to plan their careers in advance, because unexpected surprises are bound to occur in the course of their careers in ministry.

The fact that Paul indicates he will remain in Ephesus until Pentecost, the anniversary of the day the Holy Spirit came upon Peter and the other disciples (Acts, Chapter 2), reinforces the idea that one's own career planning is always subject to modification, upset, or countermanding by the mysterious workings of the Holy Spirit.

I believe the speaker made a very good point. One should not formulate a detailed plan for one's career in ministry, but should instead be open to the workings of the Holy Spirit. On the other hand, I also believe that one should make an effort to anticipate what lies ahead and not leave everything to chance or happenstance. Consider the following bit of colloquial wisdom:

> A guy named Joe finds himself in dire trouble. His business has gone bust and he's in serious financial straits. He's so desperate that he decides to ask God for help. He begins to pray. "God, please help me. I've lost my business and if I don't get some money, I'm going to lose my house as well. Please let me win the lotto." Lotto night comes and somebody else wins it. Joe again prays, "God, please let me win the lotto! I've lost my business and my house, and I'm going to lose my car as well." Lotto night comes and Joe still doesn't win. Once again, he prays. "My God, why have you forsaken me? I've lost my business, my house, and my car. I don't often ask you for help and I have always been a good servant to you. Please just let me win the lotto one time so I can get my life back in order." Suddenly there is a blinding flash of light as the heavens open and Joe is confronted by the voice of God himself. "Joe, meet me halfway on this. Buy a ticket!"

Of course, this story is not as theologically profound as the commencement speaker's words of wisdom, but it, too, makes a good point. If a graduating senior made absolutely no plans for the future, there would be no surprises, no basis whatsoever for claiming the agency of the Holy Spirit in *redirecting* one's career.

Although a graduating senior cannot know precisely what lies ahead, it isn't as though the future is completely unknowable, a sort of professional tabula rasa. Many books have been written about what congregations are like. The congregation that any given graduating senior goes out to serve will have its own style and will present unique problems, challenges, and opportunities. These books provide invaluable information and insights concerning how a congregation of 100 members differs from one having 250 members or 500 members.

A research area that lags far behind congregational studies is the study of the ministerial career itself, especially in its early phases. Seminarians often take a battery of tests designed to alert them to their own personal strengths and potential weaknesses. The Myers-Briggs Type Indicator is one of the most commonly employed instruments for this purpose. However, an issue that receives very little research attention is how a minister's career may be expected to unfold over the ensuing years. Can the overall trajectory of one's ministerial career be known in advance? Are there stages or phases in the ministerial career, and are these stages or phases more or less uniform, that is, common to almost all persons who have made ministry their chosen career?

I believe that the answer to these questions is yes, but, unfortunately, not much research is available to back up this belief. The study of the ministerial career—its long-term trajectory and its stages or phases of development—has been largely neglected. Because of this neglect, we tend to rely mainly on anecdotal accounts, such as the informal reminiscences of older ministers who are reflecting back on their own careers and on how they got where they are now. While these anecdotal accounts can be highly informative, and are often useful to persons who are at the entry stage of their ministerial careers, such accounts tend to be more impressionistic than systematic, and they are often tinged with a mixture of both positive and negative emotion. Such emotions are often illuminating, but they may also be distorting, especially if they are strongly felt at the time the anecdotal accounts are being related.

A more systematic approach would be to use a conceptual model or theory that was developed from studies of other occupational or professional groups, and to apply this model to ministers. Although such an application would undoubtedly require us to make modifications in the conceptual model, we would not be starting from scratch. A conceptual model of this kind that captured my interest more than two decades ago is the one presented by Daniel J. Levinson and his associates in *The Seasons of a Man's Life*.[1] It was based on extensive interviews with businessmen, university professors in the biological sciences, novelists, and factory workers. Because they interviewed men who were in their late forties, they were able to study in considerable depth a period in these men's careers that much older men would not be as likely to recall with as much accuracy. This is the period from age thirty to age forty, when individuals are likely to be considered somewhat "junior" in status. Their research showed that this period in one's career—especially the second half of this decade—is likely to be highly influential on the future, often determining whether the individual will be highly or moderately successful, or fail to meet long-term career goals.

Levinson and his colleagues also discovered that the early forties—which they came to call the "midlife transition"—is usually a time of reflection, questioning, uncertainty, and self-doubt, and that the man who emerges from this period seems very different, sometimes light years away, from the man who entered this phase at or near the conclusion of his thirties. In effect, Levinson and his associates identified a critical period in adult life that was comparable in terms of its life-changing effects to the "identity crisis" that Erik H. Erikson had discovered among adolescents several decades earlier.[2]

If this conceptual model applies to ministers—and the whole purpose of this book is to demonstrate that it does—then the appropriate message to graduating seniors who are in their twenties is this: "What happens to you in your thirties, especially your late thirties, is very important, for these years will be the basis on which your whole future career will be established." A corollary message, also based on this conceptual model, would be this: "At the time, you are unlikely to feel that this period in your life is as important as it will actually prove to have been. Sometimes you will feel that you are merely marking time, sometimes you will feel overworked but underutilized, and sometimes you will feel like a person in exile, despairing, demoralized, even disgusted with the way your career seems to be going." It is perhaps precisely here that the Christian idea of the Holy Spirit can be a source of encouragement, as it testifies to the fact that something more is going on than currently meets the eye. As William Stafford writes in his poem, "Bi-Focal," "So, the world happens twice— / once what we see it as; / second it legends itself / deep, the way it is."[3]

As I have indicated, Levinson and his associates based their research on extensive interviews with forty men. This was a major undertaking, so major, in fact, that the book reporting the results appeared several years after it was promised. This was also the case with his follow-up study of women, *The Seasons of a Woman's Life*, which was published two years after his death.[4] The fact that Levinson had a significant amount of research funds and several associates, yet was unable to keep the study on its projected timetable, is itself a strong cautionary note to anyone who might seek to develop and carry out a similar research study of ministers. However, a more economical and efficient way to go about it is to study biographies written about ministers. Because most biographies of ministers are about individuals who lived in earlier times, the contemporaneity of Levinson's study is necessarily sacrificed with this approach. But this approach also has some offsetting benefits. Biographies are typically about persons whose careers are completed. More often than not, they are written about individuals who are no longer living. Thus, the whole trajectory of the minister's career is known, and this contrasts with the type of study that Levinson and his associates carried out, in which the men were in their late forties. Yet, the biographer generally has information about the period that especially interests us here— the subject's late thirties—and is therefore able to provide what an older minister, relying solely on his own memory of that period, is likely either to have difficulty recalling or to misrepresent.

Another important value that the study of biographies affords, one that is especially germane to ministry, is that it enables us to recognize the similarities between what it means to be a minister today and what it meant to be a minister in an earlier historical era. Obviously, every profession changes from one generation to the next. Over time, such changes accumulate, with the result that the profession today may have few similarities to the profession as it manifested itself in times past. The profession of the physician, which can be traced back at least as far as Hippocrates (ca. 460-377 BC), is dramatically different in twenty-first century America from what it was in fifth- and fourth-century Greece. Yet, despite the differences, the profession retains its original name, and physicians continue to take the Hippocratic oath. The following anecdote by John Stuart Mill illustrates the point:

> Sir John Cutler had a pair of black worsted stockings, which his maid darned so often with silk that they became at last a pair of silk stockings. Now, supposing these stockings of Sir John's endued with some degree of consciousness at every particular darning, they would have been sensible that they were the same individual pair of stockings both before and after the darning; and this sensation would have continued in them through all the succession of darnings; and yet after the last of all, there was not

perhaps one thread left of the first pair of stockings: but they were grown to be silk stockings, as was said before.[5]

If it is true that the daily activities of physicians today have almost nothing in common with the daily activities of their early Greek predecessors, they nonetheless share a common identity. If this is true of physicians, it is also true of ministers (and not true, for example, of computer programmers, an occupation that does not have the same venerable history).

Seminarians often say that the courses they take in church history are only marginally useful in their preparation for ministry. If these courses were not required, most seminarians would probably not take them. Although I am in no position to judge the validity of these claims (and am aware of the fact that some seminarians would say that *none* of the courses they take in seminary are useful in their preparation for ministry), I *can* say that great value lies in reading the biographies of ministers who lived in earlier times. Perhaps if church history courses were more biographically oriented, many seminarians would share this conviction. However, the value of such reading is greatly enhanced when one reads these biographies with a conceptual model such as the one Levinson and his associates provide. As we will see, this model enables us to focus on a period in the life of a minister that is often overlooked precisely because it is typically a period long before the subject of the biography became sufficiently noteworthy to warrant a biography. This model also enables us to take a comparative approach, to consider the careers of several ministers together and to compare the ways in which each career unfolded. Given our special interest in the latter half of the fourth decade of the minister's life, we can compare several ministers' professional careers in terms of what occurred in this period of their lives.

I realize, of course, that Levinson's model has significant limitations. It may not be as useful for studying the careers of men who came into ministry in their forties after spending their thirties in another occupation or profession. On the other hand, the model may be useful for deepening our understanding of why they made this career change, and why it occurred at this stage of their life. Also, this model may not be as useful for women ministers. Levinson's *The Seasons of a Woman's Life* demonstrates that women's lives follow a similar alternating pattern of stability followed by transition, however, the study of women did not focus on selected occupational groups, but on women who, in their twenties or early thirties, either chose careers outside the home or chose to be homemakers. Although Levinson's research demonstrates that, for most women, this choice was not an irrevocable one, it nonetheless adds a complexity that was not encountered in the study of men, where it was a matter of which occupation would be chosen from among the many possibilities that were afforded. My own study focuses on the professional careers of five male ministers, but I believe that women may profit from reading this book because women who enter ministry are entering what has traditionally been a male profession. Thus women may find that many of the specific features of Levinson and his associates' conceptual model apply to them as well. Even if this proves not to be the case, women readers of this book may find that it provides valuable insights into the careers of the men with whom they work.

For this study, I have chosen to focus on five ministers who lived in earlier historical periods. They are

Phillips Brooks (1835-1893),
Jonathan Edwards (1703-1758),
John Henry Newman (1801-1890),
John Wesley (1703-1791), and
Orestes Brownson (1803-1876).

Why I chose to focus on five men, why I chose these particular five, and why I discuss them in the order indicated here, will become self-evident when I present Levinson's conceptual model. In presenting profiles of these five men, I will be focusing almost exclusively on the period in life on which Levinson and his associates also focus, the years prior to their late forties. I will also be making the case that their thirties, especially the latter half of their thirties, were especially decisive years. Regardless of when or where their ministry was carried out, and regardless of the peculiar circumstances of the local situation in which they ministered, the years from thirty to forty-five, but especially the late thirties, were of extreme importance to their subsequent careers.

During this life period, Phillips Brooks established his reputation as an effective and highly visible church leader; Jonathan Edwards, fresh from the exhilarating successes of the "Great Awakening" throughout New England, began to experience bitter and ultimately unresolvable conflicts in his home parish; John Henry Newman began to perceive that his days in the Church of England were numbered, and that he needed to begin a whole new career in a totally new setting; John Wesley, a relatively unknown Anglican clergyman, began to acquire widespread fame (or notoriety) as the leader of a rapidly growing network of Methodist societies in England; and Orestes Brownson came to the painful conclusion that he lacked the necessary competencies to be the minister of a local church. In each case, the decisive change—whether for better or for worse—occurred in their late thirties.

The ministers selected for this study were not chosen because of their historical significance, their contribution to theology, or because of their particular church affiliations. They were chosen strictly to illustrate the possibilities and difficulties of ministry in midcareer. I anticipate that ministers who read this book will find their own lives mirrored in one or more of these five ministers. I am also persuaded that my analyses of these five ministers demonstrate that the midcareer period will almost inevitably have a very decisive influence on the minister's subsequent professional career. Although the first five years of ministry are not likely to make or break one's career, the following ten years (roughly between age thirty and forty) are almost inevitably decisive. If marked by significant growth and progress, these years lay a solid foundation for the next twenty-five years of ministry. If marked by instability and great frustration, the following years will most likely be devoted to compensating for the disappointments of the midcareer period. This does not mean that those whose careers were marked by instability and frustration were of lesser account. Indeed, here, as in many other circumstances of life, what counts as success in the eyes of the world may be radically different from what counts as success in the eyes of God. We should be careful not to romanticize instability, frustration, or failure, but we also need to recognize the personal price that frequently accompanies success. As Erik H. Erikson points out in *Young Man Luther,* some men may be paying too great a psychic price for the good work that they are doing.[6]

Chapter 1

Levinson's Developmental Model

Daniel Levinson's theory of adult development is self-consciously based on Erik Erikson's life cycle theory. In 1950 Erikson proposed that the life of an individual proceeds through the following eight stages from infancy to old age:

1. Trust versus mistrust
2. Autonomy versus shame and self-doubt
3. Initiative versus guilt
4. Industry versus inferiority
5. Identity versus identity diffusion
6. Intimacy versus isolation
7. Generativity versus stagnation
8. Integrity versus despair[1]

Erikson locates the first four stages in infancy and childhood, the fifth stage in adolescence, the sixth stage in young adulthood, the seventh stage in adulthood, and the eighth stage in old age. Over the years, Erikson's theory has influenced our understanding of infancy, childhood, adolescence, and young adulthood. His theory has not been as influential on our understanding of adulthood. This is largely because he proposes a single stage, that of generativity versus stagnation, to capture the dynamics of a period of life that extends some thirty years or more.

Levinson's theory does not replace Erikson's view of adult development. Instead, it incorporates Erikson's insights into a more finely calibrated theory of adult development. Rather than viewing the middle adult years largely in terms of a single stage of development, Levinson has divided the years between seventeen and sixty into two major eras—the young adult era and the middle adult era—with each era subdivided into two stable periods and two transitional periods.

The stable periods encompass roughly seven years, the transitional periods five years, but variations from these norms are not uncommon. Overlap is also typical, so one should avoid thinking that each stability-transition cycle is strictly twelve years. It is never, however, less than ten years. Levinson also extends his theory to include the post sixty era of late adulthood, but his theory of development in the early and middle adult years is the major thrust of his work. It provides a theoretical formulation of sufficient complexity to take account of the variety of critical events that normally occurs in the early and middle adult years, and its division of each of these two eras into two stability-transition cycles enables us to chart and record the changes in an individual's life with considerable precision.

As noted earlier, Levinson does not apply his theory to the study of ministers. His theory is based on extensive interviews with businessmen, university professors, novelists, and factory workers. But, as I hope to show, the theory can be readily applied to the lives and careers of ministers. However the ministry differs from these other occupations, it manifests the same developmental patterns. This fact should become patently clear as we discuss the specific features of the theory.

As indicated, Levinson divides the adult years into three major eras. The early adult era (age seventeen to forty), the middle adult era (age forty to sixty and the late adult era (age sixty to eighty). He briefly discusses a fourth era, the late-late adult era, which begins around eighty and continues until death. Only the first two eras are based on actual research and are discussed in this study. The following description of Levinson's theory centers almost exclusively on the two earliest adult eras, the early and middle adult eras.

THE EARLY ADULT ERA

Levinson suggests that the early adult era consists of two major phases: the *novice phase* and the *settling-down phase*. The novice phase begins with a five-year transitional period from adolescence to adulthood (between ages seventeen and twenty-two), continues with a more stable period in which the individual enters the adult world (between ages twenty-two and twenty-eight), and concludes with another transitional period which Levinson calls the age thirty transition (between ages twenty-eight and thirty-three).

The Novice Phase

The Early Adult Transition

Concerning the first stage of the novice phase, Levinson says that the early adult transition (age seventeen to twenty-two) is a developmental bridge between the eras of pre-adulthood and early adulthood, confronting the individual with two major tasks. The first is to terminate the adolescent life structure and leave the pre-adult world. The second is to make a preliminary step into the adult world. This preliminary step involves exploring the possibilities presented by the adult world, imagining oneself as a participant in it, and testing some tentative choices before fully entering it. This stage normally involves beginning the lifelong process of separation from parents and beginning a process of change that leads to a new home base for living as a young adult in an adult world. The majority of the subjects of Levinson's study formed a life in early adulthood that was quite different from that of their parents. While few strongly rejected their origins, most began to loosen their ties to familial, ethnic, and religious traditions, and chose wives less on the basis of traditional family structures and more in terms of the ambitions, values, and interests of a pattern of upward mobility.

Entering the Adult World

The second, or "entering the adult world" period in the novice phase (age twenty-two to twenty-eight) involves constructing a new life structure different from the life structure developed in adolescence. If the previous period from seventeen to twenty-two was a period of transition, this period is one of consolidation and greater stability. This period involves exploring freely by keeping options open and avoiding strong commitments, but at the same time requires making some firm choices and taking on adult responsibilities. In some individuals, free exploration is dominant, in others making firm choices and assuming adult responsibilities predominates, but the opposite side is never absent. Moreover, regardless of which emphasis is primary, a general movement toward increasing commitment is evident as one approaches the end of this period. The liabilities of a provisional life structure are recognized, and there is an "increasing internal need and external pressure to work at the other task and to get more order, purpose and attachment into their lives."[2]

On the other hand, Levinson points out that the task of achieving such order, purpose, and attachment is exceedingly difficult. This difficulty is due in part to specific aspects of one's situation—economic recession, discrimination, the rivalries of a highly competitive world—and to emotional problems involved in committing oneself to an occupation, marriage, and to separation from parents. This difficulty is also due to the sheer complexity, even contradictoriness, of the developmental tasks encountered in this period of life. This difficulty is in turn further complicated because the individual is too young, inexperienced, and uncertain of his real interests and desires. Thus, while occupational and marital stability may provide the focal point around which a relatively integrated life structure may be established, no one escapes the feeling that the direction of one's life in the middle to late twenties is unsatisfactory in at least some major respects.

In *The Seasons of a Woman's Life,* published eighteen years after *The Seasons of a Man's Life,* Levinson, through the assistance of his wife, Judy, identified a new feature of the novice phase which he calls "the Age 25 Shift."[3] Through analysis of the lives of the forty-five women in the study, the Levinsons found that all of the women experienced some event of decisive importance in their twenty-fifth year (not before late twenty-four or after early twenty-six). They use the word "shift" because it suggests a "smaller scale" alteration or change than the word "transition" suggests, but it typically involves a more or less conscious decision to realize a more integrated life. Thus, it is consistent with the fact that the years from twenty-two through twenty-eight are ones in which a stable life structure is being formed. Whatever the event itself may be, it involves more than a single relationship or aspect of life; it is intended to make her life as a whole more integrated and satisfying. An example of such an event at age twenty-five is having a second child. To her husband and others, this event may have no unusual significance, but, in her mind, the decision to have another child may derive from a more fundamental life choice, such as choosing to remain in a difficult marriage, or putting her occupational interests aside for the time being. Another example is taking a new job that is not markedly different from an earlier one. From an external point of view, this may not be a notable event. From a subjective standpoint, however, it constitutes a major turning point, as she is choosing not merely to take another job, but to become more independent, establish a more defined occupation, and give her family a less exclusively central place in her life. Her private intentions in making this choice may not become clearly conscious for many months or even years, although the impact on her life structure is more immediately evident.

Levinson emphasizes that even though the "Age 25 Shift" usually involves one or more major life events, the nature and consequences of the shift cannot be determined merely by looking at the external event. It is essential to look as well at the personal meaning of the events and the life structure in which they occur. Although he did not identify this shift in his earlier study of men, he guesses that it may exist for men as well. He does not speculate on what the event or events may be, but the same points would also apply to men, namely, that the intentions that lie behind the event may not become self-evident for many months or years, and it is essential to look beyond the externalities of the event and probe the personal meaning of the event in the context of the life structure in which it occurs.

Age Thirty Transition (Age Twenty-Eight to Thirty-Three)

The "age thirty transition" period in the novice phase (age twenty-eight to thirty-three) provides an opportunity "to work on the flaws in the life structure formed during the previous period, and to create the basis for a more satisfactory structure that will be built in the following period."[4] During this transitional period, the sense arises that the provisional, exploratory character of the twenties is ending. Also, a greater sense of urgency is felt, that if changes in one's life are to be made, this is the time to do it before it is too late. Levinson's research indicated that the age thirty transition is more likely to be stressful than smooth. This stress is partly because, as with all transitional periods, some of the stability achieved in the earlier period is being relinquished to prepare for the creation of a life structure with significantly new elements in the next period. This stress, however, is fundamentally because, among transitional periods, the age thirty transition can be uniquely painful because it raises searching questions concerning what one has done with one's life to this point and what new directions one will try to initiate if still within the realm of possibility. Levinson likens the age thirty transition to that of a man alone

on a body of water trying to get from one island to another. He fears
that he will not reach his destination but that he has gone too far to
turn back:

> A man may experience himself as swimming alone, as rowing in
> a leaky boat, or as captain of a luxurious but defective ship
> caught in a storm. There are wide variations in the nature of the
> vehicle, the sources of threat and the nature of Past and Future.
> The critical thing is that the integrity of the enterprise is in seri-
> ous doubt: he experiences the imminent danger of chaos, disso-
> lution, the loss of the future.[5]

In short, a stressful age thirty transition was more the rule than the exception in Levinson's study. Less than one in five had fairly smooth
transitions.

Major Tasks of the Novice Phase

In addition to identifying the three major periods of the novice
phase and noting the specific demands that each of these periods
makes on the emerging adult, Levinson also describes the tasks that
are common to all three periods in the novice phase. The following
four tasks are common to the novice phase as a whole:

Forming a Dream and giving it a place in the life structure. Levinson points out that the novice phase of early adulthood involves exploration and choice strongly shaped by (a) the influences of family,
class, subculture, and social institutions; (b) his own active striving,
competence, and rational considerations; and (c) various aspects of
one's personality, including motives, values, talents, anxieties, and
life goals. Levinson's study of forty men also indicated the importance of a fourth factor, which he calls the Dream. His view of the
Dream and its importance for adult development is influenced by
D. W. Winnicott's discussions of transitional periods in early childhood. Winnicott points out that in such transitional periods the child
imagines various possibilities for himself in the future, and enacts
these imaginings in daydreams, play, and other make-believe explorations. At the beginning the Dream "is a vague sense of self-in-adult
world. It has the quality of a vision, an imagined possibility that gen-
erates excitement and vitality. At the start it is poorly articulated and
only tenuously connected to reality. . . ."[6] But during the novice

phase, the young man has the developmental task of giving it greater definition and of finding ways to live it out. The fortunate young man is the one who is able to build a life structure around the Dream. He has a better chance of personal fulfillment, though years of struggle may be required in working toward its realization. The magical or unrealistic features of the Dream will also need to be relinquished, usually during the midlife transition (age forty to forty-five). Unfortunately, however, many young men develop a conflict between a life direction expressing the Dream and another that is quite different:

> A man may be pushed in the latter direction by his parents, by various external constraints, such as lack of money or opportunity, and by various aspects of his personality, such as guilt, passivity, competitiveness and special talents. He may thus succeed in an occupation that holds no interest for him.[7]

This conflict may extend over many years and evolve through various forms. But if the Dream is relinquished or remains alien to the evolving life structure, one's sense of aliveness and purpose may be lost.

Forming mentor relationships. Finding and relating to a mentor is one of the most important and complex developmental tasks of early adulthood. The mentor is usually several years older and a person of greater experience in the world the young man is entering. The mentor's roles include

> *teacher*—contributing to the acquisition of skills and intellectual development;
>
> *sponsor*—facilitating the young man's entry and advancement into the occupation of his choice;
>
> *host and guide*—welcoming the young man into a new professional and social world and acquainting him with its value and customs;
>
> *exemplar*—exemplifying virtues, achievements, and a way of life that the younger man can admire; and
>
> *fostering the Dream*—believing in the young man, sharing the Dream, and giving it his blessing.

In Levinson's view, fostering the Dream is the most important role that the mentor can play in the development of the younger adult. In carrying out this, as well as his or her other functions, the mentor is a transitional figure. He or she is not a parent or "father figure," because the parent is identified with the life that the younger man is leaving behind. Neither is he or she a peer, because a peer cannot represent the advanced level toward which the younger man is striving. Thus, the mentor is ordinarily eight to fifteen years older than the protege. The mentoring relationship tends to last two or three years, eight to ten years at the most, but much of the value of the relationship may be realized after its termination. Although its termination may at first evoke feelings of bitterness and abandonment, the longer range result is the younger man's internalization of the admired qualities of the mentor. The personality of the younger man is thereby enriched as he makes the mentor a more intrinsic part of himself.

Forming an occupation. While an individual may "decide" on an occupation in his early twenties, the formation of an occupation is a complex, psychosocial process that extends throughout the novice phase and often beyond. An initial serious choice is usually made during the early adult transition (age seventeen to twenty-two) or entering the adult world (age twenty-two to twenty-eight) periods, but although the early choice seems to be very definite, it usually proves to represent only a preliminary definition of interests and values, and only begins to initiate a complex process of relating interests to occupational possibilities. In addition, one common feature of all occupations is that one does not complete his occupational novitiate or apprenticeship until his late twenties. Thus, forming an occupation involves most of one's twenties both because of difficulties in matching interests to occupational possibilities and because occupations are themselves so structured as to require an extended novitiate before one is considered a full participant in the occupation. Moreover, by the time the novice phase comes to a close, levels of attainment can vary considerably from one individual to another, even within the same occupation. At age thirty-three, an executive type may be at the first rung of management or near the top. A biologist may be an associate professor with a national reputation or an assistant professor just beginning to do independent research. Nonetheless, in spite of major differences in levels of attainment, the more open and formative phase is normally concluded by the end of the novice phase. Subsequent occupational tasks will build on the pattern established by the early thirties.

Forming a marriage and family. About half of the men in Levinson's study married during the early adult transition (age seventeen to twenty-two); about 30 percent married during the entering the adult world period (age twenty-two to twenty-eight). In the former case, courtship and marital choice were heavily bound up with the tasks of the early adult transition, especially with efforts to separate from parents. One's wife is chosen in part because she lacks the qualities he fears and resents in his inner maternal figure. In the latter case, the marriage is colored by the developmental tasks of the entering the adult world period, and is enriched by the developmental work done in the preceding transitional period. One's wife is chosen in part because she appreciates his emerging aspirations and wants to share in his planned life. Marriages during this period are usually consonant with the adult world one is entering, though it is often the case that the marriages that occur during this period are the culmination of a friendship begun in the earlier transitional period, when the developmental needs of the two individuals were quite different.

About 20 percent of the men in Levinson's study were bachelors until their late twenties. They felt a need to "get more serious" about marrying during the age thirty transition (age twenty-eight to thirty-three). In many respects, they were more knowledgeable about themselves and their relationships with women. This advantage was somewhat offset by the fact that they felt themselves under some pressure to marry. The decision to marry during the age thirty transition is as likely to be based on a desire to "normalize" one's life as to fulfill a deep love relationship.

In his discussion of the task of forming a marriage and family, Levinson places considerable emphasis on the relationship between one's marital choice and the formation of his Dream. One's wife may be that "special woman" who helps him shape and live out his Dream. Like the mentor, she believes in his Dream, shares it as her own, and helps to create a "boundary space" in which his aspirations can be imagined and his hopes nourished. However, if in supporting his Dream she loses her own, her development will suffer and both will pay the price later. Moreover, his need for her support of his Dream will tend to diminish over the years, a process that will come to a critical point in the midlife transition (age forty to forty-five). In other marriages, the couple may have a loving and supportive relationship but one that has little connection to his Dream. What she loves in him may, in fact, hinder or preclude the pursuit of his Dream. In time, the disparity will need to be dealt with, especially because it is most likely that the disparity is not due simply to her inability to support his Dream, but because her own Dream and his are in opposition. In Levinson's view, it is during the age thirty transition (age twenty-eight to thirty-three) that the difficulties present in the marriage are most likely to reach a critical level. Disparities between the marriage relationship and the two individuals' personal Dreams require particular attention in this transitional period.

The End of the Novice Phase

By the end of the novice phase (age thirty-three) a new life structure considerably different from the adolescent structure established by age seventeen has been achieved. By this time, one's Dream is more or less incorporated into the life structure. The character of his occupational life has taken shape. A marriage and family have been formed (in some cases, a second marriage has already been formed), and he has most likely experienced a mentor relationship. If these tasks have been carried out well, he is prepared for the settling-down period that follows the age thirty transition. If not, the settling-down period will become increasingly painful and attempts to create a more satisfactory structure will be more difficult.

The Settling-Down Period

The second major period in the early adult era, the settling-down period, normally occurs between ages thirty-three and forty. After the age thirty transition, this is a period of consolidation. It is the culmination of early adulthood and is the time for a man to realize the hopes of his youth. The major developmental task in this period is that of "becoming one's own man." This task becomes the focus of the last four years in the settling-down period, from age thirty-six to forty.

In his study of forty men, Levinson was able to identify five major ways in which the settling-down period was negotiated:

1. *Sequence A:* Advancement within a stable life structure
2. *Sequence B:* Serious failure or decline within a stable life structure
3. *Sequence C:* Breaking out—trying for a new life structure

4. *Sequence D:* Advancement which itself produces a change in life structure
5. *Sequence E:* Unstable life structure

In sequence A, life goes at least moderately well as a man advances toward his major goals. In sequence B, he fails to achieve these goals, or he suffers a serious decline from his earlier level of achievement. In both of these patterns, the life structure itself is relatively stable. In sequences C and D, a stable structure has been formed at the beginning of the settling-down period, but various internal and external forces lead to change. In sequence C, the structure formed at the beginning of the settling-down period (ages thirty-three to thirty-six) proves intolerable, so by the latter half of the period, when the task of becoming one's own man is central, a major attempt occurs to break out of the existing structure and create a new one. In sequence D, achievements in the settling-down period propel him, often unexpectedly, into a new world. In both sequence C and D, major changes occur in the life structure, but in sequence C they are normally the result of frustration, whereas in sequence D they are normally the result of unanticipated, perhaps even unsought, successes. In sequence E, a stable structure is not formed at all, usually because the previous periods of entering the adult world and the age thirty transition left the individual with major liabilities as he entered the settling-down period. So the settling-down period begins with tenuous choices that are not followed up, and the life structure remains in flux throughout the settling-down process. Because the settling-down period, with its developmental task of becoming one's own man, is of central importance in our study of the minister in midcareer, I discuss each of these sequences in some detail.

Sequence A: Advancement Within a Stable Life Structure

In this sequence, life proceeds more or less according to expectations. During the early phase of this period, when settling down is most marked (age thirty-three to thirty-six), the individual makes his primary commitments, defines his enterprises, and gradually enriches and elaborates his life structure. In the later phase of this period, when becoming one's own man is most marked (age thirty-six to forty), he defines more precisely what he hopes to have accomplished by age forty and is close to achieving these goals. Whatever the precise nature of his goals, he forms a coherent life structure in the settling-down period and maintains it throughout. When important changes occur in job, place of residence, lifestyle, or family pattern, these changes represent advancements, enrichments, or progress within the life structure and not changes in the basic structure. He may experience times of discouragement, even times when advancement itself is in serious question, but these times are generally tolerable because the individual senses that the overall trend is one of advancement.

The major difficulty confronted by individuals in sequence A is that their very success throughout the settling-down period creates new problems when they reach age forty. The top rung of the first ladder—attaining goals that represent years of striving—turns out to be the bottom rung on a new ladder as one enters a new "senior" world in which new and more complex responsibilities are presented. Nonetheless, the individual who has followed sequence A in becoming his own man usually has a strong sense of self-esteem and personal competence. Moreover, to the extent that his settling-down enterprise is consonant with his Dream, he experiences a sense of personal satisfaction and basic well-being. What he needs to guard against, however, is that his life may be providing genuine satisfactions at too great an inner cost, especially if he is gaining rewards that will prove to have little personal value for him in the long run. In addition, his strivings for advancement may be based, in part, on the illusion that reaching his goals will provide everything he ever wanted. Although this illusion is rarely conscious during the "becoming one's own man" period (age thirty-six to forty), it is often consciously recognized as an illusion in the following period (the midlife transition from age forty to forty-five).

Sequence B: Serious Failure or Decline Within a Stable Life Structure

Men whose lives follow this sequence in their late thirties either fail in obvious ways or achieve much external success but fail in certain crucial respects, which make the entire enterprise seem pointless or futile. One of the most prominent forms of failure or decline in this period is occupational, specifically when one reaches one's highest level of influence within the organization at mid-thirty. By their late thirties, it is evident to these individuals that "they have reached their ceilings: not only would they fail in their goals, but their sense of direction and their possibilities for the future were undermined."[8] Middle managers who do not move up into the high management positions and younger faculty members who are not promoted to tenured professorships are prominent examples of men who have worked hard to achieve their goals but are now forced to reevaluate these goals in light of future possibilities. These men normally engage in considerable self-evaluation in light of their own perceptions of what constitutes success, and they frequently believe they have been cheated or otherwise treated unfairly by their employers or associates. Moreover, they often subject their Dream to careful, even ruthless critique. Unlike the individual in sequence A who may be operating under false illusions as he contemplates his success in carrying out his Dream, the individual in sequence B is more disillusioned concerning his Dream.

Sequence C: Breaking Out—Trying for a New Life Structure

In sequence C, the individual recognizes that he can no longer live within the confines of the life structure he has constructed to date. In most cases, the settling-down structure involves a reaffirmation of choices made during one's twenties, but men in this sequence find that the goals which this structure represents are increasingly oppressive to them. So, just when one is most eager to become his own man and fulfill his aspirations, he feels something is fundamentally wrong with these aspirations. Yet to change or break out of this structure is to destroy much that he has built over the past ten or fifteen years. Caught between trying to live with an intolerable situation or destroying what he has put together, his personal demeanor tends to reflect much confusion: "As he struggles to make the fateful decision—to break out or to stay put—he is likely to be moody, uncommunicative, alternately resentful of others and blaming of himself."[9]

The difficulty here is partly that his life structure is indeed flawed. But these flaws have been present and tolerated for some time. Why are they suddenly so intolerable? The reason is that the developmental task of becoming one's own man is so urgent at this period of life. The flaws in his life structure that threaten this task of becoming one's own man can no longer be endured; they need to be confronted. Significantly, flaws that threaten the successful completion of the task of becoming one's own man typically involve marriage and occupation, two areas of life that are most difficult to change without serious damage to oneself and the other individuals involved. If a man attempts to terminate his occupation or marriage, it will take several years to carry through the process of separation. Before he will be able to create a new life structure, therefore, he enters the midlife transition at age forty, a period when one's aspirations and goals are vulnerable to internal critique. Thus, the new aspirations and goals to which one has "broken out" during one's late thirties are now subjected to reevaluation. In Levinson's judgment, it is virtually impossible to establish a new structure until the midlife transition ends (about age forty-five), so the man who breaks out during his late thirties must anticipate a period of considerable instability and flux, lasting eight to ten years.

In light of the enormous costs involved in breaking out, the pain it causes loved ones, and the possibility that it may not result in major improvements, the prudent course may well be to remain with the existing structure, resigning oneself to its flaws, rather than making drastic changes that entail great sacrifice by the individual and his family. However, the intense passion that normally accompanies the sense of having a deeply flawed life structure does not ordinarily lend itself to acts of prudence. Furthermore, remaining in the present structure may be experienced as a kind of living death. This indicates that, if remaining in the existing structure is chosen over breaking out, major efforts need to be made to deal with the flaws in the existing structure. Levinson's studies seem to suggest that flaws in the occupational areas may have a better prognosis than major flaws in one's marriage because occupational problems can sometimes be ameliorated by a satisfying marriage. The converse is less likely. If marital difficulties are severe, occupational satisfaction is generally not a strong enough countervailing influence. More likely, marital difficulties will also generate occupational difficulties.

Sequence D: Advancement Which Itself Produces a Change in Life Structure

In sequence A, advancement occurs within a stable life structure. Changes occur, but the basic character of the life structure remains intact. In sequence D, advancement brings with it a significant change in life structure. In Levinson's study, the advancement usually occurred in the occupational area, with a significant promotion or drastic increase in salary. At first, the increase is experienced as a tremendous blessing, an opportunity to live better and engage in long-desired activities, but this gain also thrusts him into new roles and relationships, activating new aspects of the self but forcing the termination of other, previously important ones. The net effect of these changes is a major alteration in life structure that is part blessing, part curse.

In Levinson's study, three men fit sequence D, while three others were a mixture of sequence C ("breaking out") and sequence D. The latter went through a change in life structure in their late thirties partly as a result of advancement but also partly as a result of other factors such as "breaking out." It is noteworthy that this sequence is most likely to be mixed with other sequences, especially the sequence of breaking out. This would suggest that advancement resulting in major changes in life structure may reflect previous efforts to "break out" or result in such efforts. Moreover, men in sequence D are more likely than the others to have altered their Dreams in important respects in their late thirties. While sequence A individuals sought to achieve their Dream and were largely successful, and sequence B and C men were still struggling with discrepancies between the Dream and their current reality, sequence D individuals were engaged in more extensive alterations of the Dream itself. In effect, they were being forced or propelled into a life that was different in many significant respects from the Dream they had set for themselves, but different in a pleasant way. A biologist, for example, abandoned his goal of becoming a renowned researcher when he was offered the opportunity to shape the biology curriculum at another university. Although he relinquished his earlier Dream of being recognized as a researcher, he gained considerable satisfaction from his new role as an educator and administrator, and also found more time for his family and leisure interests. The remaining question during his midlife transition (age forty to forty-five) was whether the new life based on an essentially new Dream would prove as fulfilling as the life based on the older Dream. The new Dream was sufficiently like the older Dream in that his new life was based on the hard work expended in the pursuit of the earlier Dream, but it was different enough to raise the possibility of future remorse. On the other hand, this possibility would seem to be less threatening and more manageable than the problem that another sequence D individual confronted, namely that the advancement he experienced extended well beyond his previous aspirations and projected him into a social milieu for which he was emotionally and culturally unprepared. In this case, external success was bought at too great an inner cost.

Sequence E: Unstable Life Structure

In sequence E, the life structure remains unstable and in flux throughout the settling-down period. None of the men in Levinson's study actually sought this instability. All who fit into this category attempted to settle down during this period and tried to become their own men in the process, but in each case a variety of external circumstances and internal difficulties kept the individual from achieving these goals. Moreover, those that fit this category entered the settling-down phase with major instabilities in previous periods. Thus, their work on the developmental task of becoming their own man (age thirty-six to forty) was seriously hampered by earlier failures at the developmental tasks of the novice stage, whether forming an occupation, finding a mentor, forming a stable marriage and family life, or incorporating their Dream into their life structures. Becoming one's own man requires previous success at all, or certainly most, of their earlier developmental tasks. The overall effect of these earlier failures, then, is to postpone achievement of the goal of becoming one's own man, a postponement that can prove at least as troublesome as the decision of sequence C men to "break out" at this time in their lives. In both cases, one enters the midlife transition (ages forty to forty-five) with some major liabilities and inadequate supports.

The Five Settling-Down Sequences

As indicated earlier, the settling-down period is the major focus of this study. The five sequences of the settling-down period will be used to differentiate the five ministers who are the subjects of this book. Because these sequences will be given such strong emphasis, it is important that we take particular note of Levinson's observation that many individuals do not fit neatly into one of these types, but reflect a combination of types. The task is to determine which of the sequences is dominant during the settling-down phase (ages thirty-three to forty). I will assign our five ministers to the dominant sequence during the settling-down phase.

THE MIDDLE ADULT ERA

The major emphasis of this study is the early adult era (ages seventeen to forty), especially its culmination in the settling-down period. Some attention, however, needs to be given to Levinson's discussion of the middle adult era (ages forty to sixty), particularly the years that immediately follow the completion of the early adult era. Although I will not discuss Levinson's comments on the middle adult era in as much detail as the preceding era, a brief summary of his formulation of the middle adult era follows.

The early adult era usually ends around age forty, when an individual has a sense of having become his own man. At age forty, he is in a position to evaluate the man that he has become. He will consider himself relatively successful if he has achieved his major occupational goals, has been affirmed within his occupational and social world, and is becoming a senior member of that world. He will consider himself relatively unsuccessful if he feels he has not advanced sufficiently in his occupation and has not gained the affirmation, independence, and seniority he wants. The next developmental stage is the midlife transition, a transitional period that involves three major tasks:

1. Termination of the era of early adulthood. This involves reviewing and reappraising his life during the early adulthood era.
2. First steps toward initiation of middle adulthood. Although not yet ready to start building a new life structure, he can begin to modify the negative elements of the present structure and test new choices.

3. Dealing with the polarities that are the sources of deep division in his life. These include the young/old, destruction/creation, masculine/feminine, and attachment/separation polarities.

In discussing the first of these tasks, Levinson places greatest emphasis on the need to scrutinize one's illusions. Early childhood provides a fertile ground for illusions, and illusions play a role in aspiring toward the achievement of one's Dream. However, the midlife transition is normally a period of "deillusionment," a process of relinquishing or reducing illusions about oneself and one's world. While such "deillusionment" may cause one to feel bereft, it may also have the effect of liberation, a sense of being "free to develop more flexible values and to admire others in a more genuine, less idealizing way."[10]

During the midlife transition, the second task of modifying the life structure may involve changes (occupational, marital, social, and geographical mobility), but even when no significant external changes of this sort occur, there are important internal changes. These typically include reducing the psychological hold of one's original Dream, leaving the youthful generation and becoming a mentor, and modifying one's marriage (largely by taking more personal responsibility for marital problems than one was willing to assume in the settling-down period). Internal changes also include the individuation process, which Levinson considers to be the third major task initiated in the midlife transition period.

If the early adult era culminated in the developmental task of becoming one's own man, the major developmental task in the beginning stages of the middle adult era is individuation, a process in which one achieves a greater understanding of the boundary between self and external world. Levinson does not employ C. G. Jung's own complex views of the individuation process (Jung was responsible for introducing the concept of individuation into psychology), but instead combines the views of a number of psychologists who have, in effect, identified important features of the individuation process in middle age. These views include Erikson's theory that middle adulthood involves conflicts between generativity versus stagnation, Elliott Jacques' belief that the central issue at midlife involves coming to terms with one's own mortality, and Bernice Neugarten's view that the central midlife change encompasses a growing interiority, a turning inward toward the self. These and other ideas provide the basis for Levinson's four polarities.

In Levinson's perception, the individuation process into which an individual moves in the middle adult era is largely a reintegration of these basic polarities. The young/old polarity, which Levinson considers the most important polarity in this period, involves dealing with the problem of mortality, especially in a man's concern at this age with the problem of physical and psychological decline. Although physical decline is actually quite moderate and leaves a man with ample capacities for living in middle age, it sometimes has a psychological effect of great significance as he begins to fear that he will soon lose all his youthful qualities. This problem of *decline* is accompanied by concerns about one's *legacy* as a parent and as a worker. Regarding his legacy as a parent, a man's concern at this stage about "how the children are doing" is related in part to feelings about the value of his contribution to posterity. Regarding his legacy as a worker, the midlife transition may usher in the realization that his previous successes are not as grand as he had imagined, that they are at best the prelude to his new tasks, the basis on which a more substantial project can be built. Moreover, even if the new tasks promise to be effectively accomplished, the result is unlikely to be as monumental as his Dream had led him to hope. Thus, in his desire to create a legacy as a worker, he needs to find some middle ground between an illusory sense of the lasting importance of his work and the cynical view that nothing in his labor has any real value.

The destruction/creation polarity focuses on the problem of one's own destructiveness toward others, and one's sense of having been hurt and damaged by others. Levinson emphasizes the importance of achieving some awareness of one's destructive tendencies, and sees the developmental task here to be that of achieving greater self-knowledge and self-responsibility in those areas of life in which one has the power to injure and hurt other individuals.

The masculine/feminine polarity focuses on the task of the greater integrity of the masculine and feminine components of the self, especially achieving a more adequate balance between these masculine and feminine characteristics. While the phase of becoming one's own man involved a surge of masculine strivings, an effort to achieve a more senior and "manly" position in the world, the individuation process of the middle adult era involves achieving a more balanced integration of qualities he regards as masculine and feminine (for example, achievement and nurturance, power and weakness, cognition and feeling). To the extent that he continues to view the qualities of nurturance, weakness, and feeling as feminine traits, and inappropriate qualities for a man to have, this balanced integration is yet to be achieved.

The attachment/separation polarity largely involves a shift toward greater separateness during the middle adult years in order to overcome an overbalance toward attachment in the early childhood era. In his twenties and thirties, a man is tremendously invested in the external world. Forming an occupation and a family demand this, but these external demands are accompanied by internal urges to establish his niche in society. Now, in the middle adult era, the work of reappraising his life to this point (the first developmental task initiated in the midlife transition) requires greater inwardness, more engagement with himself, in order to understand his real interests more adequately, what are, what future goals he desires, and how he feels about himself. This introspection generally results in a more critical view of the groups, institutions, and traditions that have the greatest significance for him, and the achievement of a less "tribalized" and more "universal" perspective. He is less inclined to idealize certain groups and individuals, or to condemn others. He may also look with more favor on his own origins, which in most cases he left behind in the period of entering the adult world (age twenty-two to twenty-eight), and attempt some sort of rapprochement. Thus, greater introspection is accompanied by a more universalistic perspective with regard to social groups and institutions. This does not mean that he now views society in a detached manner. On the contrary, because he is less tyrannized by his ambitions, dependencies, and passions, he is able to be involved with other individuals and perform his social roles in a more responsible way than before. He is capable of a more effective response to parental responsibilities and is able to contribute to the development of younger adults through increased opportunity and capacity for mentoring.

Modifying a Life Structure

The foregoing survey of Levinson's discussion of the middle adult era has been relatively brief, but enough has been provided to establish the basic point that, if the early childhood era is concerned with *forming* a life structure, the middle adult era is largely involved with *modifying* that structure. The developmental tasks of early adulthood all focus on formation—that is, the formation of a Dream, of an occupation, of marriage and family, and of mentor relationships. The developmental tasks of the middle adult era focus on modification of these same elements of the life structure. These modifications are largely the effect of the *reappraisal* of the life structure as formed in the earlier era, and the *individuation process* itself. The important point, however, is that the life structure achieved in the settling-down period is the structure to which such modifying efforts are directed. This means that the late thirties, when one is involved in settling down and becoming one's own man, are extremely important developmentally, for they are the basis of the midlife transition that occurs from age forty to forty-five. I have chosen this period to focus on in the following study of five ministers in midcareer, for these are clearly the formative years in the development of one's life structure.

STUDY OF FIVE MINISTERS IN MIDCAREER

The five ministers chosen for this study were selected largely because preliminary exploration into their lives and careers indicated that each represented one of the five sequences in the settling-down period (age thirty-three to forty). Since my primary interest was to explore the early adulthoods of men who have adopted careers in ministry, Levinson's sequences seemed to provide a valuable means of identifying the variety of patterns in which individual careers in ministry evolve. These sequences are precise enough to enable us to identify individuals who fit each sequence, but they are also flexible enough to permit us to note instances in which one sequence operates as the dominant pattern while another plays a subordinate role. Moreover, Levinson's sequences are useful here because they provide a perspective from which we can look back at previous periods of the early adult era and look forward to the initial periods of the middle adult era. Thus, by being able to place an individual in a particular sequence, we can explore those facets of the earlier periods which help to account for this particular pattern in the middle to late thirties.

Also, by locating an individual in a particular sequence, we can use this placement to help us account for modifications in the life structure that began in the initial periods of the middle adult era. In other words, the sequences provide a vantage point from which to view each minister's past and future.

Besides employing Levinson's five sequences, my analyses of the careers of the five ministers will be informed by other important features of his theory. The four developmental tasks of the novice phase (forming a Dream, mentor relationships, occupation, and marriage and family) will provide the focus for my discussion of the pre-settling-down years. And, to the extent possible, the four polarities (young/old, destruction/creation, masculine/feminine, attachment/separateness) will guide my discussion of the post–settling-down years. In addition, Levinson's divisions of the early adult era into two major phases (novice and settling down), each with their subphases, will be used to give coherence and structure to my discussion of each minister's development over time.

A final word about the sources of data for my discussions of the five ministers: Levinson's own study was based largely on personal interviews. Since all five of the ministers in this study have long since died, interviewing is impossible. Written documents were therefore used, with particular reliance on biographies. The danger in relying on biographies is that the biographers may be guilty of inaccuracy and distortion. In addition, all biographers attempt to place their subject's life within a convincing interpretive framework. Thus, it is possible that an individual may appear to belong in one of Levinson's five sequences because this is how the biographer chose to portray the subject's life. This danger may seem particularly serious when viewed in the abstract, however, it tends to dissolve as the reader of a biography begins to differentiate the "facts" from the biographer's interpretive schema. I am under no illusion that facts can be clearly isolated from the interpretive schema in which they occur, but it is not too difficult to identify those points in a biographer's narrative in which significant discrepancies occur between the interpretive schema and the facts this schema is intended to describe. Furthermore, the major concern in this study is not to contribute to the historical understanding of these five ministers, but to enhance the understanding of the lives of ministers in modern times. This practical concern far outweighs any interest in contributing to the historical understanding of these five individuals. For this reason, it seems appropriate to use existing biographies of these men as a major source of information concerning the major thesis of this study, which is that the latter half of a man's thirties is enormously influential on the course and nature of his whole career.

Chapter 2

Phillips Brooks:
Advancement Within a Stable
Life Structure

Levinson describes the "advancement within a stable life structure" pattern as one in which life proceeds more or less according to
expectations.[1] During the early phase of the settling-down period
(age thirty-three to thirty-six), the individual makes his primary commitments, defines his vocation, and gradually strengthens the initial
life structure. Then, during the later phase of the settling-down period, when involved in becoming his own man (age thirty-six to
forty), his personal ambitions receive external support and he continues to advance. It is true that he may experience much hardship and
suffering, but the stresses are manageable and the satisfactions out-
weigh the difficulties. It is also true that significant changes may occur during the settling-down period, but these represent advancement
(or difficulties) within the existing structure and not a change in this
basic structure.

When the settling-down period comes to a close and the midlife
transition comes into play (age forty to forty-five), the very successes
of the earlier period project this individual into a larger "senior"
world. This generally means new and expanded responsibilities that
are consonant with the existing life structure. These new responsibilities are evidences of success and indicate the continuing vitality of
the life structure formed earlier. On the other hand, Levinson points
out that the experience of success is always based to some degree on
illusion:

> Even when a man is doing well in an external sense, he may be
> gaining rewards that will turn out to have little meaning or value
> for him. His life may provide genuine satisfactions but at great

inner costs. In order to devote himself to certain goals, he may have to neglect or repress important parts of the self.[2]

However, if the individual whose life follows this sequence is more subject to illusion than those of the other types, Levinson warns against debunking such individuals. The advancement may not be worth the great costs involved in achieving it, but it is more likely that the advancement will have both its positive and negative elements, with the positive far outweighing the negative.

The minister I have chosen as representative of this type is Phillips Brooks. Brooks (1835-1893) was an Episcopalian clergyman and one of the foremost religious leaders in nineteenth-century America. He began his ministry in Philadelphia in 1859 (at age twenty-four) where he spoke out against slavery and gave strong support to the Union cause during the Civil War. He then moved to Boston in 1869 (at age thirty-four) where he became the rector of Trinity Episcopal Church in Boston. Here he gained a national and even international reputation as a gifted preacher and increasingly influential churchman. His theological views were moderate, but when he was selected by the Massachusetts Diocese to become its bishop in 1891 (age fifty-six), much controversy arose over his selection because his theological views were thought by many to be too liberal. He died suddenly, apparently of diphtheria, in 1893 at the age of fifty-eight. He is most remembered today for his preaching. Many of his sermons were published during his career as rector of Trinity Church and are readily available today. He never married.

CHILDHOOD AND ADOLESCENCE (1835-1855)

Brooks was descended from the Phillips and Brooks families. Both families had known each other from the beginning of the founding of Massachusetts Bay Colony two centuries before he was born. His paternal great-grandfather was a minister who also served in the Revolutionary War. His paternal grandfather was a businessman in Portland, Maine. His father, William Gray Brooks, left Portland at nineteen to begin a business in Boston. William spent many hours visiting in the home of his uncle, Peter Brooks, probably the wealthiest man in Boston at the time, and it was there that he met Mary Phillips, his future wife.

Mary Ann and William Brooks had six children, all sons. Phillips was the second son. The boys were initially raised in the family religious tradition of Congregationalism. When William and Mary Ann were married, they chose as their church home First Church of Boston, a famous church whose history can be traced to the founding of Massachusetts Bay Colony. The minister of First Church at the time, N. L. Frothingham, was the son-in-law of Peter Brooks. Two years after their marriage, however, Mary Ann began to have serious misgivings about the growing liberalism of First Church. In 1835, the same year that Phillips Brooks was born, Frothingham delivered an address on the thirtieth anniversary of his ordination and, on this occasion, expressed his agreement with many of the central tenets of the Unitarian views of William Ellery Channing. Frothingham said he found no scriptural basis for belief in the atonement, the doctrine of human depravity, eternal punishment, or the Trinity. It is not known whether Mary Ann Brooks was in the congregation to hear Frothingham's sermon, but it is known that she arranged to have her third son, George, baptized by a more conservative Congregational clergyman. Then, in 1840, she and her sister were confirmed in St. Paul's Church, one of the Episcopal churches in Boston. William Brooks did not immediately join Mrs. Brooks in converting to the Episcopal Church, but seven years later he too was confirmed. Phillips was twelve years old at the time of his father's confirmation. This event may have left a vivid impression on him, for from this time on he began to exhibit a very serious interest in religious matters. Moreover, the new rector at St. Paul's, Dr. A. H. Vinton, was to become his lifelong mentor. Brooks' biographer, Raymond W. Albright, points out that his "early associations with Doctor Vinton were merely the beginning of a lifelong friendship which continued to grow in later years, so that he rarely made a major decision without seeking the advice of his former rector and friend."[3]

He attended private school in Boston from age four to age eight, then attended a public grammar school until age eleven, when he was admitted with his older brother to Boston Latin School. He remained at Boston Latin School for five years, then entered Harvard College in the fall of 1851. His record at Boston Latin School was excellent, though not distinguished. He ranked third in his graduating class. His work at Harvard was similarly very strong, but not brilliant. Regarding his religious development during college, he was more open to liberal theology than would have been approved of by his mother, who had changed churches rather than submit to liberal views. Still, in his tendency toward open-mindedness during college, he also retained a strong appreciation for the beliefs and practices of the church in which he was raised. His academic pursuits were focused on English and classical literature. He developed an especially strong love for Alfred, Lord Tennyson's poetry, and Thomas Carlyle's essays. He avoided courses in elocution; his professors and classmates saw no signs of unusual ability as a public speaker, but he was recognized for the clarity of his writing. One of his more notable features was his large physical size. By the time he was eighteen years old, he reached his full height of nearly 6 feet 4 inches and weighed 160 pounds. He later gained considerably more weight and was thus an imposing figure in the pulpit.

His childhood and adolescence were, as far as can be determined, quite stable. The family was well settled in Boston and his father's business, a hardware store, was financially sound. He was sent to good schools and seemed to do well both academically and socially. He was occasionally recognized for his good conduct in school. He was evidently somewhat reserved and withdrawn during his years in grammar school and the Latin School, but not abnormally so. This reserve may have been due to physical awkwardness attributable to rapid growth. Albright also speculates on the possibility that the sense of security in his home and especially in his closeness to his mother may have limited his desire for wider associations.[4]

If there was an area of conflict in his childhood and adolescence, it was in religious matters. As noted, his mother converted to the Episcopal Church when he was five years old, and it was not until he was twelve that his father also converted. Like his father, he evidenced a similar slowness to follow his mother's desires in religious matters when he resisted her efforts to get him to prepare for confirmation. She asked Dr. Vinton to write a letter to her three older sons when they finished Sunday school, reminding them of their continuing obligation in religious matters, and she not only wrote Phillips about his own decision for the church but also asked him to remind his younger brother George of his responsibilities in this regard. Still, he was not confirmed until he was twenty-two years old, after he had spent a year in seminary.

If his childhood and adolescence reflected some conflict over his religious obligations, however, they do not appear to have been severe. His differences with his mother over confirmation, for example, were not of the sort that led to any estrangement between mother and son. Nor were his inclinations toward a more liberal theological perspective than hers during college significant enough to cause her any serious concern. By and large, he was the type of son who gave his mother little cause for worry. As he had been frequently commended at school for his "industry and good conduct," so also in his relationship to his parents, he was a son they could rely upon to do the right and proper thing.

EARLY ADULT ERA

Novice Phase

As noted in Chapter 1, Levinson divides the early adult era (age seventeen to forty) into two phases, the novice phase, which extends to age thirty-three, and the settling-down phase, which begins at age thirty-three and continues to age thirty-nine.[5] The novice phase is subdivided into three periods, the first of which is the early adult transition from age seventeen to twenty-two. It is followed by the entering of the adult world period from age twenty-two to twenty-eight, and the age thirty transition (age twenty-eight to thirty-three). I will use these divisions to structure the following discussion of Brooks' life through age thirty-three.

Early Adult Transition (1855-1859)

Brooks was just twenty years old when he graduated from Harvard College in July 1855. After graduation, he accepted an invitation to teach in the Boston Latin School. He viewed his teaching position as an opportunity to acquire some money so that he could go abroad to study in further preparation for college teaching. His first teaching job did not go well. He began with a class of younger boys but was assigned to an older class two or three months after the school year began. He evidently found it difficult to adjust to the older boys. They were a particularly unruly class, having forced three teachers before him to leave the school in frustration. He fared no better. His sixteen-year-olds locked him in his room, scattered explosive matches on the floor of the classroom, and threw buckshot in his face. He resigned his position in February, long before the year was out.

However, even if he had been able to handle the boys, he would eventually have clashed with the headmaster. In fact, he resigned immediately after the headmaster had gone to the school committee to inform them that he "had in him no single element of a successful school teacher" and asked for a replacement.[6] The committee hoped that he would stay on until his successor had been chosen, but he refused, quitting almost at once, even though he had no other prospects for work. He began to tutor several pupils in English studies and thereby earned a modest living, but his failure as a schoolteacher was deeply distressing to him, causing a wound to his ego that remained with him throughout his life. The headmaster undoubtedly contributed to his distress when he said that he had never known a man who, having failed as a schoolteacher, had succeeded in anything else.

Now he did not know what to do about his life. His earlier idea of going to Europe to prepare for college teaching now seemed rather unrealistic. Doctor Vinton invited him to come and visit with him about his future, but he at first declined. He continued to attend church with the family and kept himself busy tutoring and translating the classics, but he was reluctant to talk to Dr. Vinton about his future, perhaps because he sensed that the rector would suggest that he consider the ministry. He was also sensitive about his failure and understandably reluctant to talk about it, though not so demoralized that he was willing either to jump into the first job that came along or to simply accede to the advice of others. As he put it,

> If I am to choose a life for *myself,* which I am to live and for which I am to answer, let the choice be *really mine.* Let me say to my advisors: I receive your advice, but no dictation. Without presumption or vanity, humbly, earnestly, and firmly. I claim my own human and divine right to my own life.[7]

Having thus assured himself that he would make his own decision, and not let others make it for him, he consulted President Walker of Harvard as to what he thought he should do. Walker advised him to enter the ministry. He thereupon went to Dr. Vinton, whose earlier invitation he had not responded to, and the latter talked to him about the necessary steps involved in becoming a candidate for ministry.

In the course of their conversation, Dr. Vinton stressed the importance of both confirmation and conversion. This disturbed him somewhat, because he was consciously postponing confirmation, having resisted Dr. Vinton's earlier advice along these lines, and he could think of nothing that even remotely indicated that he could anticipate a conversion experience in the months ahead. He did not immediately accept the idea of going into the ministry either. His notebooks indicate that he was considering the three professions—law, medicine, and ministry—and in recounting the merits of each wrote, "the last is not unworthy."[8] While hardly an enthusiastic endorsement of the ministry as a calling, this comment indicates that he was at least giving the ministry some serious thought, and so his ruminations about what direction his life would take continued through the summer and early fall.

At length, he acted. Without telling anyone but his immediate family, he left Boston in late October 1856, and even though the fall term had already begun, he went down to the Episcopal seminary in Alexandria, Virginia, with the intention of entering there as a beginning student. The suddenness of his decision to go, his decision to go after the term had already begun, and the fact that he did not discuss his decision with Dr. Vinton, suggests that he was not yet certain that he wanted to enter the ministry. As he expressed it in his notebooks, he was embarking on an "experiment," one that he hoped would result in strengthening his interest in the ministry.[9]

However, he remained at Virginia Theological Seminary from October 1856 to July 1859 when he completed his studies. He was not very happy with his seminary training during the first year. The seminary was new and had a small faculty, consisting of only three men. He disliked being in the South, and reacted most strongly against the seminary's use of slaves to carry out the duties normally performed by servants. His major criticism of the seminary was that its academic standards were too low. After the broadening intellectual experiences of Harvard, he found the seminary to be less than stimulating. By early spring, he and two other first-year men were so discouraged that they began to write to other seminaries with the thought of transferring. These explorations, for one reason or another, came to nothing. All three returned to Virginia Theological Seminary in the fall.

During his first year in seminary, however, he also began to develop a vigorous social life. Shortly after his arrival in Virginia, he was invited to various parties, "each one only equaled in stupidity by the other."[10] Their stupidity aside, these parties probably helped him maintain the self-image of a young man who was still free, not yet on a course that would lead inevitably to his becoming a minister. Through these parties, he also met a young woman who invited him to remain in Virginia during the Christmas break rather than return to Boston for the holidays. This young woman, mentioned in a letter, was probably Jenny Fairfax, a member of one of Virginia's leading aristocratic families. After the holidays, he began to attend receptions at the Fairfax home and took increasing interest in Jenny. His letters to his family during the winter months contain numerous references to her attractiveness and charm. Then suddenly all references to her, and to other young women, cease. He gives no explanation for this in his letters, but does mention that on one or two occasions he went out to her home, only to find her not at home. We are led to assume she had other romantic interests.

One of the more intriguing consequences of his decision to remain in Virginia during Christmas, however, is that his mother decided to visit him instead. When his mother came to Virginia for the Christmas holidays, he made his first communion with her. This evidently initiated his preparation for confirmation which took place the following summer in Boston. His mother's visit was followed by a letter from his father requesting the necessary recommendation for confirmation from the dean of the seminary. Brooks promised to comply with this request, but added: "If it is not necessary that my name should be presented now, and if it will occasion no delay to postpone it, I should much prefer that it should be put off for a time."[11] Thus, he seems hesitant about making these religious commitments, but his parents seem determined to ensure that they will be made. Moreover, we are not told what effect his mother's visit during Christmas had on his lifestyle, either during the holidays themselves or during the subsequent months, but it is perhaps significant that his social life began to run aground after the Christmas holidays.

Disappointed in romance and under some parental pressure, he began to invest himself more in the life of the seminary. One form that this took was his participation with other Northern students in a program to teach the servants to read and write, and to petition for improvements in the servants' working conditions. The Southern students protested, threatening to tar and feather one of the Northern students if he did not leave the school. Brooks and the other Northern students stood by their colleague, and he himself issued the counter threat that, if this student was forced to leave, all the Northern students would leave together and would "publicly declare their reasons for withdrawing."[12] This threat, accompanied by a petition to the faculty requesting its assurance of their protection and freedom of speech, not only saved the student from forced withdrawal but also won faculty approval of the use of the prayer hall for free discussion.

Throughout his seminary career of nearly three years, he took considerable interest in the slavery issue. He not only assisted local blacks in securing their freedom, but also went to Washington to listen to public debates on slavery in Congress. His father responded to one of his letters in which he had commented on his work in behalf of blacks by noting that similar efforts were being made in Boston. His mother also wrote to him about the religious revival that was sweeping the country in 1858, implying that this revival, more than the slavery issue, should be uppermost in his understanding of his ministry. She asked him to write to his younger brother George about this resurgence in religious interest, hoping this would stimulate George's interest in spiritual matters, and she expressed the hope that the revival would extend as far south as Alexandria, Virginia. She wrote:

> The present religious feeling in the community seems different from the usual seasons of revival, as there is no undue excitement but almost everyone's soul seems stirred within them. They say there has not been such a state of feeling before for a hundred years. . . . The ministers here all seem very anxious and devoted in guiding such a state of things—they seem awed, as well as everyone else.[13]

She added her hope that "all the young ministers will be quickened and be filled with a double portion of the spirit to fit them for their great and holy work."[14] One senses that she included her own son in this anticipation that the young ministers would respond to this awakening. His father, however, took a more cautious view of the religious awakening in New England. He said that, at present, "it seems to be a healthy feeling and promises much good," but he added the warning that "it will require all man's wisdom to manage it properly so as not to run to excess and excitement. . . ."[15] In response, he reported back to his parents that there had been little evidence of the revival at the seminary in Virginia.

Besides his involvement in the issue of slavery, his other major activity was his engagement as a teacher during his third year in seminary. His duty was to teach thirteen men who wanted to enter the seminary but had failed to meet entrance requirements. Since he was the first to be chosen for this task, it reflected a vote of confidence by the seminary faculty. Moreover, it gave him an opportunity to prove to himself that he was capable of being a good teacher, thereby counteracting some of the humiliation he experienced in his earlier teaching failure. This vote of confidence from the faculty, and his effectiveness in his new role as teacher, also caused him to begin to think much more highly of the seminary and the training he was receiving there. He especially developed a strong affection for the dean of the seminary, Dr. William Sparrow, who recommended him for his first parish upon graduation.

Another change that occurred during the final year of his seminary training was that he became more involved in preaching. He was not pleased with his first sermon preached in the seminary chapel in October 1858, but he began to take considerable interest in the writing of sermons. As he wrote his brother William: "I can't recall many pleasanter hours than those I have spent writing my two or three first poor sermons. It seems like getting fairly hold of the plough, and doing something at last."[16] He continued to write sermons through the year, looking forward "with impatience, though with fear," to the time when he would preach to a congregation.[17]

Throughout his final year of studies, he struggled with the question of where he would go after graduation. The previous summer he had discussed the matter with his parents, and had apparently secured their approval of his decision not to return to the Boston area. Albright suggests that his reluctance to return to Boston was due to the fact that the Episcopal Church in Massachusetts was generally at a low ebb and that he had by no means forgotten that in Boston he was remembered as the Brooks boy who had failed as a teacher at the Boston Latin School.[18] We might add to these reasons the likelihood that he wanted to begin his ministry away from family influences. Ten years later, when he was considering accepting a call to Trinity Church in Boston, the fact that he would be returning to the family fold caused him some hesitation. We may assume that the hesitation was even greater for the young seminarian contemplating his first parish assignment.

It is also possible that his discussion with his parents during the summer of 1858 concerning his decision not to return to Boston created some difficulties in their relationship. While his father assured him that nothing could give his parents greater pleasure "than to have our children open their minds to us freely,"[19] his mother seems to have been rather disturbed by her son's current thinking about his future. She wrote him on his birthday in December, expressing the wish that he would "walk worthy of such calling and be faithful to your Master's work to win souls."[20] When he did not respond to his mother immediately, claiming illness and preoccupation with other matters as the reason, his father reminded him, "You have a good mother, value her."[21] This reminder, together with his receipt of Christmas gifts from the family, prompted him to write:

> If I ever can do anything to give pleasure or credit to you, a big part of the justification to myself will be in feeling that you are gratified, and are so adding to your other kindnesses that of taking my own efforts to help and improve myself as payment for your long labor to help and improve me. You may have thought it a little strange now and then that I haven't said this by word of mouth, but the truth is I can write what I feel deeply much easier and better than I can say it; but the feeling, I at least know, is none the less deep for that, let this explain a great deal of what you may have fancied is coldness in all my life, and more particularly in my new profession.[22]

This response might have gotten him off the hook, except that the letter smelled of tobacco and this disturbed his father, who expressed the hope that his suspicion that his son smokes is unfounded, but, if true, begging him that "if you value my good opinion or my wishes you will at once practice total abstinence in the matter."[23] He failed to respond to this query, so his father wrote again, and he still did not answer. He *did* respond to a letter from his brother William who, probably under prompting from his parents, suggested he take a pledge to give up smoking. He responded to William that he considered such a pledge almost absurd, given the fact that he smoked only two or three cigars per month.

This interchange, however insignificant the issue, indicates that his relations with his family were somewhat strained during his final year in seminary, the major cause probably being that he had decided not to return to the Boston area for his first parish assignment. His father, however, became reconciled to this prospect when Dr. Vinton, their rector in Boston, became rector at Holy Trinity Church in Philadelphia during Brooks' final year in seminary, and suggested to him that he would like to have him as his assistant. In serving under Dr. Vinton, his parents would at least have felt that their son was in good hands, but he was not so sure he wanted this either. He wrote his parents later in the spring that he had been invited to remain on at the seminary as head of the preparatory school and assistant in the chapel. He also mentioned the possibility of securing his own parish in Philadelphia, one for which he had been recommended by Dr. Sparrow.

In March 1859, this church, the Church of the Advent in Philadelphia, offered him the rectorship of the parish. He wrote to his father and to Doctor Vinton for advice. His father approved on the grounds that the Episcopal Church in Massachusetts was in disarray. His mother was more reluctant, but simply admonished him to be "sure and pray for God to direct you in your decision."[24] He accepted the position, assuring his family that he had "not accepted from any ambitious desire of occupying a conspicuous or responsible place."[25] He graduated from seminary the last day of June 1859, and was ordained the following day. Ten days later, he began his ministry at the Church of the Advent in Philadelphia.

His "early adult transition" came to an end with the beginning of his ministry in Philadelphia. By now, he was clearly committed to the ministry as his life's profession. Although he had entered the seminary uncertain about a career in ministry, much that occurred during his three years of seminary confirmed the appropriateness of this decision. The seminary faculty had entrusted him with a responsible teaching job, he had discovered the attractions of sermon writing, and he had become involved in the major social issue of the day in the problem of slavery. In a real sense, these three areas of interest— teaching, preaching, and social action—were to form the nucleus of his ministry throughout his life, with preaching being its central core. Thus, by the time he graduated, he had already begun to shape the contours of his ministry.

The early adult transition also involved achieving some independence from his family in Boston. The Brooks family was clearly a close-knit family. Not only was there a close relationship between himself and his parents, but also between the six brothers. His parents sometimes used the brothers' closeness to one another as a means of exerting their influence on one or another of their sons. He himself was enlisted by his mother to encourage his brother George toward a more spiritual life, and William was used by Phillips' father to attempt to terminate his smoking habit. He did not rebel against this family influence, but he did insist on making his own decision in the matter of choosing his first parish. His decision not to return to Boston was a difficult one for his family, especially his mother, to accept. On the other hand, the timing of Dr. Vinton's decision to move to Philadelphia was fortuitous, as it became an important factor in his parents' acceptance of his decision to locate in Philadelphia.

He seems to have had much respect for his father's views and sought his advice on at least one important occasion. His relationship to his mother was more ambivalent at this time. Her visit to the seminary during his first Christmas there was a generous gesture, but her decision to do this came after he had informed his family that he would be spending Christmas at the home of the young woman (probably Jenny Fairfax) he had mentioned in previous letters. Although no clear evidence supports that her visit had a direct effect on his romantic life, it did pressure him to begin thinking seriously about confirmation and to give greater thought to his vocational objectives. His mother also had rather strong ideas about what constituted good ministry. His letters relating his work with blacks were responded to with reference to the religious awakening in Boston. Having left Congregationalism for the Episcopal Church years earlier, she seems determined that her son would manifest the same passion for deep spiritual commitment and faithful communication of the Gospel that she sought and found in the Episcopal Church. Obviously, she was a deeply religious person who would not assume, merely because her son was in seminary, that he would prove a committed minister of the Gospel. His own desire to postpone his confirmation probably gave her reason to suspect that, if she were to let up, he might never make this commitment.

A less stable individual might have rebelled against this family influence. He might have decided against the ministry simply because he was subject to such influence. Instead, Brooks seems to have taken it with a grain of salt, sensing that it would not do to reject it outright. But as he had insisted before he began seminary, "If I am to choose a life for *myself,* which I am to live and for which I am to answer, let the choice be *really mine.* Let me say to my advisors: I receive your advice, but no dictation."[26] This seems to have been his attitude toward his family throughout his seminary years. As a result, it is fair to say that his decision to enter the ministry, and the type and location of ministry he decided on, was very much his decision. It is perhaps indicative of his future success as a minister that he rejected his parents' idea that he begin his ministry as an assistant under Dr. Vinton and instead moved immediately into his own rectorship, assuring his older brother William that he had not made this decision from "any ambitious desire."[27]

Entering the Adult World (1859-1863)

He remained at the Church of the Advent in Philadelphia for two and a half years. His formal duties included two sermons, a lecture, and a Bible class every week. He devoted considerable energy to the development of a good Sunday school and he greatly expanded his work in behalf of black slaves. It was rumored that he was among those responsible for helping John Brown get through Philadelphia safely and hiding him in Camden, New Jersey. Brooks entered an item in his notebook concerning Brown's death and surrounded it with a heavy black border. The following day, December 3, 1859, he wrote to his parents concerning Brown's "heroic devotion."[28] This letter frightened his parents, and his father wrote to advise him not to mix politics and religion, or to discuss political issues in the pulpit. He accepted his father's admonition, but complained that the Episcopal Church was being far too hesitant in interpreting the slavery issue.

He continued his involvement in the slavery issue during his ministry at Church of the Advent, but he was becoming even better known in Philadelphia for his preaching. His sermons were fully written out and, due to their length, he had to preach them very rapidly in order to complete them within thirty minutes. Since they were thirty manuscript pages in length (he never varied from this), he needed to preach at the rate of a page per minute. Years later, he was clocked by a shorthand expert in Westminster Abbey at 213 words per minute. This expert, Thomas Allen Reed, said he had never listened to anyone "who kept up such a continuous, uninterrupted flow of rapid articulation."[29] Pulpit exchanging was common in Philadelphia, and this contributed to his exposure as a preacher.

His popularity is perhaps best indicated by the fact that, before he had served a full year as rector at the Church of the Advent, he received at least five calls from other churches. Calls from St. John's Church in Cincinnati and Grace Church in San Francisco were extremely tempting, partly because they were offering far more remuneration than he was receiving at the Church of the Advent, but in the end he turned them down because attendance was steadily increasing, much progress had been made toward retiring the church's debt, and he got along very well with his congregation.

However, in 1861 (at age twenty-six), he received a call that he could not reject. His old mentor, Dr. Vinton, had accepted a call to a church in New York City. This created an opening at Holy Trinity Church in Philadelphia, and because he had preached for Dr. Vinton in his absence, parishioners at Holy Trinity were familiar with his skills. His father was opposed to his acceptance of the call on the grounds that Holy Trinity would be too much of a strain on the mental and physical powers of a young minister. He first declined the call, not on the grounds that the church would be too demanding (as his father had suggested) but because he had not yet gotten the Church of the Advent out of debt. Holy Trinity let the matter rest for six months, then issued a second call in which it promised to pay the remaining two-thousand-dollar indebtedness at the Church of the Advent if he would accept the call. In November 1861, at the age of twenty-six, he accepted the call to Holy Trinity, one of the most prominent churches in Philadelphia.

His acceptance of this call may be viewed as the event that marks the "Age 25 Shift." By accepting a second call, he could no longer view his decision to enter the ministry as an experiment. He was now in it "for real" and, barring some unforeseen circumstance, "for good." Also, the new situation was one in which he would be viewed as successor to his mentor. This would mean living up to his mentor's faith in him, but also meant that he was in a position to supersede him if his ministry proved successful. He was also moving to a prominent church, and this, in itself, would have important consequences for the shaping of his own vocation and his style of ministry.

He was to remain at Holy Trinity for eight years, through the "age thirty transition." Because he made no professional move between the ages of twenty-six and thirty-four, his professional life had at least greater outward stability than that of other ministers in our study during their late twenties. Furthermore, Holy Trinity Church was generous to him both in salary and in granting him a year's leave of absence after the conclusion of the Civil War in 1865. Thus, his particular church situation in his late twenties was also better, at least in external matters, than the situations of the other young men in our study. In regard to the generosity of Holy Trinity Church toward him, he was fully aware that in leaving the Church of the Advent for Holy Trinity, he was moving into a congregation of prominent social and business leaders. He acknowledged that he found in his new congregation "a mixture of snobbish aristocracy and a very great deal of wealth and luxury," but he also discovered there a "large amount of intelligence and refinement as well as of earnestness and devotion."[30] He was criticized by a Philadelphia newspaper, the *Sunday Dispatch,* for going to Holy Trinity, especially in light of his work for disadvantaged blacks, but he counteracted this criticism by immediately initiating programs for the poor sponsored by his parish.[31] He pointed proudly to the fact that more than 200 poor people were involved in the church's classes and societies, indicating that the church was not simply treating the poor as charity cases but was instead incorporating them into its activities and programs.

However, the major issue during his first years at Holy Trinity was the Civil War, which began when Brooks was involved in considering his call to Holy Trinity. When he assumed his duties in January 1862, there was much optimism among Northerners that the war would end quickly and decisively, but during the summer of 1862 the Union forces suffered severe setbacks. His brother George enlisted in the army and he himself, in September, heard that he was to be invited to become the chaplain of a new regiment being formed in Philadelphia. The invitation never materialized, and he remained in Philadelphia throughout the war. Albright suggests the possibility that leading members of his congregation intervened without his knowledge and dissuaded the regimental authorities from offering him the chaplaincy.[32]

Nonetheless, he contributed to the war effort by continuing to speak out in favor of President Lincoln's announcement in September that he would emancipate the slaves on January 1, 1863. Then, his brother George was killed in action in February, a deep personal loss that, coupled with continuing Union losses in the spring, prompted him and several other Episcopal clergymen to offer their services in behalf of the war effort. Through their efforts, more than 100 clergymen of various denominations in Philadelphia went to the mayor's office and asked to be set to work on the city's defenses. In July, it was learned that Lee's forces had been repelled at Gettysburg, so he and another clergyman went to Gettysburg to minister to the wounded. Later, in November, he preached a Thanksgiving Day sermon in support of emancipation. It was such a powerful sermon that it was widely circulated. In it, he noted that the Episcopal Church, "for the first time in her history . . . has set herself flatly, firmly, unmistakably against the sin of the nation."[33]

With the conclusion of the war imminent, his own entering the adult world period also came to an end. He was now twenty-eight years old and for the past two years had proven his ability to handle Holy Trinity Church. He had played an honorable role during the war as he supported the abolition of slavery and the war effort itself with unequivocal words and significant actions. He had been an indefatigable worker throughout the war years—preaching, teaching, organizing, and contributing to the war effort itself. He maintained this pace through the next year, and while his parish work continued to go well, he was discouraged by the political situation after the war. Lincoln had been assassinated and, in his view, the reconstruction was being badly handled by President Andrew Johnson. These disappointments, together with his heavy workload in the parish, began to take their toll. It became clear in the early months of 1865 that he needed a rest. Recognizing this, the parish gave him a year's leave of absence with full salary.

Age Thirty Transition (1865-1869)

He began the "age thirty transition" (at age twenty-nine) with a year of travel in Europe and the Holy Land. During this trip, he engaged in some brief theological study in Germany, enough to convince him that he lacked the necessary background and technical skills to be a scholar. He also visited sights associated with the life of Martin Luther, his favorite religious figure. After touring other parts of Europe, he went to the Holy Land, and while there he wrote the words to the popular Christmas hymn, "O Little Town of Bethlehem." These words were subsequently set to music by the organist at Holy Trinity, Lewis H. Redner.

On the surface, this trip did not significantly alter his understanding of his life or ministry. Unlike one of our other ministers—John Henry Newman—his trip during his age thirty transition did not result in an immediately noticeable reformulation of his view of his ministry. However, in the months following his return to Philadelphia, his general demeanor underwent a rather significant change. Perhaps it was his sense of coming to the end of his formative years with certain developmental tasks undone, especially those of marriage and family. Or perhaps it was the fact that he had found his occupational niche with such obvious success and was now in the process of asking whether it had been gained at too great an inner cost. Furthermore, in the spring after his return, he was offered, but declined, the deanship of the new Episcopal seminary in Cambridge, Massachusetts, near Harvard University. We can surmise that this position was attractive to him in many ways, but the prospect of a return to Boston at this time made it difficult for him to view the offer on its own merits.

Whatever the causes—and they were probably multiple—during the three years after his return from Europe, he did not seem quite himself. In the winter of 1868-1869, the actress Fanny Kemble, who had rented rooms in the same boarding house, took great interest in him. She invited him to take his meals with her in her private dining room. He had breakfast and dinner with her for a number of months, but the relationship eventually failed. This disappointment added to his moodiness during this period of the age thirty transition. As Albright points out,

> While Brooks continued in perfect health, he developed during these days an unusual spirit of joviality which mystified and occasionally disturbed his best friends. At times it seemed natural for him to be gay and full of fun. But again, even before or after the performance of a most serious duty, he would display an inappropriate mirth. None of his associates could explain the phenomenon; it was all the more puzzling because it seemed harder than ever to engage him in intimate conversation.[34]

Albright goes on to consider the possible reasons for this change in Brooks' behavior. He asks,

> Was he afraid that men thought less of him because of his romantic failure and was he thus trying to cover up his embarrassment? Was he trying to show a new philosophy of life or how human he could be? Was it an attempt to compensate for a natural shyness or perhaps an increasing self-consciousness? Had he tried to build a substitute for the grace of easy conversation at which he never shone?[35]

Reluctant to try to determine which of these possible explanations was the most important, Albright suspects that "Brooks had been unconsciously driven by the anguish of recent months to find his defense in this inordinate and unnatural external gaiety."[36] And he further suspects that now, at the age of thirty-three, Brooks was "forlorn about his bachelor status."[37]

Although Albright suggests that Brooks "must have found the arrangement" of taking meals with Miss Kemble "a happy one,"[38] she was, in fact, twenty-six years older than he, and would have been in her mid to late fifties at this time, old enough, one might say, to be his mother. She had divorced in 1845, reluctantly accepting her husband's terms that she relinquish all rights to access to her two daughters. He, however, had died in 1867, and she, like Brooks, was a very strong abolitionist, whereas her husband had been a Southern plantation owner. Kemble's biographer, Catherine Clinton, notes that by 1869, at the time she and Brooks shared meals together, her idealism was gone because she believed that the legacy of slavery would continue despite the victory of the Union Army.[39] Some years later, her relationships with her daughters were restored, and one of them married an Episcopal clergyman, but at the time she was acquainted with Brooks, her oldest daughter was overcome by grief over her father's death and her youngest daughter had returned to Georgia to manage the plantation in order to protect his legacy. Thus, Fanny Kemble's loss of her idealism over the slavery issue seems to have been related to the power her ex-husband exerted over her daughters from the grave.[40] Clearly, Brooks met her when she was at an emotional low ebb and may have misinterpreted their conversations as more personal and less pastoral than they actually were.

He continued to serve Holy Trinity Church well through the age thirty transition period, but was almost beseiged with calls from other churches. One of the churches that sought him was Trinity Church in Boston. He had previously been asked to come to Trinity as an assistant, but had declined. Now, in 1868 (at age thirty-three), he was being invited to serve as Trinity's rector. One of the inducements offered him was that he would continue to serve in a parish capacity but could also contribute to the development of the new Episcopal seminary in Boston. His old mentor, Dr. Vinton, was opposed to his moving to Boston and his own parishioners pleaded with him to stay. Other friends felt that some day he would leave Philadelphia, but that New York would be much better than Boston. So, after a month's deliberation, he declined the call.

The Bostonians did not take this response as his final answer. Many influential Bostonians wrote, asking him to reconsider, and his mother urged him to consider his debt to Boston "and pay it in my lifetime."[41] Trinity Church continued its campaign to secure Brooks and, nearly a year later, he finally agreed to come. However, even after agreeing to come, he expressed serious misgivings about his decision. Writing to his brother William:

> At the present moment I feel more attached to Holy Trinity than I ever did in my life and feel a corresponding dislike toward Trinity on Summer Street. . . . But I dare say the day will come when I shall like the Summer Street church quite as well.[42]

He concluded by saying, "I don't know. It's all an experiment," the word he had used to describe his decision to begin seminary.[43]

Undoubtedly, an important reason for his uncertainty about this new undertaking was the fact that it would put him back in close proximity to his family. Albright points out that although he was going to a new situation, in reality it was an old one for which he had been born and bred and for which he was even better fitted.[44] There is no doubt that he was better fitted for work in Boston now, but the fact that he was returning to the place where he had been "born and bred" may well have caused some anxiety. At least, the thought of returning to his family home was not so attractive that he jumped at the chance to return. He had rejected the deanship of the new Episcopal seminary in Boston and held out for a year before accepting the rectorship of Trinity Church. These are not the actions of a man who simply could not wait to be in close proximity to his family. Indeed, one suspects that, in deciding to return to Boston, he was reaching the painful acknowledgment that he may never establish a home and family of his own. In this respect, the return to Boston may have meant accepting his inability to find a wife and begin a family.

He left his church in Philadelphia in early August 1869, at the age of thirty-four, and began his work in Boston in October. The age thirty transition was at an end, and he was embarking on a new venture as he faced the settling-down period.

The Tasks of the Novice Phase

How well did he lay the foundations for the next period in his life? How well had he carried out the tasks of the novice phase?

Forming a Dream. It is clear that he had succeeded very well in forming a professional identity. He had great success in his ministry in two Philadelphia churches, and he became known well beyond the confines of his own parishes. He appears to have been very good at organizing the corporate life of the parishes he served and, in addition, enjoyed an excellent reputation as a preacher. Albright believes that his best sermons were, in fact, preached during the Philadelphia period.[45] At this stage of his life, his Dream did not extend much beyond his identity as a good parish pastor. He expressed much personal dissatisfaction with the general conventions of the church, and generally did not participate in them. He had little desire to become a church leader. Friends felt he was destined for major positions in the church, and were convinced he would be a bishop some day, but he did not encourage such ideas. On the other hand, being a good pastor involved, in his view, extensive civic involvements. A large part of his Dream, and perhaps still another reason for his discouragement after the war, was the view that the parish minister is involved in civic and political matters. This is evident in the fact that he viewed his move from Holy Trinity to Trinity as not simply moving from one church to another but as moving from one city, with its unique religious and social problems, to another city, with its own unique problems. Both those who argued he should stay in Philadelphia and those who urged him to come to Boston centered their arguments on the differences in the two cities. A Philadelphian argued that Boston was characterized by odd religious beliefs while Philadelphia was overcome with sin.

The implication was that Brooks' ministry could have a greater impact in Philadelphia than in Boston.

As to his preaching and its place in his Dream, it is not clearly evident that he aspired to be a great preacher. As noted earlier, he worked hard on sermons while in seminary and continued to work hard on them during his years in Philadelphia, but it was not his intention to cast an emotional spell over his listeners. Moreover, he gave much attention to the writing of a sermon but it was not until years later that he devoted serious attention to his delivery. On the other hand, the fact that he *did* devote considerable time and energy to his sermon writing indicates that he gained genuine satisfaction from writing. His ability to put his thoughts into written form, an ability that dated back to his college years, was undoubtedly one reason that he considered the possibility of becoming a college professor. In fact, if any dimension of his professional Dream remained unfulfilled, it was his desire to prove himself as a scholar. His earlier plans to go to Europe to study to become a college professor were aborted when he failed in his first teaching job at Boston Latin School. Then, during the age thirty transition, he got his chance to go to Europe and to study theology, but he now recognized that he lacked the technical skills and the years of specialization in a particular theological discipline to become a first rate theologian and college professor. Yet, throughout his career, he was offered academic positions and served academic institutions in various informal ways. What he consistently resisted, perhaps partly out of a sense of inferiority, were opportunities to become a member of a theological faculty. In light of his great success as a parish pastor, such decisions were undoubtedly wise, but in terms of his Dream, they reflect certain unfulfilled aspirations. In short, his Dream focused almost entirely on his professional life. If he had aspirations outside of his career, ones related largely to the desire for marriage and a family, they never materialized.

Mentor relationships. Brooks was able to use his mentor relationships wisely. He relied on Dr. Vinton for advice, yet he was free enough of Vinton's influence that he decided to go to Boston even though Vinton had advised against it. Dean Sparrow was also helpful to him in securing his first parish. One senses, however, that he needed relatively little help from mentors, that his own motivations and abilities were so strong that his mentors' role was largely in the area of helping him think through what he ought to do, not in telling him what to do or in pulling strings for him. After his initial parish position at the Church of the Advent, his own popularity and obvious ability generated his subsequent opportunities. If anything, the danger was that men such as Dr. Vinton would give advice that might hamper his full utilization of his abilities.

Thus, by the end of the novice period, he did not seem to need his mentors. In fact, he was beginning to serve as advisor to younger ministers, including a younger brother, in their first year of ministry. In terms of Levinson's theory,[46] this shift toward being a mentor is appropriate because he was now eight or nine years older than recent seminary graduates. They would not have turned to him, however, if it were not evident that he was successful in his own right and was already in a position to provide means of access into their chosen profession.

Formation of an occupation. I have indicated that his Dream was largely focused around his professional identity. He did not have major interests (artistic, leisure time) outside of his ministry. However, his formation of an occupation showed steady progress after his initial failure as a teacher. Even in this failure, it is evident that he was faced with a very difficult situation and was not the first teacher to quit in utter frustration. Another indication of his success in forming an occupation is that his parishioners were always anxious for him to remain and used salary increases and liberal vacation policies to induce him to stay. When he did decide to move on, his congregation could resign itself to the fact that he was destined for larger things, and that they could not expect to hold onto him indefinitely. This made his decision to move even more difficult, and is one of the reasons that these decisions were made only after much soul-searching. In each case, however, he left the church on very amicable terms.

One key to his success in forming an occupation was his ability to relate to people of different social and economic classes. Although Holy Trinity was a well-to-do church, and he was able to cope with this, he was also able to work well with the underprivileged. As he reached the end of the novice period, therefore, he had already experienced considerable success in the formation of an occupation. Still a young man, he was being sought after by some of the most influential Episcopal churches in the country.

Marriage and family. In this fourth area of marriage Brooks experienced his greatest difficulty. He had brief romances during seminary but nothing really came of them. One has the distinct impression that the termination of these relationships was not by his choice. Apparently, his later involvement with actress Fanny Kemble was also terminated not by his choice but hers. Whether it was realistic for a minister to consider marriage to an actress, or to a woman much older than himself, the fact remains that he came to the end of the novice period neither married nor with any real prospects of marriage. He had one other close relationship with a woman years later. This was from 1886 to 1890 when he had a close friend in Gemma Timmins, who was twenty-four years old in 1886. He was fifty-one. This relationship, in which he apparently did not seriously consider marriage, came to a tragic end with Gemma's death in 1890.

Although his love relationships never worked out, his relationships with his brothers and with other ministers his age remained close and congenial throughout his life. He had an excellent relationship with his brother William and his wife, whom he relied on more and more during his years in Boston to take care of his financial affairs and his house. During his novice period, his relations with his parents were not always smooth, but he was strong enough to keep his parents, especially his mother, from attempting to dominate his life. His decision to return to Boston, for example, does not appear to have been much influenced by his mother's request that he consider his debt to Boston and repay it in her own lifetime. He was not the type to submit easily to such emotional blackmail.

The only serious liability in his personal relationships, then, was the fact that his efforts to gain a wife were unsuccessful. It is difficult to determine why this was the case. Albright depicts him as shy and withdrawn, not given to easy conversation.[47] This may have been part of the problem, but it does not explain the fact that his relationship with Fanny Kemble was terminated after months of regular breakfasts and dinners together. The possibility also exists that he set his sights a bit too high. His first serious relationship was with the daughter of a leading family in Virginia. His second serious relationship was with a famous actress. It is quite possible that neither of these women felt he had as much to offer them as they had to offer him— socially, financially, and so on. Undoubtedly many eligible young women of significant accomplishment and ability in his own parishes would have valued the life he could have provided them. It is difficult to imagine Jenny Fairfax or Fanny Kemble in the role of a minister's wife.

With the exception of forming a marriage and family, Brooks had negotiated his life tasks exceedingly well. He was well established in his career and had begun to develop special skills in his profession (especially preaching and care of the parish), and had begun to serve as mentor to younger ministers just beginning their careers. As he stood on the threshold of a long and distinguished career in Boston, he had laid his foundations well. During the period of settling down, his life consisted largely of consolidating the gains he had made in the earlier period.

The Settling-Down Phase

Settling Down and Becoming His Own Man (1869-1877)

In many cases, the early settling-down period (age thirty-three to thirty-six) and the later settling-down period called "becoming one's own man" (age thirty-six to forty) mark two fairly distinct periods in the life of a minister in midcareer. For Brooks, however, the two periods are of a single piece. He was thirty-four years old when he went up to Boston and he remained at Trinity Church throughout the settling-down period. Almost immediately on his arrival in Boston, he set about the task of becoming his own man. The opportunity for this was already there for, unlike his previous pastorate, he was called to Trinity because he had a reputation as a minister who could do great things for a congregation. In his previous pastorate, he had been chosen as a young man on the way up, but he was not yet thought of as the individual who could almost single-handedly make or break a church. In coming to Boston, no one questioned that he had come to lead the church and to be responsible for its future.

Thus, very early in his ministry in Boston, he became convinced that the church needed to relocate. He had perhaps intimated this conviction to his brother William even before he came when he confessed to having little enthusiasm for the church "on Summer Street."[48] He felt that Trinity Church was too close in proximity to St. Paul's Church and was no longer ministering to the people in the community. After months of efforts, he finally persuaded the church leaders that the church should relocate. A site was chosen in early

1871, less than two years following his arrival in Boston. However, the cornerstone was not laid until 1874, when he was thirty-nine years old, and the church was not completed until 1877, eight years after he had come to Boston. The old church building was completely destroyed by fire in 1872, so the congregation met in Huntington Hall of the Massachusetts Institute of Technology for five years, until the new church was finished.

The early years of his ministry in Boston were much like his years in Philadelphia. He was besieged with requests to speak at various functions—civic, educational, and religious—and served on numerous civic and religious boards. He was a Harvard overseer, Visitor to Harvard Divinity School, a member of the State Board of Education, a member of the Massachusetts Indian Commission, a trustee of Philadelphia Divinity School, and a supporter of the Young Men's Christian Association and the Hampton Institute, a school for blacks.

He also spent much time with parishioners and nonparishioners who had personal problems. He spent many evenings at home counseling and assisting troubled individuals. His family also occupied some of his time. He regularly had Sunday dinner with his parents. However, with the exception of his brother William, his brothers were no longer living in Boston, so his major family responsibilities were limited to visiting his parents and William's family. They, in turn, recognized that he was giving himself more and more to his work, to the detriment of his physical condition. He had little time for exercise, began to grow much heavier, and was ill more often. His busy schedule was also beginning to affect his sermons. His first years in Boston were not fruitful in terms of preaching. He wrote only forty new sermons, relying for the remainder on sermons previously preached in Philadelphia. In addition, toward the end of the settling-down period, he began to suffer voice failure in his preaching, and in 1875 he began to take voice lessons to rectify the problem. All these were signs that he had become overextended, and was paying a heavy personal price for his popularity and success. In Philadelphia he had found time during the week to devote to the composition of thirty-page sermons. He was not finding time to do so in Boston, where he was subject to a much larger variety of claims on his time.

However, a continuing inspiration was Trinity's building program. The plans called for a massive structure, and he was personally involved in all facets of the planning. Also, if some of the church's leaders had been reluctant to move into a major building program at first, the destruction of the old church by fire attested to the wisdom of the decision. The major frustration for him and for the congregation was that the planned edifice was so massive that they needed to meet in an auditorium for five years. Perhaps his tendency to give less time to his sermons during this period was due partly to the fact that the church was meeting in surroundings that were not as conducive to worship, yet it is also a testimony to his leadership skill and ministerial presence that the church continued to grow during this period when it lacked a permanent place of worship.

Besides the building program, another important feature of his ministry during this settling-down period were his ecumenical activities. He cooperated with ministers of other denominations on a variety of social issues, and often participated in non-Episcopal services. He was reprimanded by his bishop for allowing a non-Episcopalian minister to participate in a wedding that he conducted. Years later, his cooperation with ministers of other denominations, especially Congregational and Unitarian, was the argument used against his confirmation as Bishop of Massachusetts. In light of his mother's earlier decision to leave the Congregational Church because of its leanings toward Unitarianism, it is not difficult to see why these ecumenical activities would create problems. It is a testimony to his parents' increased ability to allow their son his independence that these ecumenical activities did not result in family conflicts. In his ecumenical activities, as in his insistence on launching into a major building program, Brooks was clearly "becoming his own man."

The settling-down period came to a close before the new church edifice was completed, but he had accomplished a great deal during this time. In addition to increased responsibilities in the care of the parish, his civic interests were greatly expanded as he began to sit on educational, city, and state boards and commissions. Although still not greatly involved in the activities of the Episcopal Church at the national level, his ecumenical activities in the Boston area itself gave him greater exposure to church life outside his own parish than he might have gained from greater involvement in church affairs at the national level.

During the settling-down period he gave up the cultivation of the inner spiritual life, the price that the successful minister typically pays during this period. It was not so much that he had relinquished extended periods of prayer and meditation; he had never been given to the life of meditation. He had let slip through his fingers the time set aside every week for sermon preparation. Sermon preparation had provided the opportunity to think and reflect. It was the one activity in his ministry that gave him unmitigated satisfaction. Unlike the minister for whom sermon preparation is sheer drudgery, for him it was an opportunity for self-expression and was nearly conflict free. The conflict-free nature of his sermon preparation is evident in the published sermons themselves. They are very lengthy, yet can be read with minimal effort because they have natural flow and movement, and great vitality. As Erik Erikson said of Luther's lectures, the written sermons of Phillips Brooks reflect a kind of "liberated craftsmanship."[49] Thus, in relinquishing his time for sermon preparation, he was less in direct communication with the sources of his own strength and power as a minister. In a sense, he was drawing on the reserves of his preaching ministry in Philadelphia. That he was able to get away with it, to continue to be an extremely effective preacher, testifies to the excellent foundations laid in his earlier ministry.

This is not to say that his ministry in Boston was not as effective as his ministry in Philadelphia. His Boston ministry, however, was less characterized by innovative ideas, warm personal relationships, and daring political involvement, features of his Philadelphia ministry that had been the basis for a greatly expanded range of influence and responsibility, and increased access to the settings in which important community decisions are made. If his political involvement in the Philadelphia days was symbolized by his mobilization of ministers to appear at the mayor's office prepared to build defenses against Lee's army, his involvement in Boston is best exhibited by his appointment to a large number of educational committees and civic commissions. His reappointment to many of these committees reflects the seriousness he gave to these responsibilities. In a sense, his community involvements and extensive building program clearly indicate that he was planning to remain in Boston for many years, and expected to be viewed as one who had made deep and abiding commitments to the city of Boston and to Trinity parish.

His personal lifestyle changed somewhat from his Philadelphia days, but the changes were relatively minor. Because he was near his family, he spent more time with family than he had in Philadelphia. Family contacts were well regulated and, given his parents' strong interest in having him return to Boston, they involved less of his time than one might have anticipated. From time to time he would complain that he did not have the close friends he had enjoyed in Philadelphia; the boarding house and a couple with whom he spent at least an evening a week in Philadelphia provided friendships for which he was unable to find substitutes in Boston. Yet, he was no less appreciated by his congregation and was treated equally well in terms of financial remuneration and liberal vacation policies.

All in all, he was on the verge of achieving senior status as a minister and religious leader. He was still not actively involved in the general convention of the Episcopal Church, but he was a recognized spokesman for a moderate Episcopalianism that resisted liturgical formalism. Volumes of his sermons were already being published, and a number of his occasional lectures were also in circulation. Clearly, his settling-down period was one of continuing professional advancement within a stable life structure.

MIDDLE ADULT ERA

Although my primary concern here is with the novice and settling-down periods in Brooks' life, a review of his ministry in midcareer would not be complete without some mention of his middle adult era, beginning with the midlife transition (1876-1881), roughly ages forty-one to forty-six.

Midlife Transition

Albright points out that the year 1877 (when Brooks was forty-two) "marked a distinct epoch in the life of Phillips Brooks."[50] The next five years were marked by increased popularity, but he also experienced increased loneliness (suggestive of the attachment/separateness polarity). The completion of the new church edifice now afforded him an impressive setting in which to preach. Moreover, he was invited to deliver the Beecher Lectures at Yale, which gave him the opportunity to reflect on his preaching principles and to communicate them to others. When published, these lectures were very well received both in the United States and in Europe. The same year, Harvard University awarded him the doctor of divinity degree.

However, if he was enjoying greater fame in his professional life, the years of his midlife transition were filled with bereavement. His father died in 1879 and, as testimony of his deep sense of loss, he devoted his Bohlen Lectures at Philadelphia Divinity School a month later to the argument that Jesus' relation to humanity was always based on the idea of God's universal *fatherhood*. He pointed out that the truly wise man knows that the

> idea of Jesus has bound our ignorance and the knowledge of God together, and made it possible for man so to count all that his Father knows as the great region for his soul to grow in, and so to value the little he knows as the gift and pledge and promise of his Father who knows all, that he can neither be proud of his own wisdom nor be dismayed before his own ignorance; but must live, as the child lives in his father's house, the happy life of complete humility and unlimited hope.[51]

Since he wrote most of his Bohlen Lectures during advent of 1878 when he knew his father was dying (the death occurred on January 7, 1879), his emphasis on the fatherhood of God, and his comparison of the Christian life to that of the child living in his father's house in complete humility and unlimited love, was almost certainly a tribute to his own father.

The following year, on February 1, 1880, his mother died. Albright believes that her loss was a greater blow to Phillips than it was to any of his brothers; without the security that her presence and her encouraging words gave him, even in her declining years, he now felt utterly alone, and he was not fitted for such a role.[52] When friends tried to console him, he replied that she had been the happiest part of his life, that all his life he had feared and dreaded the thought of losing her and that now "with God's help she will be more to me than ever."[53] All the brothers felt the loss of their father very keenly, but the death of their mother marked the end of an era, for she had been the one around whom the family life, interest, and ideals had centered.

This was not the end of his bereavement. The following year, in 1881, Dr. Vinton also died. The death of his oldest mentor came at a very difficult time for him. He had just been offered the position of preacher to Harvard University and Plummer Professor of Christian Morals. This offer was quite remarkable because Harvard was historically related to Congregationalism and, more recently, to Unitarianism. Harvard's President Eliot assured him that he and those who voted to invite him to come were fully aware of the fact that he was Trinitarian in his doctrinal views. He was urged by many, including his brother Arthur, to accept the post. He confessed that he was not particularly desirous of the position, but wondered how he could possibly refuse the invitation, it being so attractive and appropriate to his own capacities.

Uncertain what to do, he had invited Dr. Vinton, now living in retirement, to spend Passion Week with him because he wanted to talk with him about the offer and whether he ought, this time, to accept it. Vinton did come and apparently influenced Brooks to remain where he was, for shortly thereafter, he informed President Eliot that he had decided to remain at Trinity. Then, eight days later, Dr. Vinton died. Brooks preached the memorial sermon both in Boston and in the Church of the Holy Trinity in Philadelphia, where both he and Dr. Vinton had been rectors. He was clearly melancholy both over the death of his old mentor and the death of the prospect of his return to Harvard. It was with considerable sadness that he described his meeting with President Eliot in which he made his decision known. President Eliot

> said that he was sorry and didn't know where to look; and then I came away. It was the quietest death of the pretty little project that you can conceive of, and the pretty little project never looked so pretty as it does now in death. Just at this moment I feel as if I would rather be Preacher at Cambridge than rector of fifty Trinities.[54]

Entering Middle Adulthood

The three deaths and the Harvard decision took their toll both mentally and physically. He continued working the remainder of the year but sensed his need for a long rest. Consequently, around Easter 1882 (at age forty-seven) he asked the wardens and vestrymen at Trinity Church to grant him an extended vacation so that he might regain his perspective. They agreed to his request, granting him fifteen months absence. He spent the time in Europe. On his return, the most notable change in him was his emphasis in his preaching on the necessity of witnessing to Christ. From this time on until his death in 1893, he continually returned to the theme of the incarnation of God in

Christ.[55] Viewed retrospectively, this emphasis on the centrality of Christ in the Christian faith can be traced, at least in gestation, to his Bohlen Lectures shortly after the death of his father. The painful series of deaths in 1879-1881, and the difficult decision to turn down the opportunity to preach and teach at Harvard, seem to have inspired him to preach with new determination and clarity on the fundamentals of the Christian faith. The decision not to return to Harvard, the citadel of Unitarian theology, seems to have prompted him to give much greater thought to the importance of Christ as the witness to the universal Father.

In a certain sense, Brooks needed opportunities such as the Harvard offer to help him clarify in his own mind where his convictions really lay. In much the same way that he became deeply involved in the slavery issue after the termination of his social involvement with Virginia aristocracy, he discovered his deep love for traditional doctrines of Trinity, Christology, Revelation, and Atonement after he had decided that Unitarian Harvard was not for him.

He remained at Trinity Church in Boston for eight more years, when despite some formidable opposition, he was elected Bishop of Massachusetts. In retrospect, the decision to remain at Trinity Church was important in that it is very doubtful that he would have been considered for the bishopric had he left Trinity Church in 1881 and gone to Harvard. His tenure as bishop was brief—less than two years—but in that time he distinguished himself as a bishop who took considerable interest in his responsibility as mentor to young men who wanted to enter the Episcopal ministry. As indicated earlier, his death at age fifty-eight was quite sudden, apparently caused by diphtheria, an acute infectious bacterial disease characterized by weakness, high fever, and difficulty breathing.

CONCLUSION

Brooks' life clearly reflects the sequence of "advancement within a stable life pattern." His *stability* is reflected in the fact that, in his thirty-four years of professional life, he served only three churches. The *advancement* is reflected in the fact that each move he made was a step upward in terms of responsibility and challenge. The fact that his life culminated in his election as bishop also indicates that his life was one of steady advancement in the Episcopal Church.

This pattern of advancement within a stable life pattern does not mean, however, that his life was one of constant and unrelieved satisfaction. During a brief period in his life, the age thirty transition (early thirties), he seemed to be forcing himself to act jovially when he did not feel that way at all. Although he overcame this period of exaggerated congeniality, he had another more severe period of emotional strain during his midlife transition (early forties) when he requested an extended leave of absence from his church. In this case, the deaths of his parents, his earliest mentor, and his decision to reject the offer of a preaching and teaching position at Harvard, left his life in a diminished state. Thus, while his life reflected the sequence of advancement within a stable life structure, this does not mean that it was a life of unmitigated happiness, even in his professional growth and development. Some of his most difficult times, for example, were those in which he was forced to decide between his present situation and the offer of another attractive situation. Although he may have enjoyed to some extent the attention that such offers brought him, one senses that the pleasure was greatly outweighed by the genuine agony he went through in deciding which course to take.

Significantly, much of the stability of his life pattern was because he rejected numerous attractive offers. If he had accepted more offers, his life would have manifested continuing advancement, but with less appearance of stability. His stability was therefore bought at the price of rejecting attractive possibilities for ministry, but this stability also enabled him to acquire considerable influence, first in Philadelphia and then in Boston. In both places, he acquired a leadership role in the community that would not have been possible, even for a man of his abilities, if he had made more frequent moves. Moreover, his fame as a preacher may not have been so widespread if he had not also acquired much influence in the community through his other activities. His sermons were influential partly because they were the words of an articulate spokesman for a moderate progressivism in matters of church polity and civic and national affairs.

Did Brooks fulfill his Dream? Among the five ministers in our study, his life was undoubtedly the most consistently successful. Although Wesley has had greater lasting influence as a church leader, Brooks was the most consistently effective minister in his own lifetime, among his own contemporaries. Perhaps most remarkably, he accomplished this by expressing his convictions and responding with considerable freedom to the issues of the day. He did not gain his influence by being cautious or by unquestioning submission to church leaders. He could exercise this freedom because he always enjoyed the respect and support of his own parishioners and because he had no strong desire to rise within the church hierarchy.

Much of the support he enjoyed from his parishioners was gained by tireless work in their behalf. A big man physically, he communicated a sense of boundless energy that was being expended solely for the sake of others. As many of his sermons attested, he believed that individuals have considerably more resources available to them than they realize. They are spiritually stronger than they think. They have greater possibilities and potentialities than they recognize. The situation is always more hopeful than they realize or appreciate. As their minister, he saw his task to be that of encouraging his parishioners, both by word and example, to recognize and utilize the vast store of personal and spiritual resources available to them. As one infrequent listener of his sermons observed after his death, the cause of his death was not overwork, as some had suggested, but his determination to give dramatic force to his conviction that people have enormous resources if they would only recognize them:

> I recall the curious feeling of physical exhaustion that came upon me as I left the church. It was like nothing so much as relaxation following a severe but victorious struggle in some athletic contest. And I remember wondering even then, "If this so affects me, what must it be to him, and how can he bear it all?" It must have been this which finally wore him out, rather than the pressure of what most of us call work. When he was preaching he was pouring out strength as no other man could, as well as putting the power of his listeners to the utmost strain.[56]

By exuding great personal strength, Brooks embodied his conviction that all individuals possess greater strength than they realize. Thus, a major aspect of his advancement within a stable life pattern was the fact that he was recognized as a man of great strength and endurance. Very early in his career, churches recognized that he could handle positions normally held by men of much greater experience. One must believe that much of the reason for this confidence in his ability to do the job was because he was perceived as a man who could shoulder heavy responsibility without complaint.

Chapter 3

Jonathan Edwards: Decline or Failure Within a Stable Structure

In describing the pattern of decline or failure within a stable life structure, Levinson says that some representatives of this group fail in gross and obvious ways during the settling-down period, while others achieve a good deal of external success but fail in certain crucial respects that make the entire enterprise seem pointless or fruitless in their eyes.[1] Among the subjects in Levinson's study who fit in this category, none made significant professional advances in their late thirties. A few resigned themselves to this fact and found other ways—family, community life, and so on—to gain a sense of overall progress in their lives but, in most cases, the failure to advance professionally had a negative effect on these other aspects of life as well.

Levinson does recognize, however, that for some men failure in the later settling-down period ("becoming one's own man") can be a genuine boon in that it may shake an individual out of a rut and cause him to use the midlife transition to free himself from the commitments of his settling-down period. He finds new goals and new satisfactions, and defines the ladder of advancement more broadly. The overall quality of his life becomes more important than success in a single area, for example, professional standing.

Jonathan Edwards represents a minister who suffered decline or failure within a stable life structure. Known today as one of America's finest theologians, his life as a Congregational minister must be viewed as one that came to a frustrating end. In fact, one of the major reasons that he was able to produce the work that has given him a reputation as a first-rate theologian is that his difficulties as a minister forced him to retire to his study more and more, and thus to produce these impressive scholarly works. Moreover, these theological works proved to be a bone of contention between himself and his parishioners, thus contributing to an already difficult parish situation.

CHILDHOOD AND ADOLESCENCE (1703-1722)

Before focusing on Edwards' early adult era, it is necessary to sketch the broad outlines of his earlier childhood. He was born in Windsor, Connecticut, on October 5, 1703. His father, Timothy Edwards, was a minister. Timothy had graduated from Harvard in 1691, was ordained three years later, and became the first pastor of the Second Church of Windsor. He remained in this pastorate until his death sixty-two years later.

Edwards' paternal grandfather, Richard Edwards, was a wealthy lawyer and merchant. After twenty-four years of marriage to Elizabeth Tuttle, a rich young woman from New Haven, Richard Edwards filed for divorce and, after two unsuccessful attempts, it eventually was granted. Divorce was extremely rare in Puritan New England, but Richard sought the divorce on the grounds that Elizabeth was guilty of infidelity and of threats on his life. Fourteen years before the divorce action, Elizabeth's brother had killed her sister with an axe, and another sister had killed her own son, so there appears to have been basis for Richard's fear of his wife. After being granted the divorce, Richard remarried the following year and lived quietly with his new wife until he died, twenty-seven years later.

Edwards' own father was considered a scholarly man who placed much stock in logic and rational thinking. At an early age, Timothy was placed under the tutelage of a pastor in Springfield who taught students in divinity, so evidently his father Richard always intended his son to go into the ministry. When he assumed his duties as pastor in East Windsor, his father had a house built for him as a gift. It was in this house that Jonathan Edwards was born and raised.

Jonathan Edwards' mother came from an entirely different background. Her father, Solomon Stoddard, was an extremely influential minister in Puritan New England. Stoddard succeeded Eleazor Mather, uncle of Cotton Mather, at First Church of Northampton in 1669. He married Mather's widow, who had three children, and they had twelve more children of their own. Edwards' mother, Esther, was one of these twelve children. The Stoddard children and stepchildren married into other important families in the Northampton and Connecticut Valley region, and as a result of these marriages formed an extremely influential family network of wealth and power. Esther's marriage to Timothy Edwards, a first-generation minister, might seem to be an exception, but it is important to keep in mind that he was the son of a prosperous Hartford merchant and lawyer.

Edwards' parents had eleven children, ten of them girls. Jonathan, their fifth child, was their only son. Perhaps because he was the only son in a family of ten sisters, Jonathan developed a tendency toward solitude at an early age. He was also intellectually precocious. An example of his intellectual ability is his essay "On Insects," written when he was only twelve years old. This essay was written with the intention of sending it to a European journal for possible publication. It reflected his hope, even at this young age, of becoming a noted scholar.

One year after he wrote the essay on insects, he entered Yale College. Yale College had moved from one Connecticut town to another because all the towns wanted the money that students paid for board, room, and other necessities. In the year that he entered, Yale had chosen to settle in New Haven, and a three-story building was built there to house the college. While some of the students went to New Haven, others stayed in Saybrook where the college had most recently operated. Still others, Edwards among them, went to Wethersfield to study under the tutelage of Elisha Williams. Williams was a relative of the Edwards family and thus a natural choice to tutor young Edwards.

Throughout the next three years, the Wethersfield group was subject to considerable pressure to move to New Haven. Finally, the General Assembly ordered the boys to New Haven and Edwards and the other Wethersfield students complied. One month later, all of the Wethersfield group with the exception of Edwards returned to Elisha Williams' tutelage in Wethersfield. Evidence suggests that Edwards and Williams had not gotten along well, and that this was the major reason that he did not return with the others. In any event, whatever the motivation for remaining in New Haven, he had made a good decision for six months later, illness forced Williams to close the Wethersfield branch of the college and his students returned again to New Haven. Edwards completed his undergraduate degree in 1720, at the young age of seventeen, and remained at Yale to study for the ministry. Then, two years later, at the age of nineteen, he accepted his first parish assignment. This event marked the beginning of his early adult transition.

EARLY ADULT ERA

Novice Phase

Early Adult Transition (1722-1726)

His first parish assignment was to a Presbyterian congregation in New York City. New York City had a population of 7,000 at the time. Its first church building had been erected in 1698 and the Presbyterian church to which he had been called was an offshoot of a congregation established two years earlier. Since the new church had separated from the older church because of personal disagreement with the minister, the fledgling congregation was not in good financial shape and had not yet become incorporated as a church body.

He left little record of his eight months in New York, especially of his work in the church. However, his work there was evidently well received. For shortly after calling him, the church realized it could not survive unless it united with a more prosperous congregation, but it postponed moving in this direction through the year because this would "issue in our deprivation of the much respected Mr. Edwards."[2] When he decided to accept a call to East Bolton, Connecticut, this solved the church's dilemma. For Edwards, "My heart seemed to sink within me at leaving the family and city where I had enjoyed so many sweet and pleasant Days."[3]

While in New York, he developed a close friendship with a devout leather worker, John Smith, and Smith's mother. He and Smith would go on walks together along the Hudson River, talking about their religious concerns. When he left New York in April 1723, he most regretted his parting from the Smiths.

He returned to Connecticut with the intention of assuming the pastorate of the church in East Bolton in the fall. He spent the summer in East Windsor at the family home. As late as November he was still planning to go to East Bolton where provisions were being made for him. Then he was offered a tutorship at Yale and he quickly accepted, even though it was not to begin until May 1724. His biographers conjecture that one reason he abandoned his plans to go to East Bolton and seized the opportunity to return to New Haven was the fact that a young girl, Sarah Pierrepont, lived in New Haven. She was the daughter of a New Haven minister whom he had apparently met when he was a student at Yale.

Sarah was only thirteen at the time he was offered the tutorship but, judging from the following piece written on the flyleaf of one of his notebooks while staying with his parents in East Windsor, he was already in love with her. He wrote:

> They say there is a young lady in New Haven who is beloved of that Great Being, who made and rules the world, and that there are certain seasons in which this Great Being, in some way or other invisible, comes to her and fills her mind with exceedingly sweet delight, and that she hardly cares for anything, except to meditate on him. . . . She has a strange sweetness in her mind, and singular purity in her affections; is most just and conscientious in all her conduct; and you could not persuade her to do anything wrong or sinful, if you would give her all the world, lest she should offend this Great Being. She is of a wonderful sweetness, calmness, and universal benevolence of mind; especially after this Great God has manifested himself to her mind. She will sometimes go about from place to place, singing sweetly; and seems to be always full of joy and pleasure; and no one knows for what. She loves to be alone walking in the fields and groves, and seems to have someone invisible always conversing with her.[4]

He was to marry Sarah three years later.

He continued at Yale as a tutor for two years. It was a period of considerable stress. In 1722 the college rector, Timothy Cutler, had informed the Yale Corporation that he and four other Congregational ministers had decided to return to the Church of England. This action was a shock to the college and to New Haven. The trustees of the college took turns acting as rectors, but this meant that the rector of the college was usually not in residence. When Edwards took over as senior tutor, he was, in effect, the person in charge of running the college. He and the junior tutor had sixty students in addition to numerous administrative duties. He thoroughly disliked the situation he was in, but continued working for almost a year and a half until September 1725, when he became seriously ill and nearly died. He lay ill for three months in the home of a friend in North Haven and his mother came from East Windsor to nurse him back to health.

During his convalescence in the spring and early summer of 1726, he reflected on the glory of God. Through his illness, he felt "the sweet influence of his Spirit."[5] In late summer he returned to Yale until the close of the session in September. In the meantime, his former tutor, Elisha Williams, had been appointed rector of Yale. Perhaps recognizing that his days at Yale were numbered inasmuch as he had been the only student of Williams' to remain in New Haven when the others returned to Wethersfield, he accepted the invitation of his grandfather's church in Northampton, Massachusetts, to become a candidate for a position there. The individual chosen for the position would assist the aging Solomon Stoddard and would succeed him on his retirement.

He went up to Northampton to preach in August and in November was chosen for the position. Three months later, in February 1727, at the age of twenty-three, he was invited to settle in the parish, an invitation that signaled his and the church's intention that he would remain for many years to come, possibly for life. As his biographer, Ola Elizabeth Winslow, puts it, "Except for the fact that he was continuing a family succession which might entail troublesome loyalties, he began with almost everything in his favor."[6] With this invitation to join his grandfather Stoddard in Northampton, his early adult transition came to an end. He was now embarking on a journey that would not only take him to one of the most prominent parishes in New England, but also would thrust him into the adult world.

Entering the Adult World (1726-1731)

Five months after settling into Northampton parish, he married Sarah Pierrepont. They were married in New Haven and then immediately returned to Northampton. Life in the parsonage in Northampton would prove to be quite different from life in the New Haven parsonage in which she had spent her childhood and adolescence. Although the setting in Northampton was more rural and rustic, she and her young husband did all they could to provide the parsonage in Northampton the comfort and convenience of a parsonage in town. Winslow notes that Sarah was used to living an aristocratic life and made certain that her life would not be significantly less comfortable in Northampton.[7] Years later, one of the complaints the congregation lodged against him was that his family lived too luxuriously.

He continued as his grandfather's assistant until the older man's death in 1729. During the two years that he worked as an assistant pastor, he took care of many parish matters that had been neglected during the last ten years of his grandfather's ministry. The young people had become disorderly in worship. Not enough attention had been paid to catechetical instruction. Family prayer had generally been neglected. He devoted much attention to these matters so that by the time his grandfather died, he had already assumed most of the normal responsibilities of the pastor. Now, with his grandfather's death, he was about to assume full responsibility for one of the most important parishes in western Massachusetts. At the time of Stoddard's death, the congregation numbered over 600 members.

Because he succeeded his grandfather at age twenty-six, this event may be viewed as the "Age 25 Shift." Unlike Brooks, who accepted a call to another parish at this point in his career, Edwards remained where he was. He was now, however, fully in charge of the church he served and now that his grandfather was gone, he was free to take initiatives that were prohibited during the older man's lifetime. As noted earlier, however, the person experiencing the "Age 25 Shift" may not be fully conscious at the time of the longer range implications of this event. In Edwards' case, the fact that he was already performing most of the pastoral functions of the church due to his grandfather's infirmity, and that he initially continued to carry out his grandfather's own legacy, may well have given the appearance of little if any change. Subjectively, however, this event was momentous, and in time, this became apparent both to him and to his congregation.

Stoddard's fame had been largely due to his liberal views regarding church membership. As early as 1677 he began to admit people to full church membership, including communion, even though they could not present evidence that would prove they were in a state of grace. In effect, he required only a profession of faith and repentance of sins for admission to full standing in the church. Stoddardeanism, or the "Stoddard Way," was adopted throughout all of western Massachusetts. This liberalism was tempered, however, by his vigorous preaching against adultery, drunkenness, and extravagant clothes. He also believed strongly in religious "awakenings," and on at least four occasions in his ministry in Northampton had presided over hysterical revivals.

Edwards was expected by the congregation to follow in the Stoddard tradition, and during the first years of his ministry in Northampton, he seems to have fulfilled this expectation very well. When studying for the ministry at Yale, he had read about the church membership issue and had then sided with his grandfather Stoddard. So it was not difficult for him to adopt his grandfather's traditions. He was somewhat more solitary than his famous grandfather, however, inclined to visit in members' homes when there was a special need rather than as a matter of routine. When he examined the results of parents' tutelage of their children, he did not do so by going house to house, but examined the children in meetings in the church. He devoted considerable attention to sermon writing, which also meant much reading and study. Winslow describes his presence in the pulpit as follows:

> His tall, spare figure and his deliberate manner gave him a commanding presence. The piercing eyes went everywhere; the thin tones reached the dim corner of the gallery. Every word was distinctly spoken. . . . As a speaker, his chief asset was the quality of his voice—a little languid, with a note of pathos . . . too low for a large assembly, but very distinct and strangely arresting.[8]

Unlike his grandfather, who was thoroughly opposed to the use of sermon notes, the young Edwards preached from a manuscript. His content was quite different also. While equally as opposed to sin, he was less specific than his grandfather in singling out particular types of sin. If he related his sermons to what was occurring in the community, it was not to identify specific community evils but to view tragedies such as fires, drought, and illnesses in the light of God's will. (It was just such a tragedy in Northampton that led to his role in the religious awakening of 1734.) In later years, he did begin to preach against specific community evils, but this was after he and his congregation had begun to quarrel. In the early days, his sermons focused on the overwhelming power of God in the lives of his people.

He remained very close to Northampton and his parish duties for two years following the death of his grandfather. Then, in 1731, at the age of twenty-eight, he was invited by the Boston clergy to preach at the public lecture on July 8. This was his first venture outside of Northampton since he came to the region four years earlier. In light of the instant fame this sermon brought him, it may be taken to symbolize his full entrance into the adult world and, at the same time, ushered in his age thirty transition.

Age Thirty Transition (1731-1735)

The event that ushered in his age thirty transition was a sermon that focused on the traditional Calvinist view of the sovereignty of God and the helplessness of man. It was a solid attack against a growing tendency in New England toward Arminianism, which emphasized the capacity of humans to cooperate in their own salvation. Under urging from the ministers who heard the sermon, he agreed to its publication. The publication of the sermon was a great compliment in itself, but, in addition, it introduced him to other New England clergy and established his lifelong reputation as one who preached "evangelical doctrines." It also enhanced his standing with his own parishioners, persuading them as nothing else could that, in Jonathan Edwards, they had chosen a most worthy successor to Solomon Stoddard.

One direct outcome of his preaching success was that he was asked, along with two other ministers in the area, to formulate a written protest to the county court against growing vice, immorality, and bad manners. This request encouraged him to redouble his efforts in his own parish to combat moral laxity. During the next few months he preached in rather general terms against immorality, but in the fall of 1733, he noticed that the young people in his congregation were beginning to respond to his efforts to get them to examine their lives in order to uncover their sins. On one occasion he preached in quite specific terms against the evils of partying and keeping company on Sunday evening. This sermon so impressed them that they gave up these practices. He continued throughout the fall of 1733 and winter of 1734 to preach on similar topics relating to the need for an "awakening" from the life of sin. He talked about the despair of those who have waited too long to put their sinful ways behind them. He also preached on the necessary steps to be taken by sinners convicted of their sins and in need of forgiveness. These sermons were making their mark. Beginning with the young people and spreading to adults, parishioners began to examine their lives.

However, although these sermons were having a major impact on his parishioners and were beginning to "awaken" his congregation, the event that proved the greatest catalyst to the awakening of 1734-1735 were the sudden deaths of a young man and a young woman in the community. These deaths greatly disturbed their young companions and Edwards, quickly noticing this, organized the young people into small groups for private meetings designed to keep their thoughts on religious concerns throughout the week.

These two deaths created a tense atmosphere in the community at large, and he responded to this tension with sermons intended to point to the action of the sovereign God in these events. In one of his sermons, "The Justice of God in the Damnation of Sinners," he referred to specific sins that displease God: irreverence in God's house, disregard of the Sabbath, neglect of family prayer, disobedience to parents, quarreling, greediness, sensuality, and hatred of one's neighbor. It was an extremely effective sermon because hardly anyone could claim exemption from all the sins on his list. But, as Winslow points out, he was to pay a price for this sermon.[9] Its immediate effect was to open the floodgates of an "awakening" in Northampton. Parishioners would come to his parsonage on Monday morning, confessing that they had not been able to sleep the night before in anguish over their sins. Years later, however, they were to deeply resent his suggestion that such behaviors as quarreling, greediness, and hatred of neighbors were more serious than the sins that Solomon Stoddard had enumerated: drunkenness, adultery, and fancy clothes.

In December 1734 (Edwards was thirty-one years old) the first conversions of the awakening of 1734-1735 occurred. One of the first converts was a young woman who had a bad reputation in town. This gave the awakening the impetus it needed, and after that the revival moved forward on its own momentum. Young people at first, then their elders, became deeply concerned for their sins. People came to the parsonage day and night as those who had experienced salvation came to report the news and those who continued to feel condemned sought the pastor's help.

In the beginning, he kept emotions within manageable limits by holding singing meetings in which emotions could be expressed in an orderly manner. He met with his members in small groups, and encouraged them to meet in small groups in their homes. As a result, the awakening proceeded with reasonable calm, and without disruption of regularly scheduled services. Moreover, a new spirit seemed to pervade the town. The "party strife" that had always divided Northampton was, at least temporarily, halted. Neighbors who had carried grudges against one another for years settled their differences. Edwards himself was exhilarated by what was happening. As Winslow points out: "He had seen revivals in his father's parish as a boy, but nothing like this. To him, it seemed almost the millennium, and was the happiest time in all his ministry."[10]

Richard Bushman suggests that one reason for his personal satisfaction during this period was because he was seeing the fruits of his own earlier struggles with the same kind of personal and spiritual problems that his congregation was now facing.[11] Bushman bases this judgment on Edwards' early essay on insects, which he believes reveals Edwards' deepest and most enduring personal and spiritual conflicts. Bushman also believes that Edwards began to deal with these conflicts in his early twenties, first in his involvement with the Smith family in New York and then through his illness during the time that he was a tutor at Yale College. Since Edwards' ministry at Northampton through the awakening of 1734-1735 was informed by his own conflicts and efforts to cope with them, Bushman's analysis of the essay on insects is valuable for our attempt to understand Edwards' early success as the minister of Northampton parish.

In the essay on insects, Edwards develops three themes that Bushman says are central to his lifelong personal and religious conflicts. The first of these themes, based on observation of spiders, is that *rising leads eventually to destruction.* Young Edwards notices how spiders emit a fine web that carries them upward, floating higher and higher toward the sun. There is considerable pleasure for the spider in this ascent, but, sadly enough, these pleasures prove shortlived. As the spiders mount toward the sun, they are caught in the winds and carried out to sea. There they join other insects and suffer the same violent end, burial in the ocean. Thus, the pleasant rise toward the sun leads to eventual destruction.

The second theme is *vileness under attractive appearances.* While the spider gives the appearance of sagacity and effectiveness, its violent burial at sea is warranted because, beneath its pleasant appearance, the spider gives off nauseous vapors. If large numbers of spiders were to die inland in winter, their smell would be unendurable. Thus, under attractive appearances, the spider conceals its essential vileness.

The third theme is that spiders are *ill-disposed to being manipulated.* Edwards notices that spiders are very sensitive to being jarred by the experimenter and, when jostled, quickly spin a web and drift off. They possess a delicate nervous system that causes them to resist manipulation and close contact with other beings.

In Bushman's view, young Edwards was actually describing his own personality through these three themes. Thus: (1) Edwards aspired to fulfill high family expectations; but (2) the pleasure and excitement of success was counterbalanced by a fear of destruction due to inward corruption; and (3) his tendency to be fretful and uneasy around other people made close personal relationships difficult to sustain. Although the psychodynamic origins of these themes in his earlier childhood are difficult to determine, it appears that the first theme of high aspirations was influenced by the fact that his maternal forebears were extremely prominent leaders in Puritan New England. Much was expected of the only son of one of the Stoddard daughters. The second theme of the sense of vileness underneath attractive appearances may have its motivational roots in the fact that his own father was a minister. It was incumbent on his family to maintain public respectability whatever the domestic reality. The third theme of tenuous relations with other people may have had its psychodynamic origins in the fact that he was the only son among ten sisters. Although this situation undoubtedly afforded him considerable attention and perhaps solicitude by his sisters, it also prompted the desire to escape from the omnipresence of others.

Bushman suggests that he resolved many of the conflicts these themes reflected during his early through middle twenties. Concerning the high aspirations reflected in his first personal theme ("rising leads eventually to destruction"), he relinquished his desire to excel intellectually. He gave up his dream of becoming a philosopher with a European reputation, and he accepted the fact that he would follow in the footsteps of his minister father and grandfather. Concerning the second theme ("vileness under attractive appearances"), his illumination experience—of "the sweet influence of the Holy Spirit"—during his serious illness while a tutor at Yale gave him a sense of the purity and loveliness of God. This replaced his inner sense of uncleanliness with new "delights" of a "pure, soul-animating and refreshing nature.")[12] With regard to the third theme ("ill-disposed to being manipulated"), he overcame to some extent his uneasiness around people. He still envisioned himself "alone in the mountains, or some solitary wilderness, far from all mankind, sweetly conversing with Christ, and wrapt and swallowed up in God,"[13] but he now began to value loving relationships with other committed Christians. In another poetic vision, he pictured the soul of a true Christian as "a little white flower" standing "peacefully and lovingly, in the midst of other flowers round about."[14] His relationship to John Smith and Smith's mother in New York created this deeper sense of the value of loving relationships, and overcame to some extent his uneasiness around other people.

In Bushman's view, Edwards' personal themes corresponded with the themes of his congregation. Thus, corresponding to his own high aspirations in intellectual endeavors, parishioners entertained high aspirations of economic and social success: "Examples multiplied of small storekeepers who became wealthy merchants and of thrifty farmers who doubled their estates through speculation."[15] But this economic situation was highly volatile. Dramatic success was often followed by destruction: "Commercial and agricultural expansion depended heavily on risk-laden speculations: natural disasters, debt foreclosures, and unforeseen calamities of various kinds could wipe out farmers and traders."[16] In this highly unstable economic climate, increasing attention was paid to the sense of internal corruption underneath appearances of economic and social success. The theme of vileness underneath attractive appearances, therefore, was reflected in this fact: the average parishioner could not take solace in the proposition that personal success demonstrated divine favor: "At one moment he rested in the assurance of his virtuous diligence and of the prosperity heaven had bestowed. At the next a warning from the pulpit started fears that the lust for gold had hopelessly corrupted his soul."[17] This uncertainty led, in turn, to the third theme. Relationships between neighbors and friends became increasingly brittle: "Economic expansion increased occasions for misunderstanding and ill feeling. The competition for land and trade and for every conceivable economic advantage made enemies of former friends. . . . Even relations with neighbors deteriorated as expansion multiplied the occasions for hard feelings."[18]

Thus, the same themes with which Edwards had struggled personally were prominent features of the lives of his parishioners. Through the awakening of 1734-1735, his congregation moved toward the same resolutions of the conflicts reflected in these themes that he had moved toward in his earlier years. Parishioners renounced their economic ambitions. They acknowledged their inner impurity and, through these acknowledgments, gained a new sense of inner calm and divine acceptance. They pledged neither to defraud their neighbors, default on debts, nor feed a spirit of bitterness, ridicule, and ill will.

It was not long before Edwards became the victim of a backlash against the awakening. In late spring 1735, a man committed suicide. Several weeks later, his own uncle "cut his throat on the Lord's Day morning"[19] and died immediately. In the following weeks, many others attempted suicide, and though few succeeded, it was clear that the awakening had created a thoroughly unintended side effect, and that for all intents and purposes the awakening was over. By the end of 1735, both Edwards and his parishioners were lamenting the loss of religious interest in the town, and the community was again in dissension. In 1736, some members of the congregation persuaded him to print some of the sermons he preached during the awakening in the hope that this might stir a new revival, but the enterprise had little effect. The awakening was clearly over, ending as suddenly as it had started.

The tangible effect of the awakening, however, was that 300 people had been converted, and the meeting house was not large enough to hold everyone. Thus, in November 1735, the congregation decided to build a new church and two years later the new building was ready for use. In effect, the new building was a living testimony to the awakening. For, although the awakening was over, the congregation had increased dramatically in membership, and most of the converts remained to become valued members of the congregation.

Thus, his age-thirty transition came to an end. The period from his preaching of the sermon in Boston in 1731 to the decision to build a new church in 1735 had been, to say the least, a dramatic period in his life. He had gone from being Solomon Stoddard's grandson to the major catalyst of a religious awakening in Northampton. Although tragic events were largely responsible for the beginning (as well as the ending) of the awakening, he had already been laying the groundwork for a spiritual renewal among the young people in the community. Moreover, when these events occurred, he followed his usual practice of interpreting events in light of God's sovereign will, and now his parishioners were clearly ready to respond to these interpretations of events. Winslow, however, also indicates that his preaching underwent a significant change during this period. Whereas he had preached on man's sinfulness in previous years, he had been reluctant to talk about specific sins. Now he was talking about the kinds of sins he had seen in himself when younger (ambition, inner impurity, touchiness around other people) and was noting their existence among his parishioners. Furthermore, unlike his grandfather who was inclined to talk about sins of which *other* people are guilty (adultery, drunkenness, ostentatious clothing), his list of sins pointed the finger at each member of his congregation, and challenged the long-standing mores of the community. Quarreling, greediness, hatred of one's neighbor, personal self-aggrandizement—these were sins that his parishioners had not wanted to consider serious sins. But when he implied that the recent tragedies in the community were due to sins of this nature, he made his parishioners extremely uncomfortable. It became clear to them that they needed salvation.[20]

Edwards could not have foreseen the tragedies the awakening caused—the deaths by suicide, but he could probably have anticipated that he would be subject to adverse criticism for his role in the awakening. The major criticism, which began to mount during his settling-down period, was that he expected greater "saintliness" than ordinary people should be expected to muster.

The Tasks of the Novice Phase

How well did Edwards lay the foundations for the next period of his life? How well had he handled the developmental tasks of the novice phase?

Forming a Dream. It is clear by the end of the age thirty transition that he felt he truly belonged in the ministry. His first pastorate was short-lived, but not because he was not successful there. When he returned to Connecticut, he chose teaching at Yale College over a small parish, and this might indicate that he would have desired a career in teaching. This indication is reinforced by the fact that he returned to tutoring after his illness even though his two years at Yale had been extremely frustrating. Moreover, we can surmise that the only reason he left Yale to accept an assistantship under his grandfather was that his old tutor, Elisha Williams, was the new rector at Yale College. Recognizing that he did not have a bright future at Yale under Williams, he made plans to depart. In so doing, he also began to relinquish any hopes he had entertained of being recognized someday as a great philosopher.

On the other hand, he was extremely fortunate to have been chosen to succeed his grandfather at Northampton, and seemed thoroughly capable of moving into his grandfather's parish and working effectively in what could have been a very awkward situation. After his grandfather's death, the transition from the older man's leadership to his own appears to have been smooth. The congregation had had the foresight to arrange for a smooth transition from pastor to pastor. In the next two years he began to establish a solid reputation for himself without simply copying his highly respected grandfather. However, it was not until his Boston sermon and the awakening of 1734-1735 that one could say that his decision to enter the ministry had been strongly confirmed. Without a real mentor (a minister not associated with his family) to help him enter the profession and ensure his sense of belonging to it, Edwards did not know whether he really belonged in the ministry until his sermon in Boston brought immediate confirmation from fellow ministers, and his overwhelming success in the awakening of 1734-1735 brought similar confirmation from his own parishioners.

If there was any continuing evidence of difficulty in incorporating his Dream into his life structure, it was that he viewed himself as a scholar and, at times, may well have preferred to be working in a setting in which his scholarly abilities would be more recognized and valued. Although he had opportunity to pursue his scholarly interests at Northampton, he was removed from the seats of learning in Boston and New Haven. The close attention he gave to catechetical instruction is perhaps an indication, too, that he missed his work as a tutor. Much of the focus of his early ministry was on the training of youth in Christian faith and morality. Thus, while no evidence supports that he resented not being recognized as a scholar and gained great satisfaction from his ministry, when he did begin to experience difficulty in his ministry in his late thirties, he instinctively gave increasing attention to his scholarly interests. In the meantime, however, he gave himself unstintingly to the work and duties of the parish ministry and, as evidence that both he and his congregation recognized that he was doing a good job, he was very well paid for his work.

Forming mentor relationships. Edwards was far more under the influence of his family than that of mentors. He does not appear to have been overly subject to his father's views on ministry (later he was to reject his father's emphasis on rational theology in favor of a theology of the affections), but the fact that he was the grandson of Solomon Stoddard was an extremely important factor in his early career as a minister. His only mentor outside the family circle was Elisha Williams, a distant relative, and this relationship seems to have come to grief rather early in Edwards' undergraduate career. When a student at Yale College in New Haven, and later as a tutor, there was a lack of more seasoned faculty with whom he might form a positive mentor relationship. Thus, throughout his twenties and early thirties, he was more or less deprived of the mentoring that might have enabled him to achieve greater independence of family members and their understandings of ministry. As it turned out, his belated efforts when in his late thirties and early forties to secure such independence were the major reasons for his failures. A good mentor relationship, from outside the family, may have saved him from some of the difficulties he encountered in his middle thirties. Departures from the practices of his father and grandfather could have been more easily initiated if they had the support and encouragement of a mentor.

Forming an occupation. There is no question that he had begun to prove himself a capable and effective minister. Given his tendency toward solitude and his uneasiness around people, he had overcome these liabilities in various ways. Although reluctant to go to the homes of his parishioners, he developed an effective catechetical program in the church. He was not an extrovert in the pulpit, yet his distinct speaking voice was very effective. Uncomfortable in large crowds, he made very good use of the small group both in his own home and in the homes of his parishioners. Thus, potential liabilities did not become an excuse for inaction but rather prompted him to seek ways to compensate for them. In many ways, these compensatory measures (using the church more for meetings, quiet but distinct speaking voice, the use of small groups) gave his ministry its distinctive style and were thus responsible for much of its success.

Forming a marriage and family. In contrast to Phillips Brooks, Edwards was successful in this developmental task. In choosing Sarah Pierrepont, he selected a young wife who was familiar with life in a parsonage. He married her after his career choice was made, when he was already established in his first major parish position, so she was well aware of her responsibilities as a wife. Moreover, when he became involved in religious awakenings, much evidence indicates that she deeply shared his desire for awakenings. (He later used her own awakening to illustrate the fact that awakenings are not merely the effect of emotional hysteria.) Thus, even though she was quite young (sixteen years old) when he married her, he was in the period of his life ("entering adult world") when his professional plans were clear. She could marry him knowing what his Dream for his life was and understanding how she could contribute to it.

On the other hand, even in their first years at Northampton, the discerning observer might have recognized the initial signs of future problems—not primarily between Edwards and his wife, but between the Edwards family and the congregation. For one thing, when Edwards was chosen to succeed his grandfather, he was single. The parishioners of Northampton did not know Sarah Pierrepont and she had not met them. When he married her and brought her to Northampton, he was bringing in a young woman from outside the community and even the region, and one who was of a higher cultural (if not necessarily economic) background than most of the inhabitants of Northampton. As years went by, the fact that the Edwards family lived better than most of the other townspeople became a matter of contention. It was not the issue that created friction, but when friction occurred on other grounds it was easy for disgruntled parishioners to seize on this issue and use it against the Edwards family. Sarah was particularly vulnerable to such criticism because her penchant for nice clothes clearly violated Solomon Stoddard's view that ostentatious clothing is one of the major sins.

In light of this future conflict, it is instructive to read Edwards' description of the young thirteen-year-old Sarah in his notebook. Here he depicts Sarah as a young girl who has no care for anything but to converse with God. We suspect that he is expecting more of Sarah here than anyone has the right to expect, even as later on the parishioners expected their minister's wife to relinquish her personal desires in favor of divine conversation, even though they were generally unwilling to do the same. A more revealing segment of his description of Sarah, however, is the statement that she has a "wonderful sweetness, calmness and universal benevolence of mind *especially after this Great God has manifested himself to her mind.*"[21] This seems to imply that she has a certain tendency toward less desirable traits before these divine manifestations calm and settle her mind. Thus, these descriptions of Sarah, together with the fact that their courtship was not always smooth, suggest that the couple could have problems.

Nonetheless, in terms of the family and church situation at the conclusion of the midthirty transition, there is no reason to assume that Edwards had not handled the task of marriage and forming a family very well. If, in later years, there was to be conflict not only between Edwards and his parishioners but also between the Edwards family and the congregation, more evidence suggests that Sarah was the victim of a difficult situation rather than a major cause of it.

In general, then, Edwards had handled well the tasks of the novice stage, especially those over which he could exercise some control. At age thirty-two, the conclusion of his age thirty transition, he was the pastor of an influential church in western Massachusetts who had added to the prestige of the church by means of a very successful awakening. Having inherited a large church of 600 members, he had now added 300 more. To all appearances, he was a young man who was clearly on the rise. With the exception of a mentor relationship whose assistance in the difficult years ahead might have helped him avert failure, he had succeeded very well in the developmental tasks of the novice period.

The Settling-Down Phase

Settling Down and Becoming His Own Man (1736-1744)

Besides commenting on the continuing work that was being done on the new church building, Winslow has little to say about the early phase of his settling-down period (1736-1739) when he was thirty-three to thirty-six years old. On the surface at least, it was a period in which he and his congregation recovered from the awakening of 1734-1735 and devoted itself to the tasks of church building. However, incipient troubles were indicated for Edwards in the two events during this period that the biographers *do* report.

The first was the notorious Breck case of 1735-1736. Robert Breck, a young Harvard graduate, had been called by the Springfield, Massachusetts, congregation to be its minister. The Hampshire Association, a consortium of ministers in the county, opposed his ordination because they questioned his orthodoxy. Resenting interference in its affairs, the Springfield congregation called a council of Boston ministers to weigh the charges and, if they could be proven false, to ordain Breck. However, when Breck arose to answer the charges, he was arrested by the civil authorities at the instigation of the Hampshire Association and placed in jail. A great protest arose against the jailing of a minister and, before the affair was concluded, the Massachusetts General Assembly officially censured the Association. Edwards was not present at any of the meetings in the Breck case, but he agreed to draft the defense of the Hampshire Association after the General Assembly censured it. He was not only sharply criticized for this act of support of the association at the time, but because he was the author of the written defense, his role in the affair was to be remembered long after the names of the other members of the association, the primary instigators of the action against Breck, had been forgotten.[22]

A second event during this period was the collapse of the front gallery of the old church building in March 1737. No one was killed. More than seventy persons were seated directly underneath, but were protected by the high pews. Edwards interpreted this event, as was his custom, as a "rebuke of God and a loud call to repent."[23] But if the short-term effect of the accident was to cause the congregation to worry about their souls, their long-term reaction was to congratulate themselves for having begun a building program for a new church more than a year earlier. The accident simply inspired them to greater efforts to complete the new building.

Neither of these two events by itself should be taken to indicate that Edwards was losing his influence in the community. But together, they suggest that he was somewhat out of step with the mood of the day. Inhabitants of Hampshire County were more concerned that Robert Breck's basic liberties had been violated than by the suspicion that his religious views were unorthodox. The collapse of the front gallery was not a sufficient catalyst to impel Edwards' congregation to a new religious awakening. They had had their awakening in which 300 new members had been gained, so why would the pastor want to stir up another one? The Breck case, however, was to prove the most damaging to Edwards. When he was replaced in the pulpit of Northampton parish in 1753 (at age fifty), it was Robert Breck who officially welcomed his successor.[24]

The second phase of his settling-down period (1740-1744), from age thirty-seven to forty-one, began auspiciously. Before it was over, however, his ministry in Northampton was virtually at an end. In 1740, the English preacher, George Whitefield, then twenty-six years old, came to the United States. He arrived in Boston on September 18 amid much publicity and was enthusiastically received by most of the Boston clergy. After a ten-day triumph in Boston, Whitefield came immediately to Northampton and spent four days as the house guest of Jonathan Edwards. Edwards had looked forward to Whitefield's visit, having recently complained of the "sorrowfully dull and dead time" in his own parish.[25] Edwards himself left no record of Whitefield's first visit to Northampton, but Whitefield described what happened when he preached in Edwards' church that Sunday:

> When I came to remind them of their former Experiences, and how zealous and lovely they were at that Time, both Minister and People wept much; and the Holy Ghost enabled me to speak with a great deal of power.[26]

Whitefield remained in Northampton four days, preaching four times in the church and one in the parsonage, and observed that he had greater success in Northampton than in his previous meetings in Boston. He particularly noted how Edwards wept "during the whole time of exercise" on Sunday morning.[27] When he departed on Monday, Whitefield proceeded south through Connecticut and, at every stop, stirred the churches as he had stirred Edwards' congregation in Northampton. The Second Great Awakening of 1740-1741 was underway.

The religious excitement reached its peak during the spring and summer of 1741. The ministers in New England were traveling to other towns, preaching sermons that they could not preach in their own pulpits. Edwards' sermon preached to the rural congregation in Enfield, Connecticut, on July 8, 1741, (exactly ten years later to the day of his earlier influential sermon to the ministers in Boston) played a major role in sustaining the awakening. His theme was the wrath of God and the imminence of everlasting punishment. Isaac Watts, the English clergyman and author of the words of such well-known Christian hymns as "Joy to the World," "O God, Our Help in Ages Past," and "When I Survey the Wondrous Cross," called it "a most terrible sermon."[28] An eyewitness, Stephen Williams, described its impact on the congregation:

> Before sermon was done there was a great moaning and crying out through the whole house. What shall I do to be saved? Oh I

am going to hell. Oh what shall I do for Christ, etc. etc. So that the minister was obliged to desist. The shrieks and cries were piercing and amazing. After some time of waiting the congregation were still so that a prayer was made by Mr. W. and after that we descended from the pulpit and discoursed with the people, some in one place and some in another, and amazing and astonishing the power of God was seen.[29]

This sermon, titled "Sinners in the Hands of an Angry God," established Edwards as the acknowledged leader of the Great Awakening of 1740-1741. In this sermon, he reverted to the spider image of his youthful essay, representing humans as hanging like spiders on their fragile webs over the hot flames of hell.

While Edwards was traveling and preaching in other New England churches, his pulpit was filled by ministers who were doing the same. Sarah Edwards worried that a visiting minister might make her husband look inferior by making more converts in his own church than he had been able to make, but after praying about it, she was able to say that she was willing, if God pleased, that "some other minister should convert more people than her husband."[30]

The ministers involved in the awakening soon came under severe criticism from ministers who considered it a crass exploitation of parishioners' fears and anxieties. One of the most vocal opponents of the awakening was Thomas Clapp, the minister who had led the fight against Robert Breck in Springfield, but since that time had become the rector of Yale College. Edwards encountered Clapp on the way to a ministerial convention and when Clapp soundly criticized him for his involvement in the awakening, he decided to defend himself in some public forum. In September 1741 he defended the awakening and his role in it at the last Yale commencement he ever attended. He later expanded his New Haven sermon into a much larger defense of the awakening, using his wife's experiences, without naming her, as evidence that the awakening appealed to mature Christians.

Although he was defending the awakening in sermons and treatises intended for fellow ministers, his congregation in Northampton had begun to grow weary of this awakening, much as they had grown weary of the awakening in 1734-1735. Some in his congregation had resisted the awakening from the beginning. Others were irritated when he insisted on preaching a series of sermons in 1742-1743 distinguishing between false and true religious emotions. Thus when two fairly minor disputes between Edwards and members of the congregation erupted in 1742 and 1744 he lacked the broad backing and support he needed to help him weather these conflicts. Unlike the earlier awakening in 1734-1735 when he stayed in close contact with his parishioners, the awakening of 1740-1741 in Northampton had occurred while Edwards was absent for extended periods. Whereas the earlier awakening culminated in the decision to erect a new church building, this second awakening culminated in a dispute over his salary, a dispute that he could ill afford given his recent absences and the feeling of some influential members of the congregation that he should never have encouraged a second awakening in Northampton in the first place.

He had experienced a series of minor skirmishes with the parish over payment of his salary during the 1730s, but in each case, the reason for the conflict was that the town constables were slow in paying his salary. In 1742 the issue was different. The previous year he had taken his case before the town and asked for more money than had been agreed upon. The town responded favorably to this earlier request, but the following year, when he was granted another fifty-pound increase in salary, a "great uneasiness in the town" arose regarding his expenditures.[31] The townspeople complained that he was living on a lavish scale, that his family wore expensive clothes, and that he could support twice as many children on his present salary. To prove their point, they forced him to make his family budget public. Among the itemized budget items was an expenditure of eleven pounds for his wife's new locket and chain.

A year later the town book contained the item: "The question was put whether the town will pay the charge of bringing Mr. Edwards his daughter from Brookfield and it passed in the negative."[32] Winslow observes that this was certainly "an ungracious gesture in response to what would seem a strange pastoral assumption. Why should he have allowed such a question to be put at a time when feeling was so inflamed against him?"[33] The following year he asked for a fixed salary instead of an amount to be determined annually, but the town refused his request. This dispute over salary dragged on for six years until, in 1748, the town finally agreed to his request for a fixed salary. By this time, however, so much bad feeling existed over the dispute that this was hardly a personal victory.

The second dispute involving Edwards occurred in March 1744. This is the so-called "bad book" case.[34] It was important because, similar to the salary dispute, it contributed directly to the parish resentment that culminated in his subsequent dismissal. In this case, five or six boys in town got hold of a book of instructions for midwives and passed it around to other young teenagers. Before long a large number of teenagers had either perused the book or been informed of its contents. For teenagers in Edwards' day, a midwives' manual would be the closest thing to pornographic literature. Some of these teenagers were from the town's better families and members of the church. When Edwards heard of the situation, he informed the congregation after the regular service what had occurred, and asked it to authorize an investigation. When such authorization was given, he then read a list of the names of young people who were to appear at the investigation, but failed to differentiate between those who were accused and those who were being called as witnesses. His failure to distinguish accused from witnesses thoroughly upset many members, because some of their own children's names were on the list.

The investigation dragged on for two months with twenty-two witnesses implicating eleven teenagers. Finally, two boys confessed to contemptuous behavior against the authority of the church, and this closed the investigation, but ill feeling toward Edwards continued. Church members asked: Was this a private matter and not the minister's business? Was there a limit to the church's interference in matters of conduct? Does pastoral authority take precedence over parental authority in the disciplining of children? In addition to these quite legitimate questions, more emotional issues were also involved. A major one was the fact that Sarah Edwards and some of the Edwards children testified against the children of parishioners. Even though only two boys (from the total of eleven accused) were actually charged, the fact that the names of others were brought before the investigation by the minister's wife and children did not set well with the parishioners involved.

Edwards discussed the controversy over his handling of the issue with his father, who had recently withheld communion from the entire congregation in East Windsor because of a dispute regarding his refusal to baptize the child of a couple who had failed to secure the consent of the bride's parents before marrying. The result of this discussion is not known. What is known is that Edwards continued to preach about the young people's neglect of religion. Whereas his efforts to create a religious sensitivity in young people ten years earlier had contributed to the awakening of 1734-1735, this time his warnings fell on deaf ears. Resentment among church members toward him regarding the salary dispute and "bad book" investigation ran deep. It was already clear that his ministry in Northampton could no longer be effective, but the contention and hostility continued for another six years before the congregation succeeded in dismissing him from the Northampton pulpit.

He was thirty-nine years old when the salary dispute erupted, and forty-one years old during the "bad book" conflict. These two controversies mark the conclusion of his "settling-down" period, and indicate quite clearly that his career as a minister was undergoing serious decline, if not outright failure, despite very promising beginnings. Undoubtedly, some of the reasons for this decline were larger than the local controversies of Northampton parish. Throughout New England, congregations were challenging pastoral authority. The fact that the charges eventually leveled against the two boys who were disciplined in the "bad book" case were not for circulating the book among fellow teenagers but for contemptuous behavior against the authority of the church illustrates the difficulty ministers were having throughout the region in maintaining authority in their congregations. Still, it is clear that Edwards made some serious errors in judgment. As Winslow points out, he "made the initial mistake of reversing traditional practice, and instead of first dealing with offenders in private, bringing the whole affair before the congregation of the outset."[35]

The trouble can probably be traced to the Second Great Awakening itself. Edwards' absences and the fact that he was not personally responsible for much of the awakening that took place in his own parish made it difficult for him to regain an effective mastery of the situation in the aftermath of the awakening. His efforts to keep the awakening alive beyond his congregation's endurance by means of a series of awakening sermons was resented by many of his members. However, the congregation could not easily direct their resentment against his choice of sermon topic, especially a topic as fundamental to the Christian faith as this. His family's extravagant ways, which had earlier been accepted or at least tolerated, became a convenient target of this resentment. Judging from the available evidence, there was some basis for the congregation's complaints in this regard. On the other hand, they conveniently overlooked the fact that earlier in his ministry in Northampton the church was frequently late in paying his salary. This had been a recurring problem that unquestionably sowed the seeds of subsequent conflicts between Edwards and the parish over salary matters. Moreover, although Sarah Edwards' purchase of a locket and chain for eleven pounds appears to have been very extravagant, it should be noted that the purchase of valuable jewelry was one of the few ways that New England families had of saving for a rainy day; jewelry could be sold relatively easily in the case of an emergency, and its value was less susceptible to economic vicissitudes than cash.

His mishandling of the "bad book" case undoubtedly was partly triggered by his own resentment against the congregation in the salary dispute. If his family finances had been the object of *their* criticism in the salary dispute, their handling of their teenage children was the object of *his* criticism in the bad book dispute. It is noteworthy that his wife and children appeared before the congregation as witnesses against some of the parishioners' own children, as though to suggest that if the church members wanted to criticize the Edwards family then the Edwards family was prepared to criticize them, and on the same issue of how to manage family affairs. Thus, if he used poor judgment in his handling of the bad book dispute, it may well be that this was not entirely unintentional. A curious irony occurs in the fact that the church members felt the real concern in the bad book dispute was the issue of whether the church should exercise authority in matters that could be handled privately by individual families. Because they were dependent on the parish for their livelihood, the Edwards family was not accorded the same right to manage their own affairs where money was involved, whereas the congregation felt they themselves had such rights in the matter of disciplining children.

In contemporary times, the minister might simply have recognized the writing on the wall and sought another appointment. With Edwards, the situation was more complicated. His grandfather had spent his whole career at Northampton and it was customary for ministers and congregations to view their situations as permanent—terminated only by serious illness, death, or perhaps a change of vocation (such as Thomas Clapp's appointment as rector of Yale College). As with the matter of pastoral authority, changes were also occurring in this policy of lifetime tenure, and other ministers in New England were being dismissed from their parishes. Still, even if this was occurring in the region on a small scale, Edwards was not a run-of-the-mill pastor. He was still recognized throughout New England for his effectiveness in the two religious awakenings, and he was still the grandson of the church's revered former pastor. For these and many other reasons, his eventual dismissal was protracted and extremely bitter. It was not until 1750 (he was forty-seven at the time) that he was eventually voted out of his position and not until 1751 that he left Northampton. Moreover, the church had great difficulty in finding his replacement because the controversy over whether to dismiss him had created a deep and enduring rift in the church. As indicated earlier, his replacement did not arrive until 1753.

Although my primary concern has been to trace Edwards' career through the "settling-down" period, beginning with the decision to build a new church and concluding with the bad book episode, I will give some attention to the period of the middle adult era in order to show that the decline begun in the later phase of the "settling-down period" in the early adult era continued into the next era of his life. He never recovered from this decline.

MIDDLE ADULT ERA

Midlife Transition

Winslow declares flatly that "The years 1744-1748 were barren years."[36] The salary dispute continued, not a single new individual sought membership in the church, and the whole parish waited for an occasion that would force his removal. He began to turn inward during the first two years of his midlife transition (reflecting the attachment/separation polarity), spending considerable time on his *Treatise Concerning Religious Affections*, published in 1746. In this treatise, he wrote for his fellow ministers, contending for the view that religion is not a matter of rational exercise but "true religion consists very much in affections."[37] He also contended that "All who are truly religious are not of this world."[38] This contention may perhaps be recognition of his own alienation from the ordinary world of human affairs.

In 1748, his seventeen-year-old daughter Jerusha died. David Brainerd, to whom she was betrothed, had died of tuberculosis four months earlier. She contracted the illness in nursing Brainerd even though his situation was virtually hopeless. Five days after her funeral, Edwards spoke a eulogy before the congregation. In thanking members of the congregation for supporting the Edwards family in their grief, he strongly implied that many had failed to support them. As he put it, "at least many of you were so pleasant and comfortable while God continued it. . . . Some of you have shown affection on occasion of her death."[39] The implication is quite unmistakable that some had not even put away their animosity toward the Edwards family in their time of bereavement. Edwards continued his writing projects by setting himself to the task of editing David Brainerd's diary and writing a brief biography to accompany it. Because Brainerd had been a missionary to the Indians, the publication of his life and diary was highly successful in dramatizing the need for increased missionary work among Indians. In carrying out the project, he responded to Brainerd's dying request that he edit and publish the diary, and he undoubtedly met some of his own emotional needs, perhaps relating to the young/old polarity, by contributing what he could to the cause for which his daughter had given her life.

Four months after the death of Jerusha, Edwards suffered the death of Colonel John Stoddard, the leading citizen of Northampton and his staunchest supporter. The loss of Stoddard made him more vulnerable to those who sought his dismissal, but his adversaries still lacked the big issue they required to initiate dismissal actions. Within months, he had given them the issue they had been waiting for, doing so with full awareness that he was inviting his dismissal.

Entering Middle Adulthood

The issue, simply, was that he felt he could no longer subscribe to his grandfather's liberal approach to church membership. For some time, he had felt that he had been wrong in accepting his grandfather's practice of allowing people to become church members without recognizable signs of grace, but it was not until 1748 that an application for membership forced the issue. He informed the appropriate church committee that he wanted to set forth his views on admission to membership in print, and his request was granted. His treatise on the matter was published in 1749. In it, he denied the allegation that he himself wanted to be the judge of an applicant's degree of piety. He also pointed out, both in the treatise and in statements before the church, that he did not even insist that candidates be able to state the manner or time of their conversion. What he asked simply was that church members be able to profess sincere belief in their change of heart rather than simple assent to the doctrines and moral prescriptions of the church. At issue here, as in his treatise on religious emotions, was his contention that genuine religion is a matter of the affections, not merely (as his own father believed) of rational assent. Thus, he argued against the policy of his grandfather that the Lord's Supper should not be limited only to those who had the assurance of regeneration.

His views on the issue were rejected by the committee of the church even though he submitted four different forms of public profession of faith that he would find acceptable. In response to this rejection, he offered to resign from his position as minister if, after the parish had read his treatise on the matter, they still wished him to go. This offer was also rejected, apparently on the grounds that the majority wanted him to go without having to read the treatise itself. In fact, feeling against the treatise ran so high that only twenty copies were circulated in Northampton, and some parishioners would not even allow it into their homes. If the book on midwifery had caused a scandal in 1744, his own book caused an even greater scandal five years later. However, he would not give up. His next move was to ask permission to preach his views on the matter of church membership to the whole congregation. At first this request was rejected but then, in the midst of growing tension, he was granted permission to deliver five public lectures in March 1750. Unfortunately, the people who opposed him failed to attend the lectures, so his hope that he could change the minds of his opponents never had a chance.

In the following months a complex dismissal procedure was set in motion and, on June 22, 1750, he was formally dismissed. His supporters in the congregation were outnumbered ten to one and, as Edwards himself observed, most of his remaining supporters were women. On July 2, he delivered his farewell sermon, but this was not the end of his involvement in Northampton affairs. At the age of forty-six, he felt he was past his prime and, in any case, had no prospect of a suitable position as yet. So he remained in Northampton, and for better than a year he explored alternative situations. As the congregation sought his successor, he filled the pulpit on numerous occasions at the request of the supply committee. His continuing presence in Northampton gave rise to his supporters' hope that he would consent to be pastor of a second church in Northampton comprised of people sympathetic to his views. However, his opponents were so thoroughly angered by this idea that they began to vilify him in public, accusing him of attempting to split the church. He informed his supporters that he did not want to consider the possibility of remaining in Northampton.

Age Fifty Transition

By late 1750 he had received several offers, one that particularly interested him. This was a position at the Indian Mission at Stockbridge, Massachusetts. After some delay, due largely to continuing dissension in Northampton, he and his family moved to Stockbridge. Stockbridge, beyond the frontier, consisted of 12 white families and 250 Native American families. His work among the Native Americans was successful enough, but he suffered continuing frustrations because the most influential governors of the mission were the Williams family. They were directly related to his old college tutor, Elisha Williams, and were also related to one of the chief opponents in Northampton against his new proposal for church admissions. A number of his plans for the mission were frustrated by the Williams family's failure to cooperate with him.

He continued his work in Stockbridge for six years when, quite unexpectedly, he was asked by the trustees of New Jersey College (later to become Princeton) to succeed his son-in-law, who had died suddenly, as president. He was heartened by this sudden turn of events, pleased to be considered for the position, but also concerned that he not assume responsibilities he could not handle at his age. He set down some conditions on which he would accept the position, these were agreed to, and all was set. He and one of his daughters went to Princeton in February 1758, with the rest of the family planning to join them in the spring when the president's house was ready. However, a week after his arrival in Princeton he was inoculated for smallpox and, within another month, on March 22, 1758, he died. His wife was on her way to visit him, but she did not arrive in time. Honor had at last come to him, but it came too late. He had no opportunity to use the presidency of New Jersey College to rehabilitate his career. The honor of being chosen to head the college was a vindication, but it could not erase the bitterness he felt toward the church in Northampton, nor make up for his nearly seven years in virtual exile in Stockbridge. As Henry Bamford Parkes notes in his biography of Edwards, "Edwards died apparently a failure. Nobody except [Joseph] Hawley wished him back in Northampton, the Stockbridge Indians were unconverted, Princeton was scarcely touched."[40]

CONCLUSION

I have judged Edwards to be in the category of serious decline or failure within a stable life structure. There was considerable stability in Edwards' life as evidenced by his long-term pastorate in Northampton. His secure family life, including his marriage to Sarah Pierrepont and their involvement in child raising, was another. Still another source of stability was his continuing relationship to extended family members, both on the Edwards and the Stoddard side.

Yet a serious decline occurred—if not outright failure—within this stable life structure. To some extent, this decline was the other side of the coin. The factors that made for stability in his life also contributed to the decline. His immediate family proved almost his sole comfort during his midlife transition, but they were also implicated in the problems that contributed to the decline in his late thirties. Similarly, his extended family gave invaluable assistance both in his securing the Northampton parish and in seeing him through difficult days (the role of Colonel John Stoddard was especially important in this regard). At the same time, these connections contributed to his difficulties. One wonders, for example, if his late decision to dissociate himself from his grandfather's position on church membership was an unconscious admission that his family ties had done him as much harm as good. The fact that he raised this issue after the death of Colonel Stoddard lends some weight to this possibility.

The long-term nature of his pastorate, a real source of stability, also became a source of difficulty. This is not to say that long-term pastorates will inevitably develop serious difficulties, or that the Northampton church was one of those churches in which a long pastorate was ill-advised. After all, Solomon Stoddard managed quite well in Northampton for sixty years (1669-1729). But one reason that Grandfather Stoddard managed to fare as well as he did was that his views on the matter of church membership were far more compatible with the views of his congregation than with those of the New England ministerium of the day. In effect, he had championed the viewpoint of the people. Edwards was different from his grandfather in this respect. Although he initially followed his grandfather's policy in regard to church membership, he broke with this policy at a time when he could ill afford to do so. His personal disposition was to work toward increased, rather than reduced, pastoral authority. As Winslow points out, he was taking an unpopular position on the issue of authority, one calculated to create disagreements and dissension between the pastor and church leaders.[41]

Another source of difficulty was his success in the awakenings of 1734-1735 and 1740-1741. The first awakening brought in 300 new members and prompted a major building program completed three years later. But it is quite possible that either this increase in membership or the major building program, or both together, caused the church to lose its momentum. Apathy is usually not the result of failure but of success. As indicated, Edwards himself referred to this church building period as one in which the church seemed "dull and dead."[42] The second awakening in 1740-1741 afforded him an opportunity to be effective in other pulpits besides his own, but after it was over, the prospect of returning to his former activities in Northampton parish were something of a letdown. He tried to keep the awakening spirit alive by preaching on themes of awakening, but this did not work. It was also almost immediately after the awakening of 1740-1741 that the church became embroiled in major disputes, a sign that, whatever else it accomplished, the awakening did not succeed in an outpouring of Christian charity.

Probably the best answer to the question, "Why did Edwards eventually fail at Northampton parish?" is suggested by Bushman's article on Edwards' personal conflicts. As noted earlier, Edwards' resolution of his own personal conflicts provided an excellent model for his congregation's resolution of their personal conflicts. The first awakening in 1734-1735 enabled the congregation to resolve, on a corporate level, the same conflicts that he had earlier resolved in his personal life. The congregation learned that they could renounce their economic ambitions as he had renounced his ambitions to be a scholar. They acknowledged their inner impurity and need for salvation as he had acknowledged his own, and they pledged to relate to their neighbors in terms of Christian love even as he had discovered, through his relationship with John Smith and Smith's mother, the deep joys of mutuality between Christian friends. One could argue, however, that it was the latter conflict that the congregation had most difficulty with, even as it had been the most difficult for Edwards personally. His essay on spiders indicated that difficulties in establishing close interpersonal relationships are due to resistance to manipulation. Perhaps, in his demand for saintliness greater than his congregation could muster, Edwards had reverted to the grand experimenter (trying to manipulate the people) instead of continuing to be the great awakener (evoking hidden qualities). As young Edwards discovered in his study of spiders, the urge to manipulate the object of one's attention becomes almost irresistible when that object threatens to drift away from one's orbit of influence. Something similar to this happened in Edwards' ministry.

However, if the most dramatic controversy over Edwards' demand for greater saintliness than his people wanted was his effort to institute more stringent admission policies, the recurrent issue throughout his ministry in Northampton concerned the teenagers in the congregation. From the first awakening in 1734-1735 to the bad book episode, he gave great attention to the spiritual and moral development of the youth. If he became manipulative in his efforts with the youth, he sensed that they—like the spider—are also the most likely to resist the efforts of the church and to drift away from its orbit of influence. In directing his efforts toward the youth, he took a very great risk. He was extremely successful in the first awakening of 1734-1735 when youth and their parents responded to his call for greater saintliness. He failed miserably in the bad book dispute when parents sided with their teenage children against their minister.

Chapter 4

John Henry Newman: Breaking Out— Trying for a New Structure

Levinson suggests that the breaking out sequence is likely to be the most dramatic example of the late thirties as a time of crisis.[1] Just at the point in which this individual is most eager to become his own man and fulfill his adult aspirations, he feels that something is fundamentally wrong with his life and he needs somehow to break out of this structure. In earlier periods of his life, he undoubtedly felt some dissatisfaction, but now, at age thirty-six or thirty-seven, he feels the urgency of the need to do something about it. His life, or a major segment of it, has become intolerable.

Levinson acknowledges that this feeling that life is intolerable can happen anytime. It is certainly not confined to the settling-down stage, but what makes it distinctive in this period is that it was just a few years earlier that the individual had committed himself to building a life structure that was to serve for a long time. Now, just when he ought to be beginning to enjoy the fruits of this labor and he is on the verge of becoming his own man within this structure, he wants to break out of it. The choice he confronts, therefore, is whether to break out, tearing the very fabric of his life, or resigning himself to living the balance of his life with what he himself acknowledges to be a flawed structure.[2] If he does make the decision to break out, he can expect that the process of breaking into another life structure will be emotionally demanding and will likely take a number of years to complete. It will definitely continue well into the period of the mid-life transition (ages forty to forty-five).

My example of a "breaking out—trying for a new structure" type is John Henry Newman. Newman was reared in the Church of England and was one of the founders of the Oxford Movement. At the age of forty-four he converted to the Roman Catholic Church. His decision to convert is prima facie evidence of his concern to "break out" of an unsatisfying life pattern, but my concern here is to penetrate beyond the act of conversion itself and to determine what occurred during his novice and settling-down phases to prompt this act of breaking out and trying for a new life structure. Discussion will begin with a brief account of his childhood and adolescence.

CHILDHOOD AND ADOLESCENCE (1801-1819)

Newman was born February 21, 1801, in London, England. He was the eldest of six children, three sons and three daughters, all born within a nine-year period. His youngest brother, Francis, went on to gain a solid reputation as a philosopher and classics scholar; Francis's religious odyssey carried him from the Church of England to various small Protestant sects and finally to Unitarianism. The middle brother, Charles, was considered the family misfit—incapable of holding down a job and possibly mentally disturbed. The two older daughters, Harriet and Jemima, married in their early thirties after the death of Newman's mother, and Harriet went on to gain a reputation as a novelist. The youngest daughter, Mary, died suddenly at the age of nineteen.

When Newman was born, his parents were caught up in the general optimism of a nation standing on the threshold of a new century. They were recently married and his father was engaged in establishing a banking firm in London. Mr. Newman had purchased a home in a well-to-do section of London for the purpose of becoming acquainted with persons who might become investors in the bank. He had been in the banking business for some years, having begun as a clerk in a bank owned by relatives of Newman's mother. It is reasonable to assume that Newman's parents met through this connection. However, Newman's father came from considerably poorer stock than his mother. Mr. Newman's father was a London grocer who died almost penniless; Mrs. Newman came from a family of wealthy paper manufacturers whose banking interests were secondary.

Newman's paternal grandmother was an extremely important influence in his early childhood. His parents owned a second home in Fulham where his grandmother and aunt lived year-round. He spent a considerable amount of his first four years in Fulham with his grandmother. Apparently, he was left with his grandmother for extended periods of time because his parents were so involved in developing the banking enterprise and in childbirth (starting with John, the Newmans had four children within five years). His biographer, Maisie Ward, points out, "There was a grandmother—his father's mother—at Fulham, with whom he apparently lived, or anyhow stayed for considerable periods."[3] This grandmother played an important role in his religious development. Many years later he recalled being in Fulham "and grandmother taking me on her knee to look at the Bible."[4]

He was sent off to boarding school at age six and remained there, with the exception of vacation periods, until he went up to Oxford University at age sixteen. One year before he went to Oxford he had a conversion experience that caused him to make a decision to enter the ministry. This experience occurred in August 1816 following what he later called a "keen, terrible illness" whose nature he did not reveal.[5] The experience occurred only three or four months after the collapse of his father's banking business in the spring of 1816, and was probably related to it. During the financial uncertainties that followed the bank failure and his father's efforts to begin a new career as manager of a brewery in Hampshire, his parents left him at school during the late spring and early summer months. He later attributed his conversion experience to the fact that he remained at school for six months longer than he originally planned. During this period, he became intimate with Reverend Walter Mayers, his classics tutor. Mayers gave him theological books to read, mainly written by authors who adhered to the Evangelical wing of the Church of England, and spent many hours discussing religious matters with him. As a result of his readings and conversations with Reverend Mayers, as well as his brief but apparently painful illness, he was prepared for the conversion experience in August.

He did not then, or subsequently, describe his conversion experience in any real detail, but he did comment that the experience was instrumental "in confirming me in my mistrust of the reality of material phenomena, in making me rest in the thought of two and only two absolute and luminously self-evident beings, myself and my creator."[6] The fact that he speaks here about his "mistrust" of the reality of material phenomena leads a biographer, William Robbins, to observe: "Perhaps the tendency to such mistrust has already been confirmed by the failure of his father's business in March of the same year, the change from banking to brewery, and the move from London to Hampshire."[7] Newman's adoption of an Evangelical perspective would be consistent with this mistrust of the material as opposed to the spiritual world because what impressed him about the Evangelical writings that Reverend Mayers encouraged him to read that summer was their emphasis on unworldliness, their mistrust of the world. Even after he abandoned Evangelicalism some twelve years later, he spoke admiringly of its renunciation of the world.

After his conversion experience, his perception of a conflict between the "spiritual" and "material" world affected his relationship to his parents. In a journal entry written shortly after his conversion experience, he pointed to the gulf between himself and his parents in matters of "conscience," and expressed the hope that he would be able to present "my scruples with humility and a due obedience to my parents."[8] He said that his parents lacked a real understanding of him. If they had it, they would appreciate his desire to lead a more spiritually dedicated life:

> The beginnings of sin are small, and is it not better, say, to be too cautious than too negligent? Besides, I know myself in some things better than you do; I have hidden faults, and if you knew them, so serious a protest could not appear to you strange. . . .[9]

The conflict with his parents over his religious commitments continued into the following year, when he began his studies at Oxford University. In reference to a letter that he had written his parents from Oxford, his father complained: "That letter was more like the composition of an old man, than of a youth just entering life with energy and aspirations."[10] Then he predicted that his son would abandon his Evangelical views in two or three years, and added: "Men say and do things, when young, which they would fain retract when older, but for shame they cannot."[11]

When he went up to Oxford at age sixteen, he was enrolled in Trinity College, one of Oxford's more "gentlemanly" colleges. His parents were aware that they had chosen a gentlemen's college, as indicated by the fact that they sent him far more money than he required. In addition, his mother urged him to participate fully in college activities, warning him that his Evangelical scruples against "worldliness" would hinder his making friends.

He resisted the wine, women, and song that his mentor, Reverend Mayers, had warned him against, but he struggled against his "dreams of secular ambition."[12] If his conversion experience had caused him to anticipate going into the ministry, he now began to think about a secular profession. This shift in thinking was partly the result of the fact that his father was influencing him toward a law career. In November 1819, when he was eighteen years old, his father entered his name at Lincoln's Inn, the college of law, with the intention that he would go there after completing his BA at Oxford. He later acknowledged that it was not simply his father's ambitions for him that led him to think about going into law, but that he found the idea attractive as well: "In 1819 and the beginning of 1820, I hoped great things for myself, not liking to go into the Church but to the law."[13] What happened next—the reversal of these carefully laid professional plans—inaugurated the "novice phase" in his development, his first major step into the adult world.

EARLY ADULT ERA

Novice Phase

Early Adult Transition (1820-1822)

By 1820, his final year in college, all that stood in the way of the realization of these "secular ambitions" were his examinations for the BA degree. Since he had been an outstanding student who had already been awarded a Trinity College scholarship, he decided to stand for honors. At nineteen, he was a year younger than most students standing for their degrees, but he felt that his scholarly diligence would offset any age disadvantages.

The examinations were scheduled for the final week in November, and as the time approached, he became more and more agitated. His diary entries reveal a deep preoccupation with his sins and personal deficiencies. Because of his "former sins," which he did not identify, he found he could not anticipate the examinations with equanimity. Two or three weeks prior to the examination he wrote in his journal:

> The time draws near. I have had anguish in my mind. Yes, and all owing to my former sins. My soul would have been light and

cheerful, I could have rested in the loving-kindness of the Lord. I should have been of good courage, but He seems to be threatening retribution, and my enemy takes occasion to exult over his prey. Yet, through the thick cloud of heaviness which is on my heart, the gracious Lord at intervals darts His beams and shows that He has not forsaken me.[14]

He confessed that his anguish was related to his desire to achieve honors and especially to his fear that gaining honors could result in spiritual harm. In a letter to his brother Francis, written three months prior to the examinations, he explained: "It is my daily, and I hope my heartfelt prayer that I may not get any honors if they are to be the least cause of sin to me. As the time approaches and I have laboured more at my books, the trial is greater."[15]

The examination began on November 25 and continued for six days. At the conclusion of the examination period, he was awarded his degree but his bid for honors had been a miserable failure. As he explained it, "my nerves quite forsook me."[16] A biographer, A. Dwight Culler, describes his feelings of deep depression during the examinations:

> On November 25, a day sooner than he expected, he was suddenly called into the schools and found himself so nervous that he could not answer half a dozen questions. The examiners gave him every consideration, but nothing would do. Whenever he approached the room a great depression came over him. He was nervous in the extreme, a thing he declared he had never before experienced and did not expect. His memory was gone; his mind was altogether confused, and he dragged on a sickly examination from Saturday to Friday, when he was finally obliged to retire from the contest.[17]

This miserable showing on the examinations meant that the plans for his continuing his education at Lincoln's Inn must now be scrapped. Anne Mozley points out that his failure made the "prospect of rising in a difficult profession doubtful."[18] His father withdrew his application to Lincoln's Inn at considerable monetary loss.

A variety of explanations have been offered for his examination failure. Some biographers argue that he was mentally exhausted from too much studying. Others suggest that his preexamination anxieties were due to his failure to study adequately. Others blame the fact that he was thrown off guard because the examiners called him in on the weekend, which was atypical. His mood and demeanor during the examinations—his extreme nervousness, his deep depression, his inability to talk—would suggest that a deeper conflict was involved, that perhaps he had become overwhelmed with guilt for having replaced his earlier resolve to go into religious service with secular ambitions. Thus, his failure on the examination might be viewed as a means of resolving this conflict. This interpretation of his failure is supported by the fact that the immediate consequence of his failure was that his thoughts about his future now turned back to a religious career. When his father raised the issue of his future during the Christmas holidays, he reports in his diary that "My father this evening said I ought to make up my mind what I was to be. . . . So I chose; and determined on the Church. Thank God, this is what I have prayed for."[19]

If I am correct in viewing Newman's failure as a means of resolving the conflict between pursuing a religious or a secular profession, we may ask why he was incapable of resolving the conflict in a manner that would have been less destructive to himself. The humiliation of failure on the examinations could not have helped his self-esteem. Why, then, could he not have simply confided in his father that he had serious misgivings about a secular career, that he felt called to a religious career? An episode that occurred only two months prior to the examination may explain why he was unable to go to his father and attempt to resolve the conflict in a more rational, less self-destructive way. One Sunday in September, Mr. Newman had asked Newman's brother Francis, who had also been led to an Evangelical conversion by Reverend Mayers, to copy a letter for him. Francis refused on the grounds of the Evangelical principle that it is unlawful to work on the Sabbath. A heated argument followed. Mrs. Newman asked John to arbitrate between Francis and his father, but Newman supported Francis. It is not known what happened next, but evidently their father lost his temper. As Newman wrote in his journal that night, "A scene ensued more painful than any I have experienced."[20] An account of this episode also occurs in Francis Newman's autobiography, on the second page.[21] No longer an Evangelical at the time of his writing of the autobiography, Francis does not defend the idea of not working on the Sabbath, but he does say that his father "attempted to deal with me by mere authority, not by instruction; and to yield my conscience to authority would have been to yield up all spiritual life. I erred, but I was faithful to God."[22] With this episode vividly in Newman's mind, it is perhaps no wonder that failure in the examination was a less painful means of resolving his conflict over his professional future than a candid talk with his father would have been.

How to plan a religious career now became the crucial issue. Within weeks following his examination failure, he decided to enter the competition for a coveted university fellowship offered by Oriel College at Oxford. At the time, this was considered the foremost college in the university in terms of its intellectual standards. In April 1822, he won the fellowship by examination over extremely stiff competition. As he anticipated this new examination, he worried that his "evil passions" of secular ambition would revive themselves: "After my failure last November, I thought that they would never be unruly again."[23] In fact, by gaining the fellowship, he was again in the position to pursue a career in law, but this time he was reasonably secure in his own mind that his intention was to use the fellowship to assist his pursuit of a career in ministry, and Oriel College fellows normally proceeded to holy orders.

Entering the Adult World (1822-1828)

When Newman took his place at age twenty-one among the resident fellows of Oriel College, he recognized that his association with Oriel would play a significant role in the formation of his religious vocation. He was perhaps less prepared for the role that certain Oriel fellows would play in his life as mentors, yet one of the most important features of his life over the next few years was the formative role of his mentors. Among the five ministers in this study, Newman was the most subject to mentoring, both in its positive and negative dimensions.

His first relationship with an Oriel College mentor began rather inauspiciously. Shortly after his election as Fellow, his new colleagues began to question the wisdom of their choice—not that he was disappointing to them intellectually, but that he was excessively reserved and solitary. They decided to rectify the situation by appointing Richard Whately, a promising logician some eight years Newman's senior, to draw him out. Whately took this assignment very seriously.

He had the open, easygoing personality necessary for the task of drawing Newman out and, in time, he was speaking enthusiastically of his success in overcoming his protege's reserve. Newman concurred in Whately's assessment of success. As he wrote in his autobiography many years later: "While I was still awkward and timid in 1822, he took me by the hand, and acted toward me the part of a gentle and encouraging instructor. He, emphatically, opened my mind, and taught me to think and use my reason."[24]

This mentor relationship continued to develop over the next three or four years. In 1826 Whately took over the headship of a university hall and immediately selected Newman to assist him, yet in the same year, signs of difficulty between them also emerged. That year Whately published his *The Elements of Logic*. The book was well received, considerably enhancing his reputation as a logician, but in writing the book, he borrowed from some papers Newman had written earlier, acknowledging Newman's contribution in the preface. Newman was disturbed by this. Although it might be expected that he would be flattered that Whately used his work and gave him credit for it, Newman was troubled because Whately used material he had written a couple of years earlier, which Newman considered not representative of his current abilities. When Whately responded to this concern by saying that he would include an explanation of the circumstances under which his material was written in subsequent editions of the book, Newman felt he had missed the point, and was being "unfair."[25]

This episode indicates that he and Whately had begun to drift apart, but what effectively ended their relationship was an episode that occurred in 1831, when Newman was thirty years old. In that year, Whately had been promoted to Archbishop of Dublin. Newman was taken with the idea of accompanying Whately as a member of his staff, but was not certain whether he should accept Whately's invitation if it were forthcoming. In the end, the decision was made for him, because Whately never extended him an invitation. Newman confessed in a letter, "He knew me better than I know myself."[26] But when they happened to pass each other on the street in Oxford some time after Whately had moved to Dublin, he refused to acknowledge Whately's presence. Relating his avoidance of Whately to a friend, he is reported to have said, "Ah, Rogers, you don't understand, what anguish it was to me to pass Whately on the street coldly the other day."[27] Obviously, the mentor relationship was over, ending in misunderstandings and hurt.

Whately was not his only mentor during his early years at Oriel College; another important mentor was Edward Hawkins, who was twelve years Newman's senior. His close relationship with Hawkins began to develop two years after his election as Fellow of Oriel College, and hence two years after the beginning of his relationship with Whately. This mentor relationship with Hawkins played an extremely important role throughout Newman's novice phase. I will continue to comment on it as I trace his vocational development.

In 1824, two years after his election as Oriel College Fellow, Newman accepted a position as curate in a parish located in a poor section of Oxford. The rector, John Gutch, was in his eighties, so it was expected that Newman would handle most of the parish responsibilities. Having accepted the position, he needed to become ordained as a deacon. The following month he was ordained, but the only member of the family who attended the ceremony was his brother Francis, who was a student at Oxford at the time. Newman had visited his parents the week prior to his ordination and while at his family home wrote in his diary that he felt "more and more happy" about his ordination. After he returned to Oxford, however, he confessed to "an unwillingness to take the vows, a dread of so irreparable a step, a doubting whether the office is so blessed, the Christian religion so true."[28] Moreover, some of his anxiety about his ordination is reflected in his argument with his brother Francis after the ceremony. When the ceremony was over, Newman, presumably suspecting his brother's lack of interest in the proceedings, asked Francis if he had remained through the whole ceremony. Francis confessed that he went out a short while, but that he was present when the laying on of hands took place. Newman says in his journal that Francis undoubtedly left the service "for the purpose of praying for me, *me* who at the time was so hard and so miserable."[29] Later that evening, when he and Francis were reading the Bible together, Newman broke down crying and confessed to himself, "O the evil of my heart, so vile, and so proud. How I behave to him!"[30] He also wrote in his journal that night that he felt "melancholy at the idea of giving up all for God" and compared himself to "a man thrown suddenly in deep water."[31] One suspects he would have felt better had his family expressed greater support by attending the ceremony.

His mentors were also causing difficulties for him. For example, the Sunday following his ordination he preached his first sermon at the parish of Reverend Mayers, his former classics tutor. Mayers was extremely upset with the sermon's doctrinal implications. He is reported to have fumed, "What was that he said about the conversion which exists among all who are baptized, just as if baptism was of any avail, if we were not 'converted.'"[32] Newman may have been hurt by Mayers' reaction to his sermon, but this was only one of two negative reactions the sermon provoked in his mentors. The other sermon critique was offered by Edward Hawkins who, during the summer that Newman assumed parish duties and "was full of the difficulties of a young curate," was "a kind and able adviser."[33] However, like Reverend Mayers, Hawkins was also very critical of Newman's maiden sermon. Mayers had thought the sermon denied the necessity of conversion for salvation; Hawkins felt it denied the efficacy of baptism in effecting regeneration.[34] Apparently, Newman had sought to steer a middle course between conversion and baptism and in the process satisfied neither Hawkins nor Mayers. This problem of how regeneration occurs troubled him throughout the summer. In August he wrote, "The question of regeneration perplexes me very much."[35]

Thus, in his very first weeks in the parish ministry, he had problems. First, his parents did not attend the ceremony of his ordination. Although there may well have been a very good reason for this, it nonetheless deprived him of an important parental blessing of his decision to enter the ministry. His behavior toward his brother Francis the evening of his ordination might also be viewed as his way of taking out on Francis his frustration for his parents' failure to attend the ceremony. Second, his mentors gave him conflicting advice. Reverend Mayers, an Evangelical and the minister responsible for his initial decision to enter the ministry, felt he had strayed from basic Evangelical tenets, especially the fundamental Evangelical view that conversion is necessary to salvation. How could this young protégé so water down the importance of conversion when he had had such a decisively important conversion experience himself? Hawkins, a moderate Anglican, felt that he had denied the regenerative powers of baptism and had thus weakened the traditional Anglican view of the sacraments as means of grace.

A young man who was deeply convinced that he was called to the ministry may have been able to slough off these conflicting words of advice, but Newman had his own doubts about the ministry, questioning whether it was really such a high calling, and had gone against his father's wishes in deciding to become a minister. Thus, when confronted with his mentors' differences of opinion, he was sorely tempted to abandon the ministry because it had brought him nothing but conflict and trouble. Less than a month after his ordination, he visited the church missionary house in Oxford to inquire about going abroad as a missionary. By the end of the summer, he was "so distressed and low" that he began contemplating getting out of the ministry altogether.[36]

A resolution to these vocational conflicts soon came in a most unexpected but painful way. In the throes of his vocational problems, he was summoned home in late September with the news that his father was gravely ill. When he arrived home, his father was still conscious but he was dying. Newman described their reunion: "He knew me, tried to put out his hand and said, 'God bless you.'"[37] Sometime during the day his father asked him to read to him Isaiah 53, the suffering servant passage. Toward evening, "he said his last words. He seemed in great peace of mind. He could, however, only articulate, 'God bless you, thank my God, thank my God'—and lastly, 'my dear.'"[38] Clearly, Newman was deeply impressed and moved by his father's demeanor on his deathbed. If he and his father had quarreled before, especially over the matter of religion and his religious vocation, the fact that his father asked him to read the Bible appears to have conveyed a belated but heartfelt parental blessing on his chosen vocation.

Newman certainly took it as such, for during the next few months, he became more reconciled to his choice of a career in ministry. In January 1825, he felt the problem of regeneration could be resolved simply by placing those who affirm the view that regeneration is truly transformative of the individual, whether such transformation occurs in baptism or in conversion, against those who consider regeneration "a mere opening of new prospects."[39]

On the other hand, he was not completely reconciled to his vocational choice until May 1825, when two events occurred in very quick succession—the death of his paternal grandmother and his ordination as priest. His grandmother died on May 22. Newman attended the funeral and exclaimed in his journal, "Thou hast made her my earlier benefactor, and how she loved me!"[40] The following Sunday, May 29, he was ordained a priest. In his grandmother's death, he lost the person who had provided for his physical security and spiritual growth in his earliest childhood. In the wake of this loss, he seemed far more content with his ordination as priest than he had felt regarding his ordination as deacon a year earlier. On the evening of the ceremony, he said that the service of ordination "has a fragrance in it; and to think of it is soothing and delightful."[41] Perhaps he felt that he was completing a phase of spiritual development begun years earlier when he sat on his grandmother's knee as she read the Bible to him. This view is suggested in a poem he wrote to his brother Francis the following year,[42] in which he encouraged Francis to follow him into the ministry so that, together, they would "prove her prayers were not in vain."

Some months following his ordination, he decided to leave St. Clements where he was assisting the rector and accept the offer to become a full-time tutor at Oriel (his "Age 25 Shift"). His decision to leave St. Clements was aided by the fact that the choir had recently quit en masse over a dispute with him concerning a policy matter. Moreover, there were unfounded rumors that he was about to marry the rector's daughter. His mother was against his return to Oriel as a tutor because she felt he had been called to give comfort to many, not to the privileged few at Oxford. Because this view of Oxford differs considerably from her earlier desire to see him make good in a gentlemen's college, we must conclude that either her views had been changing since he was an undergraduate or that possibly she wanted him to stay at St. Clements in order that his marriage to the rector's daughter might materialize. It was during his St. Clements' period that she expressed the wish that she would see him married before her own death; she said this, in fact, on the day of his father's funeral.

In defending his decision to return to Oxford, Newman invoked the memory of his deceased grandmother. He recalled her prayer that he might always experience the presence of God in enemy territory. As he wrote in his journal:

> And now, O Lord, I am entering with the new year into a fresh course of duties (viz, the Tutorship). . . . May God be with me, according to the prayer of my dear grandmother, 'as he was with Joseph,' and may I see the fruit of my labor.[43]

Here he suggests that he was not abandoning a career in ministry for a scholarly career, but was instead taking his ministry to a foreign land even as Joseph had done great works in the land of the Egyptians.

His decision to accept the tutorship at Oriel College may be viewed as the event that marked his "Age 25 Shift." Viewed purely from an external point of view, this decision was not a major change. After all, his curacy was in Oxford, so he would not be making a change in location. Also, the tutors at Oriel College were clergymen, so it was not as though he would be abandoning the ministry itself by returning to the university. Subjectively, however, it was a major shift, as it meant that he would be leading the life of a scholar, and it was his scholarly investigations that led eventually to his view that the Church of England was established on heresy. Also, he would necessarily be postponing marriage because tutors were required to be single and were expected to give up their tutorships if and when they married. It is impossible to know how much the necessary delay in marriage figured into his decision to accept the tutorship, but the fact is that he never married. He had a close friendship with Maria Giberne, a young woman he met in 1826, and she joined him in converting to the Catholic Church in 1845. Biographer Sean O'Faolain, however, suggests that she was more attracted to women than to men,[44] and, in any case, he seems never to have thought of her as a possible wife. To him, she was more like a sister, a replacement for the void he felt following the death of his favorite sister, Mary, in 1827, the year he settled into his tutorial responsibilities at Oxford.

His return to Oriel College on a full-time basis opened up a whole new dimension of ministry. Shortly after assuming the tutorship, he also became curate under Hawkins, who was the vicar of St. Mary's Chapel, the official chapel of the university. In the months following his appointment as tutor and curate of St. Mary's, he became increasingly popular with students, a fact that both pleased and disturbed him. Writing in 1827 he said, "Much has happened in the past year to make me conceited and vain. My pupils have, or I take care to fancy they have, a high opinion of me. . . . I am becoming somewhat worldly; thoughts about livings, the Provostship, promotion etc. come before my mind. . . . I *do* struggle against this, but how difficult it is."[45] His popularity had evidently inspired him to believe that promotions were within his grasp. However, given his long-standing views against the "material" world, and his contention that he had returned to Oxford to serve the Lord in an alien territory, he wanted to hold firm to his conviction that he had not accepted the tutorship position in order to further his own professional advancement. He had justified leaving his parish position and accepting the tutorship on the grounds that the university was as much in need of spiritual help as the poorest Oxford ghetto.

In late 1827 an episode occurred that revealed the intensity of his conflict over his forbidden desires for promotion. In November of that year he was examining graduating students for their degrees. He had been released from his other duties that fall in order to prepare several "young candidates of distinction for their trial."[46] He was anxious to acquit himself well after his own examination failure at Trinity College seven years earlier. Thus, he was already under strain when, during the examinations, an important piece of news reached him. Edward Copleston, the provost of Oriel College, had just been promoted to a bishopric, and would need to be replaced. This news came in the midst of his thinking about livings, the provostship, and promotion, and at a time when his popularity with students was growing. The news was too much for him. Already in a state of anxiety concerning the examinations, he suffered an "attack" manifesting itself in a "confusion, an inability to think or recollect."[47] As he puts it: "This completed my incapacity. I heard of it on the Friday (November 23), when I was in the Schools—dreamed of it that night, and (I believe) the next—drooped during the Saturday, which was my leisure day—and on Sunday felt the blood collect in my head; on Monday found my memory and mind gone, when examining a candidate for the first class . . . and was obliged to leave the Schools in the middle of the day."[48]

He himself noted that this "attack" occurred on the anniversary of his examination failure seven years earlier. There is perhaps nothing too remarkable in the fact that it occurred during the same week in November, since the examinations were scheduled for the same time each fall, but there was significance in the fact that seven years had elapsed, since this is reminiscent of the seven year divisions in Joseph's interpretation of Pharoah's dream (Gen. 41:25-36). If Newman had accepted the comparison of his situation with Joseph's, as suggested in his grandmother's prayer, his new "failure" in an examination may suggest the end of an old era and the beginning of a new one. Perhaps a more significant comparison of the two examination failures (one as a student, one as an examiner) is that in both a vocational crisis was at issue. It was a vocational issue involving his own professional future that in both cases caused him to lose his capacity to keep his mind on the examination itself. The vocational issue in the examination "failure" in 1827 centered on the fact that Copleston's promotion from the provostship of Oriel College to a bishopric meant that a change in Oriel's leadership was inevitable. Such a change could directly affect his own professional future. Culler captures the vocational implications of his nervous attack when he points out that Newman "saw a field of promise suddenly opening before him and he dreamed about it for two nights in a row."[49]

Newman was not in line for the provostship itself, but by the time the dust had settled the following spring, he had gained a significant promotion from the whole affair—the vicarship of St. Mary's Chapel, the position that Hawkins had held. Perhaps this was the "living" he had been dreaming about after the news of the vacancy of the Provostship came to him. In any event, during the months following Copleston's promotion to the bishopric, Newman exerted considerable influence in the election of the new provost. Edward Hawkins, his mentor, was one of the leading candidates; John Keble was the other. Newman strongly supported Hawkins and later explicitly acknowledged that Hawkins' election was largely the result of the efforts he expended in Hawkins' behalf. As Meriol Trevor points out:

> Hawkins largely owed to Newman his election to the Provostship which he was to hold through half a century, dying in 1882 at the age of ninety-three. . . . In helping to put Hawkins rather than Keble at the head of his college, Newman was unknowingly cutting his own throat, for the Provost was to prove one of the stiffest of his opponents. For Keble, it meant a lifetime of obscurity in country parishes.[50]

Hawkins' election as provost left his vicarship of St. Mary's vacant and Newman, as Hawkins' curate, was selected to succeed him.

Years later, Newman's support of Hawkins was the matter of much controversy and much soul-searching on his own part. For, as it turned out, the candidate who was defeated for the position of provost, John Keble, was a major inspiration behind the Oxford Movement, and Hawkins became one of Newman's bitterest enemies. The question was often raised, therefore, how Newman could have been such a poor judge of character that he would have supported Hawkins over Keble. One answer, of course, is that Hawkins was his mentor. He was acquainted with Keble and had even commented at the time of his election as Oriel College Fellow that he could hardly bring himself to look at Keble, so overwhelmed he was with the thought of being in Keble's company. But Hawkins was his closest mentor during this period. How could he work against the interests of his mentor? Another answer is that he recognized that Hawkins' promotion to provost would leave his vicarship of St. Mary's Chapel vacant. If he assisted Hawkins in becoming the provost, how could Hawkins overlook him when the decision on the vicarship was being made? Thus, in this case, as in so many cases, the mentor relationship was advantageous both for the protégé and for the mentor himself. If Keble had been elected provost, neither Hawkins' nor Newman's situations would have changed. The opportunity for advancement that Copleston's departure had made possible would have been wasted.

Newman's "entering the adult world" period concluded with his appointment as vicar of St. Mary's Chapel. He was now securely placed within the Oxford University community. At twenty-seven, he was a young man who was clearly on the rise, with a bright future before him.

Age Thirty Transition (1828-1833)

Levinson points out that, during this transitional period, there is the sense that the provisional, exploratory character of the twenties is ending. There is also a greater sense of urgency, that if changes or additions are to be made in one's life, this is the time to do it. The age thirty transition is more likely to be stressful than smooth. This stress is partly because, in all transitional periods, some of the stability achieved in the earlier period is being relinquished in order to prepare for the creation of a life structure with new elements. This stress is also due to the unique problems and difficulties of the age thirty transition because one is beginning to reflect seriously on what new directions one will try to initiate in the years ahead.[51]

Newman's age thirty transition was stressful for these very reasons. Although he had reached a significant professional plateau in 1828 with his appointment as vicar of St. Mary's Chapel, it was not long before his life underwent drastic changes that were to have great influence on the settling-down phase of his middle through late thirties.

The first indication of changes to come were his difficulties with Edward Hawkins soon after Hawkins assumed the provostship in 1828. Although he had strongly supported Hawkins for the position, Newman began to work with two other tutors who had been students of John Keble in revising the college curriculum. They instituted the major change of placing poor students in large classes, thus saving the tutor's time for the better students, who were put into small lectures with their own tutors. When Hawkins found out about these changes he was extremely upset, and this led to a series of memoranda between the tutors and the provost that ultimately led to Newman's dismissal as tutor.

In the same year that these curricular changes were being made, apparently without Hawkins' knowledge, Newman became involved in a political campaign on campus whose purpose was to defeat Mr. Peel, Minister of Parliament representing Oxford, who was standing for reelection. Peel was defeated, but at one point in the campaign, Newman feared that Hawkins, their "meddling" provost,[52] might be able to win enough support for Peel to secure his reelection. Clearly, Newman and Hawkins were on opposite sides on this issue as well.

Of the two conflicts with Hawkins, however, the most important for Newman's professional future was the curriculum revision matter. As indicated, this conflict was not settled amicably, but instead led to his and the other tutors' dismissals. By March 1829, six months after the changes were instituted, the conflict between Hawkins and the three tutors had reached such an impasse that Newman sent Hawkins an "ultimatum" demanding his approval of the changes or dismissal of his tutors. In June, Hawkins informed the three tutors that he would not assign them any new students. This meant that they were being dismissed, an eventuality for which he and the others seem to have been utterly unprepared. This was especially true of Newman, for Hawkins had been his mentor and he had helped Hawkins gain the provostship. He simply could not believe that his mentor would turn on him in this fashion. One year later he had completed his work with the students assigned to him prior to the altercation with Hawkins, and this ended his tutorial work at Oriel College. He continued in his post as vicar of St. Mary's Chapel, and he was still a Fellow of Oriel College, but his work with students was over.

In addition to his conflicts with Hawkins, he became involved in one other dispute in 1830 that also had at least indirect implications for his mentor relationships—his dismissal as secretary of the Church Missionary Society in Oxford. As a consequence of his inquiries into missionary work in 1824, when he was frustrated in his work at St. Clements parish, he had become a member of the Church Missionary Society. This was a society that was strongly dominated by members of the Evangelical wing of the Church of England. As secretary of the society, he devised a scheme intended to attract non-Evangelicals to the Oxford chapter, so that moderates could take control. When word about the scheme got out, he was dismissed as secretary and he immediately resigned from the society. Some of his friends at Oxford thought his scheme was unethical, even if ingenious, while others concluded that this was just the kind of boldness the Church of England needed. For him personally his scheme signified that he no longer considered himself an Evangelical.

By 1830, then, he had broken his ties to the two mentors who had taken the greatest role in shaping his views in matters of doctrine and ecclesiastical polity. Having cut himself off from the personal influence of Hawkins, and of Mayers' Evangelicalism, his expectation in 1831 that Richard Whately might invite him to join his staff in Dublin is quite understandable. Whately was his last remaining mentor. But, as noted previously, when Whately failed to invite him and Newman subsequently snubbed Whately on the street, this relationship was also finished in a decisive, irrevocable way. It seems noteworthy that these relationships were not simply allowed to die a natural death. Rather, he felt a need to repudiate these relationships in no uncertain terms, either by challenging the mentor personally or by vigorously rejecting the cause for which the mentor had given his life. In any case, his experiences bear out Levinson's observation that mentor relationships often end in mutual feelings of betrayal.[53]

Relieved of his tutorial duties, he still had his vicarship to keep him occupied at Oxford. He was also writing a book on the Arian controversy of the fourth century. When the book was finished in 1832, he accepted the invitation of Hurrell Froude, one of the tutors whom Hawkins had released, to accompany him and his father, Archdeacon Froude, on a tour of Italy and Greece. Hurrell Froude was going on the trip for health reasons; he was in the initial stages of tuberculosis, which was to claim his life in 1836. Newman agreed to go out of a vague sense that the trip would increase "my usefulness and influence . . . a preparation and strengthening time for future toil."[54] In addition, Thomas Mozley, a supporter at the time, points out that "the tour he was about to make was in those days more of an epoch in a man's life than it is now, and it might be a turning point in his career, as many have since felt that it really came to be in Newman's. But he was now just over thirty. A man has made up his mind at thirty, if he ever made it up, he used to say."[55] Mozley also observes that Newman at this time circulated among his friends, mostly former students, a collection of poems titled *Memorials of the Past,* which included "a motto that showed that a change was passing over him, and he was entering upon a future."[56]

Besides anticipating that he was preparing for a new future in his professional life, he also saw this trip as an opportunity to put some emotional distance between himself and his mother and two sisters. They had come up to Oxford to live so that they would be closer to him, but by this time he felt the decision had been a mistake. In a letter to his sister Jemima shortly after his mother's death in 1836, he noted that he had taken "a false step" in wishing that his mother would be with him in Oxford, for the geographical closeness that it enabled them to have led to greater emotional distance, particularly because

> of late years my Mother has much misunderstood my religious views, and considered she differed from me; and she thought I was surrounded by admirers and had everything my own way— and in consequence, I, who am conscious to myself I never thought anything more precious than her sympathy and praise, had none of it.[57]

He assured his sister, however, that he was no more lonely now in the wake of his mother's death than previously, for

> God intends me to be lonely. He has so framed my mind that I am in a great measure beyond the sympathies of other people, and thrown upon Himself. . . . God, I trust, will support me in following whither he leads.[58]

While traveling with the Froudes, he thought about his desire for independence from his family. In a poem titled "Wanderings" written during his trip, he confessed that he was finding it increasingly difficult to respond to his mother's and sisters' kindness. In fact, home had lost its appeal because "parent's praise and sisters' smile stirred my cold heart no more."[59] He also wrote a poem titled "Melchizedek" in which he compared himself with those who are "fatherless, homeless, reft of age and place."[60] But it was in a letter to his mother that his sense of emotional distance from her and his sisters was most explicitly communicated. He noted that his traveling companions would frequently go out visiting and leave him to his own devices. He then complained that even St. Paul traveled with a companion and was never entirely alone. Then, in the next breath, he noted that he had borrowed a book on marriage from the local library, adding: "Don't smile—this juxtaposition is quite accidental. You are continually in my thoughts, of course. I know what kindness I should have at home; and it is no new feeling with me, only now for the first time brought out, that I do not feel this so much as I ought."[61]

This letter is extremely interesting precisely because it brings marriage and his relationship to his mother and sisters into "juxtaposition." His solitude had prompted him to borrow a book on marriage. Then, recognizing that this seemed to imply that he was thinking more about the kindnesses he might have from a wife than about the kindnesses he had received from his mother and sisters, he immediately assured his mother that his thoughts were continually on the family. Then, in a sudden burst of candor, he acknowledged that his inability to feel the full force of this kindness was not a new experience but one of which he was only now becoming fully aware. Clearly, he was struggling with his feelings about his mother and sisters, especially his desire for greater independence from them. During this trip, he was not only contemplating his professional future but also giving thought to his family relationships, recognizing that he wanted to break away from his mother and sisters but not seeing a practical way to do so.

The trip began in December 1832. He and the Froudes toured Greece and Italy, arriving in Rome in February 1833, the last stop on the tour before returning to England. Rome was to be the climax of the tour for both Newman and Froude, but especially for Froude who used the occasion to engage local Catholic officials in discussions concerning the reunification of the Churches of England and Rome. After their stay in Rome was concluded, Newman surprised the Froudes by announcing that he would not be returning home with them, that he had decided to postpone his return and tour Sicily again, this time accompanied only by a guide. The Froudes were apparently opposed to his remaining behind, but they left without him. He started out immediately for Sicily, and while touring there, he contracted typhoid fever in early May and was forced to stop traveling.

As he lay ill, in danger of dying, he recognized that his illness had some "meaning" for his life, including his professional future. He later noted that it was one of three major illnesses that profoundly affected his future:

> Another thought has come on me, that I have had three great illnesses in my life, and how they have turned out! The first keen, terrible one, when I was a boy of 15, and it made me a Christian—with experiences before and after, awful, known only to God. My second, not painful, but tedious and shattering was that which I had in 1827 when I was one of the Examining Masters, and it too broke me off from an incipient liberalism—and determined my religious course. The third was in 1833, when I was in Sicily, before the commencement of the Oxford Movement.[62]

The third, since it directly threatened his life, was the most serious of the three illnesses.

Why God permitted this last illness, however, was not immediately clear to Newman. At first, he thought it was because he had insisted on coming to Sicily against the Froudes' better judgment. Then he began to consider some deeper reason for the illness, and fixed on his obstinacy toward Hawkins in the curriculum dispute. He thought it significant that May 5, the day on which he had sent his ultimatum to the provost, was just at hand. He bitterly blamed himself for his insubordination toward the provost. This confession of guilt led to even more searching questions about his future course of action and what the illness meant in that regard. As he put it, "I felt God was fighting against me."[63] His personal inclinations, as best he could discern them, were to return to Oxford and, except for his work at St. Mary's, lead a quiet, scholarly life. On the other hand, he felt that God was calling him to engage in a more public life, that he had a larger "mission" to carry out.

He knew that efforts were underway at Oxford to organize for church reform. His experiences in the curriculum dispute caused him to be wary of the personal consequences of efforts to reform the existing system. On the other hand, as he began to recover from the fever, he sensed that God does not visit such serious illnesses on a man and then see to his recovery unless he has great hopes for that individual. As he regained his strength and began his return trip to England in June, arriving home in early July, he wrote the poem, "The Pillar of the Cloud," which was to become the popular Christian hymn, "Lead, Kindly Light." In the first stanza of this poem, he confesses that he does not know where events will lead, but that he is willing to take the initial step, trusting in God's guidance: "I do not ask to see / The distant scene; / one step alone for me." In the final stanza, he refers to the "power" that "hath blest me," expresses confidence that it "will lead me on," and concludes with what appears to be an allusion to his grandmother and his sister Mary, "O'er moor and fen, o'er crag and torrent, till / The night is gone; / And with the morn those angel faces smile / Which I have loved long since, and lost awhile."[64]

Newman's age thirty transition concludes with a tacit decision to reinvest himself in efforts toward church reform, recognizing that this could well involve paying a heavy personal price. But Hurrell Froude was encouraging him to become involved in the efforts that were being made for church reform, and his own work on the Arian controversy (the topic of the book he had completed before embarking on the tour) had given him insight into the contrast between the apathetic church of his own day and the "fresh, vigorous power" of the church of the first three centuries.[65] Thus he saw the need for reform efforts. On the trip home, he wrote another poem in which he described Jonah's effort to resist the will of God by taking passage on a ship sailing away from the city of Ninevah.[66] He pointed out in the poem that Jonah overcame his resistance to his duty and returned to Ninevah. In sensing that God was fighting against him through his illness in Sicily, Newman could readily compare his situation to that of Jonah, who had also attempted to flee from his duty but was confronted by God in his "shipwreck" on the Mediterranean Sea and went on to do the will of God.

The Tasks of the Novice Phase

As we consider Newman's handling of the four developmental tasks of the novice phase, there are some early indications that he might be prompted later to break out of the life structure that was formed in his late twenties. Indications also suggest that, if certain objectives and aspirations could be met in the early stages of the settling-down period, it should not be necessary for him to break out of this structure.

Formation of the Dream. The dreams Newman had for his life began to blossom following the deaths of his father and grandmother. His father, on his deathbed, seemed to give his blessing to the life pattern that Newman had chosen, and in the wake of his grandmother's death, Newman had a stronger sense that he was living his life in accord with the deeper spiritual commitments and aspirations first evoked in him by his grandmother. He was still struggling at that time against the dreams he had put behind him, dreams of ambition and worldly attainments. By the end of the age thirty transition, however, he had begun to infuse his professional role as minister with dreams that were no less ambitious, but more related to the church than to the secular world. In a sense, his earlier secular ambitions had become translated into religious zeal, and he was beginning to envision great things for the church. He had begun to ask: Why is it not possible for the church of today to reflect the power of the church of the first centuries? And what greater ambition and aspiration can a person like himself entertain than the recovery of this fresh and vigorous power? In effect, he had gone beyond the stage of resigning himself to the fact that the ministry is no longer a respected profession to deciding to show what a dedicated minister can do. Thus, he had moved toward the fusion of his calling as a minister and his Dream, a fusion that was clearly lacking when his Dream reflected a strong and continuing desire for secular attainment.

Mentor relationships. Newman's mentor relationships were an indication of a possible desire to break out of his earlier life structure. Mentor relationships had played a major role in his life, but in each case he felt victimized or betrayed. At the conclusion of the age thirty transition, he seems to have felt that nothing further could be done about the termination of his relationship to Whately, but the Hawkins relationship and his sense of betrayal by Hawkins was another matter. Hawkins had come to symbolize for him the problem of the church's leadership, that persons in positions of authority were not responsive to the aspirations of the persons they control. On his return to Oxford, Newman would make an open attack on the bishops of the Church of England, contending that they were not being responsive either to laity or to the common parish pastor. His altercation with Hawkins had made him both frustrated and bold enough to mount this larger attack on men in positions of authority.

In addition, as the age thirty transition came to an end, he had begun to assume the role of mentor himself. In the curriculum dispute, the Peel campaign, and the Church Missionary Society episode, he was dismantling his own mentor relationships but in the process was projecting the image of a young minister who was not afraid to take on the establishment. A supporter, James Mozley, described him as "perfectly ferocious in the cause, and proportionately sanguine of success."[67] If two of these three engagements had resulted in failure and defeat, many young men sensed that these were merely preliminary skirmishes, and that perhaps next time he would prevail. No longer a tutor, he would play a different kind of mentor role, that of championing the cause of young ministers who felt their church had been taken away from them by an indifferent and insensitive leadership.

Forming an occupation. Newman had greater difficulty than the other ministers in this study in becoming reconciled to his decision to enter the ministry. But once this struggle was behind him, he began to make significant advances in his chosen profession. Even though dismissed from his tutorship, he was the vicar of St. Mary's Chapel, a prestigious position for a man so young. As he anticipated his return to Oxford, he knew that his vicarship placed him in an excellent position to appeal to the hearts and minds of the younger men who would form the nucleus of the movement. By the end of the age thirty transition, therefore, he had decided to remain at Oxford indefinitely, rather than to take a parish. A major reason for this, related to his Dream, was that his reading of church history had persuaded him that many of the greatest changes in the history of the church occurred in centers of learning such as Oxford. Thus, he had made significant progress in the formation of his occupation through his appointment as vicar of St. Mary's, but he now intended to make greater use of this position to secure support for the reform movement. This plan was obviously risky. If he were thinking only of his own personal advancement, he would not use his position as vicar in this way. Recognizing the risk, he was careful not to use the pulpit itself to address controversial issues directly but, as we will see, used his series of "tracts for the times" for this purpose. On the other hand, the biblical texts he selected as the basis of his sermons could be "heard" by the discerning listener as having relevance for the times and as providing guidance with respect to current controversies. In this way, his habit of interpreting biblical texts as having meaning for his own personal struggles provided a method for preaching on the issues of the day. His sermons, therefore, fell midway between Brooks' tendency to preach sermons that provided encouragement for whatever the individual parishioner was facing in his or her life, and Edwards' tendency to make very direct allusions to a current event (such as the collapse of the church gallery) and the purposes of God.

Forming a marriage. Newman had made no progress by the end of his age thirty transition toward forming a marriage relationship. Unlike Phillips Brooks, who tried unsuccessfully to find a marriage partner, Newman gave little thought to marriage. He notes in his autobiography that in the autumn of 1816, at the time he experienced his conversion (he was fifteen), a

> deep imagination . . . took possession of me,—there can be no mistake about the fact;—viz. that it was the will of God that I should lead a single life. This anticipation, which has held its ground almost continuously ever since,—with the break of a month now and a month then, up to 1829, and, after that date, without any break at all,—was more or less connected, in my mind, with the notion that my calling in life would require such a sacrifice as celibacy involved; as, for instance, missionary work among the heathen, to which I had a great drawing for some years.[68]

His single status, and the fact that he was the eldest son, left him vulnerable to the demands of his mother and unmarried sisters on his time and emotions, and he sorely desired some relief from these relationships. When his mother died in 1836, he recalled what had happened one evening when he had fainted from overwork and opened his eyes to find his mother stooping tenderly to raise his feet to the sofa. He immediately drew away from her, unable to "endure" her kind touch. He said, "I saw she was hurt, yet I did not know how to set things right."[69] All he could offer in explanation of his reaction against her solicitude was that he "always had some dread or distress" of "being the object of attention."[70] Thus, his thoughts at the conclusion of the age thirty transition were centered on the need for independence from his mother and sisters rather than on the formation of a family of his own.

The Settling-Down Phase

Early Settling-Down Period (1833-1837)

When Newman returned from Sicily in 1833, a reform movement was already under discussion. The initial meeting of the group, which included Hurrell Froude and John Keble, took place two weeks after Newman returned home. This group decided to form an association that would write formal petitions against governmental interference in church affairs (the issue that had rallied forces against the reelection of Mr. Peel in 1828). Significantly, Newman did not attend the meeting but instead wrote a tract intended for distribution to clergy throughout England. This was the first of a series called *Tracts for the Times* that he and other friends wrote over the next six years. Some members of the association objected to his tracts while he objected to a national association. Eventually, an uneasy truce was reached when the leaders of the association accepted his assurances that his tracts would not interfere with their objectives, and he affirmed his support of small local associations rather than a large national one.

Within months, however, it was evident that his tracts had caught the enthusiasm of the rank-and-file clergy in the country, and that the association would play a very secondary role in the reform movement. He also began using the pulpit at St. Mary's to further the cause of reform, not however by discussing specific issues but by contending for a religious faith based on self-sacrifice and self-denial similar to that of early Christianity. Large numbers of undergraduates attended his services at St. Mary's Chapel on Sunday afternoon, and his personal following at Oxford was steadily growing.

In his new enthusiasm during the first months after his return to England, he also decided to become a candidate for the university's moral philosophy professorship. In view of the fact that he had been dismissed as a tutor, this decision was, as he confessed at the time, "a most audacious scheme."[71] One senses that he had in mind his earlier "audacious scheme" of standing for the Oriel College fellowship within a year of his examination failure. As in the earlier case, he felt that the chances of his election were extremely good and had even instructed his publishers to add the title to his name in his forthcoming volume of sermons. He had reason to be optimistic: "First, because no one else is standing; next, because the estate which feeds the professorship is bankrupt, and the office is a sinecure of trouble. . . . I have very little earnestness for the office except the name is a good thing."[72] However, others in the university, mindful of his involvement in the campaign against Peel and his more recent activities as a tract writer, felt that this was one scheme that ought to be thwarted. Another man, R. D. Hampden, was nominated at the last minute and was elected. Newman said he was "floored as to the professorship. I heard of no other candidate till the day before . . . when the Principal of Mary Hall (Hampden) was named, and has succeeded."[73] Clearly, Hampden was nominated and elected not because he wanted the position but because there were many in the university who wanted to prohibit Newman from gaining increased influence through a permanent professorship.

He seems to have retained his self-confidence, at least initially, considering his defeat for the professorship a minor and temporary setback for the Tractarian (or Oxford) Movement. By 1836, however, his attitude began to change. In that year he placed his name in candidacy for the Regius professorship of divinity but, because he felt his own chances were slim, he supported John Keble for the position. As he stated in a letter to Hurrell Froude in January of that year,

> For myself . . . I think I may say with a clear conscience I have no desire for it. . . . I have the unpopularity, the fame of being a party man . . . the care of tracts and the engagements of agitator. I am more useful as I am; but Keble is a light too spiritual and subtle to be seen unless put upon a candlestick.[74]

Newman also noted that it might be good for the reform movement if R. D. Hampden were elected, because this would release his two official positions. Then, perhaps, Keble could succeed Hampden as head of St. Mary's Hall and Newman might, after all, become moral philosophy professor. As it turned out, Hampden was elected Regius professor but neither Keble nor Newman was elected to the posts he vacated.

This disappointment occurred in February 1836. By the middle of February, Hurrell Froude's death was imminent. He died on February 28, on the same day that Newman was writing Keble to inform him that, although the archbishop had interceded in Keble's behalf for the headship of Mary Hall, the decision to appoint another man had already been made. Thus, in February 1836 Newman's hopes for the movement at Oxford were profoundly crushed both by public events and personal bereavement. He described Froude's death as a loss having very long-range implications for his own career. Prior to Froude's death, Newman wrote: "I am soon to lose dear Froude—which, looking forward to the next twenty-five years of my life, and its probable occupations, is the greatest loss I can have."[75] Having suffered the blow of defeat in the recent elections, and with the death of Froude only one week away, he preached one of his most celebrated sermons on February 21 titled "The Ventures of Faith." The same uncertainty that he expressed in his poem, "Lead, Kindly Light," on his return from Sicily was evident in this sermon. Yet, he advised his listeners to make a similar venture: "Our duty lies in risking upon Christ's word what we have, for what we have not; not doing so in a noble, generous way, not indeed rashly or lightly, still without knowing accurately what we are doing; not knowing either what we give up, nor again what we shall gain."[76]

But even though the ventures of faith sermon ended with the stirring words—"we are able"—which his supporters took to be a new battle cry and reaffirmation of the cause of reform both at Oxford and in the church at large, Newman was given to occasional outbursts of despair due, in part, to the fatigue that was the inevitable consequence of several years of religious "agitation." Also, as C. Brad Faught points out,

> The Tractarians had been collecting serious enemies since shortly after the trumpet call of July 14, 1833. In 1836, Thomas Arnold, father of the poet and the most famous schoolmaster in English history, called them malignant in the *Edinburgh Review*. His animus was based on the shoddy treatment given Renn Dickson Hampden by the Tractarians over his hotly contested appointment as Oxford Regius Professor of Divinity in that year.[77]

Of course, Newman had also received rather "shoddy treatment" when his bid for the moral philosophy professorship was thwarted at the eleventh hour.

Newman's despondency over Froude's death was also compounded by the circumstances of the death of his mother in May. Shortly before her death he had prayed that God would provide him some means of improving his financial capacity to care for her or "remove the necessity" through a legacy which there was some chance his mother might receive.[78] Now, with the necessity removed through her death, he felt deep remorse both for his prayer and for the fact that he and his mother had not had a good understanding in recent years. Also, as he became increasingly disaffected from the Church of England in his mid to late thirties, his sisters, who had married two brothers who were both clergymen and friends of Newman in their earlier days at Oxford, professed to finding their older brother difficult to understand. When he eventually converted to the Roman Catholic Church, one of his sisters broke off all ties with him for many years. The other remained in touch with him but kept her distance.

Yet, in spite of these new personal and professional setbacks, he took two major steps to sustain the momentum of the movement. His first act was to publish Froude's private papers, believing that they would inspire his younger followers to redouble their efforts in the movement's behalf. This proved to be a large tactical error. The general public was offended by Froude's references to his severe religious austerities—fasting, subjecting his body to extreme temperatures, and the like. Newman's second step was to draw Edward Pusey, a Regius Professor of Divinity and Fellow of Oriel College, into the movement. Besides his financial support in taking on the monetary responsibilities previously assumed by Froude, Pusey gave the movement "a name, a form, and a personality."[79] The movement now had its Regius professor of divinity and the national press began to call it the "Puseyite" movement.

However, Pusey's name and prestige was bought at a price, because he recommended changing the propagandistic form of the tracts into theological treatises. R. W. Church notes that Pusey's first tract, a treatise of more than 300 pages, "was like the advance of a battery of heavy artillery on a field where the battle has been hitherto carried on by skirmishing and musketry. It altered the look of things and the condition of the fighting."[80] The "tracts" became more scholarly, but they lacked the propagandistic style that had made them widely read. Newman's closest friends and supporters strongly resisted the change from tracts to treatises. They also fought against another of Pusey's ideas, the publication of a "Library of the Fathers" under the coeditorship of Pusey and Newman, with translations to be done by the younger members of the movement. There is reason to believe that these translation assignments were deliberately intended by Pusey and Newman to ward off the impetuousness of the younger men, to drain off their energies in scholarship, and the younger men resented it.

However, with these changes in leadership and direction, Newman kept the movement alive. In fact, it had greater national visibility than ever. Then, in 1838, a new threat to his leadership was precipitated by two Balliol College men, Frederick Oakeley and William Ward, who were among the newer members of the movement. Oakeley and Ward were far more impulsive than Newman and were serious threats to his leadership at Oxford because they exerted influence over the younger men who were more favorable toward the doctrines and practices of the Roman Catholic Church. This presented him with a difficult dilemma, one that was to force his hand and cause him to decide to "break out" of the life structure he had formed during his twenties and consolidated in his early thirties.

Becoming His Own Man (1838-1841)

In effect, Newman, now thirty-seven, was being pressed by Oakeley and Ward to take a position closer to Roman Catholicism. Fearing the loss of the younger members of the movement, he took steps in that direction by confessing that he was no longer as confident in the tenableness of Anglicanism. In late 1839, he began to cast his lot with these younger men, thus offending his older friends, many of whom were in parishes and no longer in close geographical proximity to Oxford. He later confessed that he felt temperamentally closer to his older friends, but his primary concern was to keep pace with the younger group which "was sweeping the original party of the Movement aside, and was taking its place."81 He recognized that he was splitting the movement apart, but he felt that his major responsibility lay with the younger and more impressionable men whose passions needed to be reined in and tamed.

He realized, of course, that he was risking a great deal personally. He knew he could not rely on the "firmness of purpose" of the younger men, but he felt "an intense sympathy" for them and "when the new school came on in force, and into collision with the old, I had not the heart, any more than the power, to repel them; I was in great perplexity, and hardly knew where I stood; I took their part."[82] For his own professional future, this was a momentous decision. If the older members of the movement had understood its purpose to be reform of the Church of England, the tendency of these younger men to voice the possibility of conversion to the Roman Catholic Church struck the older members, now in their thirties, as a total betrayal of the movement's basic objectives. The basis of the movement had been its effort to restore catholicity to the Church of England which, to Newman himself, had meant the recovery of the church of the first three centuries. If it now took seriously the possibility of conversion, it would be playing into the hands of those who had been arguing all along that the movement was never serious about reform of the Church of England, that it had always been secretly "papist" in its orientation and intentions.

For their part, the younger men were willing to acknowledge that reform of the Church of England was the movement's original objective, but they contended that it had failed in this regard because the church did not want reform. The younger men were more deeply alienated from the "establishment,"[83] the term that Newman used to describe the political and ecclesiastical structures of the church and the university. The older members had by now either committed themselves to parishes or had gone into other professions; in most cases, they had married and were dependent on their parishes for their livelihood. The younger men were still at Oxford, either as undergraduates or graduates awaiting ordination, and most were unmarried. They were less bound by the extenuating circumstances of professional and familial obligations, and Newman was the only one of the three major leaders of the movement (Pusey and Keble were the other acknowledged leaders) who was similarly unencumbered by a parish church, family, or both.

What he did next needs to be viewed in terms of his commitment to these younger men. Having made his decision to maintain his influence on them, even at the risk of offending some of his older friends and supporters, he felt that he now needed to take concrete steps to restrain them from precipitous conversions to Catholicism. He decided to write a tract on the Thirty-Nine Articles of the Church of England, which had been formulated at the time of Henry VIII's reformation, showing that they could admit a Catholic as well as a Protestant inter-pretation. His point would be essentially that, while the framers of the articles conceived them in Protestant terms, the language of the articles could bear a Catholic sense as well. If this view of the Thirty-Nine Articles were acceptable in principle, then there would be no necessity for conversion to the Roman Catholic Church. Thus, he considered the reception of this tract, the ninetieth in the series of tracts, to be a critical test. By way of underscoring the critical impor-tance of the tract for his own professional future, he decided before-hand that he would resign his vicarship at St. Mary's if the tract was censured by the bishops.

Resignation of his position as vicar would be a decisive step to-ward "breaking out" of the life structure formed in his late twenties and consolidated in his early thirties. His vicarship (which also in-cluded a small country church at Littlemore, near Oxford, which had been founded by his mother and a number of friends) was his only of-ficial position at Oxford and in the Church of England. On the other hand, while St. Mary's Chapel was the key to his continuing influ-ence at Oxford and in the church of his birth, he was quick to ac-knowledge that his work at St. Mary's had not been going well for some time. For months, the heads of houses at Oxford, who believed his sermons were calculated to undermine the established order, had sought to curtail his influence by instituting a policy of holding Sunday evening dinner at the same time that his services were being held. As Meriol Trevor points out,

> Of course Newman's unpopularity with the Heads of Houses only increased his appeal to the younger generation. The author-ities' fear of him was so acute that some actually changed the times of dinner in hall to prevent the undergraduates attending St. Mary's evening service. In after years someone, explaining why he had not gone to hear Newman, hastened to add that it was *not* because he did not want to miss his hot dinner.[84]

Noting the "pettiness of the opposition" and their "underhanded methods," Trevor adds that their

> unfairness reacted against them. [Newman] was just the right age to exert influence on young people growing up—not to be

classed with the elderly and dull, but strong in that maturity so much desired by the young, positive in idea and action.[85]

This very popularity with young students came at a price, for influential members of the Oxford University community, including the vice chancellor, began to stay away from services at St. Mary's. In November 1839, Newman observed in a letter

> I should not wonder if my situation got unpleasant at St. Mary's. Had I my will, I should like giving up preaching . . . the prospect is gloomy. The Heads of Houses are getting more and more uneasy. I should not wonder if the Bishop got uneasy, in which case I suppose I should resign the living; and I expect the country clergy will be getting uneasy."[86]

His *Tract 90* appeared February 27, 1841. The bishops immediately tried to silence the matter by getting him to suspend further publication of the tract, thus avoiding outright censure of it. He initially agreed, then later warned the bishops that if the tracts were suppressed, he would resign as vicar of St. Mary's. The bishops' response was somewhat ambiguous. They feared that his resignation would inflame matters, so they agreed to the tract's continued publication if he would agree to discontinue the series of tracts. He accepted this counter proposal, but then claimed that some of the bishops violated the agreement when they began publicly to denounce the tract. His more cautious supporters thought his objection was ill-advised, for in effect, he had won the victory he sought when the bishops did not formally censure the tract. But he also acknowledged that it was not simply the fact that some bishops denounced the tract that troubled him. Nor was it the public outcry against it. Rather, it was his "secret misgiving of heart" that the bishops *ought* to denounce the tract, "for I have neither lot nor part with them."[87]

He remained in the pulpit at St. Mary's for two more years and kept the tract in print. So his own settling-down period (at age forty) came to an indecisive end in 1841 with continuing controversy with the bishops and continued involvement in St. Mary's. Yet, unquestionably he had taken major steps toward breaking out of the life pattern formed in his late twenties, especially in the professional area, with the completion of the breaking out and the formation of a new life structure extending throughout the midlife transition. When a young man in the movement converted to the Roman Catholic Church in 1843, Newman resigned his vicarship, feeling he no longer had the right to preach to Oxford undergraduates. In 1845 (at the age of forty-four) he followed a number of the younger men with whom he had cast his lot in 1838-1839 and joined the Roman Catholic Church. In 1846, the end of his midlife transition, he was in Rome with a number of other English converts, preparing for Catholic ordination.

CONCLUSION

When Newman went up to Oxford as a young Trinity College undergraduate, no one would have predicted that some twenty-five years later he would be converting to Catholicism. Not even ten years later, when he was the young vicar of the university chapel, could this have been anticipated. What, then, occurred during his thirties to influence him to break out of the life pattern he had established years earlier? Probably the best way to understand what happened during this period is to take a closer look at the four developmental tasks of the novice phase and see what he did with them in his thirties. To a significant degree, these developmental tasks hold the key to his decision to break out of a life structure that, by his late thirties, had become untenable.

Mentor relationships. We have seen how Newman's relationships with mentors in his twenties had ended with much hostility and repudiation. Unlike Phillips Brooks, who had simply grown beyond his need for his mentor, Dr. Vinton, Newman's mentor relationships had involved open quarreling, and deep feelings of resentment and betrayal. As he entered the settling-down period, he did not feel that he owed his mentors any loyalty or continued respect. The only position he held at Oxford—indeed, the highest position he was ever to attain in the Church of England—was his vicarship, and he had gotten this by helping Hawkins gain a far more prestigious position. One senses that Newman repudiated these mentor relationships because they had meant far more to him than he had meant to them. Perhaps because he had initially entered the ministry against his father's wishes, he wanted his mentors to play more of a fatherly role toward him. He commented, for example, on the "strangeness" of the fact that Whately's role had been to help him become *more* independent. He wanted to relate to them in terms of filial obedience and when they did not understand this, but related to him with a certain professional distance, he was hurt and frustrated and, out of this hurt and frustration, lashed out against them.

Having learned from his own mentor relationships, he performed his own mentor role in a much different style. As a mentor, he was far more willing to be influenced by younger men and to allow them to exert an influence on his own personal and professional life. It is noteworthy that, even though he was the acknowledged mentor of the group of young men who converted to the Catholic Church, most of them converted months before he did and then began exerting pressure on him to do the same. Also, many of his difficulties at the university stemmed from his tendency to entrust younger men with responsibilities that they did not always handle well. For example, the vice chancellor began to boycott his worship services after a young man preached in Newman's absence on the virtues of fasting, and did so even though he had cautioned his protégé against preaching on controversial issues. Thus, he was a different kind of mentor than Hawkins or Whately, who appear to have placed their careers above their relationships to younger men like himself. In a certain sense, his mentoring was more like that of Reverend Mayers. Like Mayers, he was the kind of mentor who could command such loyalty in younger men that they would follow his leadership even if it meant alienation from their families. Also like Mayers, his very willingness to relate to his young supporters on a familiar basis made it difficult for them to reject his influence for fear of hurting him. As we have seen, it was not until Mayers' death that he could openly reject the views that he had acquired from Mayers but had since outgrown. Many Oxford undergraduates found it similarly difficult to break away from Newman even when they desperately wanted and needed to.

Formation of an occupation. The major change in Newman's professional life during his thirties was that he was denied the promotions he sought. As noted, the highest position he ever held in the Church of England was his vicarship, and he had attained this position at the age of twenty-seven. Throughout his thirties, he was continually thwarted in his efforts to gain appropriate recognition and influence in his profession. While successful as an agitator, his failure to gain a promotion at Oxford was extremely frustrating to him. The depth of this frustration can hardly be exaggerated, especially when these thwartings were politically motivated and had nothing to do with qualifications or his ability to do the work involved. We should not be surprised that a man whose upward mobility in his chosen organization ended at the age of twenty-seven began considering "breaking out" after ten years of suffering the indignity of continuing as well as concerted efforts to thwart his advancement.

Forming the Dream. I noted earlier that Newman began to incorporate his concern to recover the power of the first centuries of Christianity into his professional identity, but that he was able to do this only as an avowed reformer. The church as he found it did not provide regular opportunities to live out of this model of early forms of Christian witness. In writing and circulating his *Tract 90,* he was developing the proposition that the Church of England could at least formally accommodate this vision of Christianity. Although this proposition was not overtly rejected by the bishops, he sensed that the Church of England of his day was really not compatible in any fundamental way with this vision. Hence, he recognized that the issue was not whether the bishops denounced *Tract 90* or not, but that whatever their response to the tract, they did not share the same Dream. In contrast, his intense sympathy for the cause of the younger men in the movement was based on the fact that, whatever their personal and theological differences, they shared the same dream and the same growing doubts that the church in which they had been born and reared could accommodate it.

Marriage and the formation of a family. It becomes increasingly clear by Newman's mid to late thirties that his desire to "break out" was partly related to the continuing incompatibility of his life structure with traditional family life. The young men with whom he associated in his late thirties were largely unmarried. Critics of the Oxford Movement have argued that the younger men with whom he cast his lot in the late 1830s were homosexual and that Newman was either homosexual himself or at least very tolerant of it. There is basis for the view that some members of the movement were homosexual. Froude's private papers contained references to his efforts to overcome his homosexual inclinations.[88]

I believe Newman's own attitudes toward homosexual behaviors were similar to his attitudes toward his mother's tenderness—namely, a mistrust of all physical intimacy. At least, an episode in 1875 involving his close friend Ambrose St. John, who had converted with

Newman, suggests this. The episode occurred the evening of Ambrose's death. Ambrose had suffered a stroke a few days earlier and had lost his speech. However, he was showing remarkable signs of improvement and on that very day the members of Newman's religious community were "jubilant" about his recovery. But, as Newman related in a letter two days after Ambrose died,

> When he was sitting on the side of his bed, he got hold of me and threw his arm over my shoulder and brought me to him so closely, that I said in joke, "He will give me a stiff neck." So he held me some minutes, I at length releasing myself from not understanding, as he did, why he so clung to me.[89]

But then Ambrose "got hold of my hand and clasped it so tightly as really to frighten me, for he had done so once before when he was not himself."[90] Newman summoned another member of the community to free him from Ambrose's grasp, "little thinking that it was to be his last sign of love."[91] As Newman rose to leave the room, Ambrose "smiled on me with an expression which I could not and cannot understand. It was sweet and sad and perhaps perplexed, but I cannot interpret it. But it was our parting."[92] In a letter written a few days later, Newman again described Ambrose's actions toward him that evening, and added, "I little dreamed he meant to say that he was going."[93] Ambrose died during the night. The friend who came to help Newman free himself from Ambrose's grasp later reported to Newman that Ambrose had called for Newman to return after he left the room, but Newman had apparently not heard him. When Newman died fifteen years later, he was buried, according to his instructions, in Ambrose St. John's grave.[94]

It is not entirely clear that Newman's reference to the time that Ambrose was "not himself" implies a homosexual advance, but it is difficult to account for Newman's failure to understand Ambrose's real "meaning" in grasping his hand unless the thought of the threat of a homosexual act had crossed his mind. His resistance to Ambrose's efforts to cling to him reflect a strong determination to hold sexuality of any kind at arm's length. Moreover, his summoning of another friend to pry Ambrose's fingers loose suggests that he was both very much in control of his own emotions and able to deal with the situation without disgust or even undue embarrassment.

To evaluate the role that Newman's failure to establish his own family played in his decision to "break out," one would need to consider the pluses and minuses of marriage, friendship, and mentor relationships. Although Newman lacked a marriage relationship and had detrimental mentor relations, he did have close friends. Levinson says that in his study of forty men, "friendship was largely noticeable by its absence."[95] Among his friendships, Newman's relationship to Hurrell Froude was the most influential on his life during his late twenties and thirties. Newman's mother and sisters did not like Froude very much, partly because they felt that Froude had hurt him professionally by encouraging the curriculum changes that led to his dismissal as tutor. Newman viewed things differently. Froude had given him the moral support and financial backing necessary to continue publication of his tracts, and although they had differences of opinion on theological and ecclesiastical matters, Froude shared his longing for a deeper spirituality in the Church of England. Moreover, Froude seems to have given him a self-confidence he lacked both before they met and after Froude's death in 1836. So while his friendship with Froude had some negative effects on his career, it was not more detrimental to his life and career than his relations with mentors or with his mother and sisters. In fact, his conversion to the Catholic Church with a small group of trusted friends secured the independence from family that he had earlier longed for but did not know how to achieve apart from getting married. As he and many of his friends discovered, one of the most effective ways to sever unsatisfactory relationships with family members is to convert to a church that one's family despises!

Chapter 5

John Wesley:
Advancement Produces Change
in Life Structure

Levinson compares the sequence of advancement that produces a fundamental change in the life structure to the first sequence in which advancement occurs within a stable life structure.[1] As noted in the case of Phillips Brooks, advancement in the first sequence does not change the basic life structure. The minister may move to a larger church and take on expanded obligations, but the basic contours of life and career remain unchanged. His professional activities and the nature of the context in which they are carried out are largely the same as they had been before the advancement. In contrast, the sequence that I will be discussing in this chapter involves some fundamental changes in life and career. As a result of new opportunities in the settling-down period, a new way of life, a new career pattern, begins to emerge. Although still a minister, the basic functions of ministry have changed, or the context is so different from what it was that the same functions, carried out in a new context, have a very different set of expectations and goals.

These changes may be quite similar to those of the "breaking out" sequence but differ from them in that the motivating force behind the change is not that one's earlier goals are being frustrated, but that successes open up some unanticipated opportunities (and problems). Levinson's cases indicate that while these successes are often the result of official recognition (e.g., by one's employer), some are the by-product of routine promotion or acquisition of seniority. For example, one may become eligible for a much higher and more responsible position in a medium-size company through routine advancement in a larger firm. The smaller company offers the opportunity for a much more dramatic advancement than would ever be possible in the larger firm. This happens in academia when a professor or dean at a large university becomes the president of a small university or college. In other cases, advancement may be largely self-initiated, perhaps the result of taking some professional risks that open up new forms of professional activity. In other words, advancement may occur in a variety of ways in this life sequence.

An excellent representative of this type is John Wesley. Wesley was an ordained minister in the Church of England throughout his life. But, unlike Brooks, who moved from a smaller to larger church in his settling-down period, Wesley, during the same period in his life, became involved in itinerant preaching and group meetings that led to the formation of Methodist societies. His advancement from a relatively obscure Church of England minister to the director of Methodist societies was largely the result of his own initiative and that of friends rather than the result of recognition for his earlier work by Church of England officials. However, his standing as an ordained minister in the Church of England gave his work as an itinerant preacher its legitimacy and, at least during the period of his life that concerns us here, he sought to form and maintain his Methodist societies within the structure of the Church of England. Thus, his "advancement" was the result of his willingness, and to some extent the necessity, to take some professional risks. The consequence of this risk-taking was not a breaking out of the life structure which he had already established. Rather, it was a matter of success in his outdoor preaching leading to major changes in his professional career as an Anglican clergyman. His work centered on the formation and maintenance of his societies, and this involved a whole new set of expectations, goals, opportunities, and problems.

CHILDHOOD AND ADOLESCENCE (1703-1720)

John Wesley was born June 17, 1703. He was the son of a Church of England clergyman, Samuel Wesley, who served for nearly forty years as rector, until his death in 1735, of the unattractive parish of Epworth in the Isle of Axholme in Lincolnshire, England. As a younger man, Samuel was known as something of a rake in London society. When he was twenty-five years old, a collection of his poems was published under the title *Maggots, or Poems on Several Subjects Never Before Handled*. While the word "maggot" can mean odd or whimsical ideas, the fact that the frontispiece contains an engraving with a large maggot on Wesley's brow suggests that the engraver had in mind the more common meaning of maggot—a wormlike insect larva often found in decaying matter. The titles of his poems may suggest why, for they include "On a Supper of Stinking Ducks," "A Pindarique, On the Grunting of a Hog," "On a Discourteous Damsel That Call'd the Right Worshipful Author 'Saucy Puppy,'" and "A Tame Snake Left in a Box of Bran Was Devoured by Mice After a Great Battle." His work is featured in three recent books on very bad poets and writers.[2] Eighty-eight poets are represented in these three anthologies, and only seventeen are included in all three. This places Samuel Wesley in the top 20 percent of the world's worst poets. In fairness to him, however, he did attempt to write serious religious verse in later years, and in 1713, when he was fifty-three years old, he published a long poem "An Hymn on Peace, to the Prince of Peace."

Samuel and his parishioners were frequently at odds with one another, particularly over his view that the marshlands on which Epworth was built should be drained, an improvement that many parishioners felt would hurt their own livelihoods. As a result, he was the probable victim of arson and suffered the destruction of his crops and cattle. Still, he thought it would be cowardly to move to another parish where his training and learning might be put to better use. Wesley's mother Susanna, like his father, was raised a Puritan but made the transition to Anglicanism when she married Samuel. The Wesleys had nineteen children in all, but only ten, seven girls and three boys, survived infancy. The oldest son, Samuel Jr., was thirteen years older than John and was away at school during most of John's childhood. Five of his sisters were older than John, and two sisters and his brother Charles were younger. Thus, like Jonathan Edwards, Wesley was raised in a family in which sisters predominated.

Of two important episodes in Wesley's early childhood, the first involves the circumstances of his birth. Apparently, a year and a half prior to John's birth, his father and mother got into an argument about a political matter and his father, angered by the conversation, went up to London where, as Wesley tells it, "being convocation man for the Diocese of Lincoln, he remained without visiting his own house for the remainder of the year."[3] When he returned home, Wesley was conceived, prompting him to consider himself as a "child of reconciliation."[4] In later years, he viewed the circumstances of his birth as a sign of the special meaning and purpose of his life.

A second important episode, when he was six years old, also contributed to this view of his life as filled with special meaning. The incident was the rectory fire of February 9, 1709. John, then nearly six years old, was left sleeping in the house when it was evacuated. His father tried in vain to force his way up the burning staircase. A few moments afterward, John appeared in the bedroom window. Neighbors pulled him out just as the roof fell.[5] Wesley's mother referred to him as "a brand snatched out of the fire" (from Amos 4:11 or Zech. 3:2), a metaphor that he also used in later years to describe himself. What caused the fire is not known, but an earlier episode in which parishioners shouted and fired pistols and guns in the yard outside the manse amid threats to drive the Wesleys from their home indicates the probability of arson.[6]

Wesley was largely under his mother's tutelege during his early childhood. His mother Susanna had very definite ideas about the raising and nurturing of children, and laid particular stress on the importance of conquering one's will and keeping one's emotions in check. Spanking was avoided in favor of encouraging the children to control themselves and to voluntarily confess their transgressions. At age eleven Wesley went to Charterhouse, a boarding school located in London. His admission to Charterhouse was due to the support of the Duke of Buckingham, a patron of Wesley's father. Six years later, he left Charterhouse to attend Christ Church, Oxford.

EARLY ADULT ERA

The Novice Phase

Early Adult Transition (1720-1725)

After four years at Oxford, Wesley took his BA degree, and immediately made plans to enter the ministry. His original plan was to assist his father after his ordination. Samuel Wesley had added the curacy of the village of Wroot to his charge, and could employ his son there as its curate. However, his father also encouraged him to take enough time to study for ordination, taking more than a year if necessary. His mother meanwhile encouraged him to move toward ordination as quickly as possible, perhaps anxious for him to return to Epworth and begin assisting his father. He completed his studies for ordination as deacon in September 1725 at twenty-two years of age. In the following weeks he preached in a number of small villages near Oxford. He did not return to Epworth immediately but instead remained at Oxford with the hope of receiving a college fellowship. There was a vacant fellowship at Lincoln College that was open only to candidates from Lincolnshire. He studied for the examination through the year and, on March 17, 1726, was elected to the fellowship. His father, who was extremely proud and happy for his son, dined in the college halls that evening. Although he did not know whether he himself would still be at Epworth by the end of the summer, Samuel also observed that, "Wherever I am, my Jack is a fellow of Lincoln."[7] His mother was also pleased, though more restrained than his father: "I think myself obliged to return great thanks to Almighty God, for giving you good success at Lincoln."[8] One senses that his father felt John would now have an alternative to going back to Epworth if he chose to leave his rectorship there, whereas his mother feared that this might influence John to stay away even longer.

In 1725, while he was studying for the fellowship, Wesley became intimate with the Kirkham family. The elder Kirkham was the rector at Stanton, where Wesley had preached on occasion, and Wesley developed a close relationship with the four Kirkham children who were close to him in age. He became especially fond of Sally Kirkham, but realized that with no money and poor prospects at the moment, he could not propose to her. Moreover, if he were to marry, he could not hold a fellowship. She married the local schoolmaster in December 1725, three months before his successful bid for the fellowship. But, as his biographers point out, he and Sally remained very close friends after her marriage. V. H. H. Green recounts an incident that occurred one evening when he was with Sally and her sisters, in Sally's husband's absence. He "leaned on her breast and clasped her hands in his."[9] She reacted by saying that she would certainly inform him

> if my husband should ever resent our freedom, which I am satisfied he never will; such an accident as this would make it necessary in some measure to restrain the appearance of the esteem I have to you, but the esteem as it is founded on reason and virtue

and entirely agreeable to us both, no circumstance will ever make me alter.[10]

Although Sally Kirkham's husband never objected to his close relationship to her, Sally's sister Damaris had a suitor who felt Wesley was trying to steal her away from him, and Damaris encouraged his jealousy by flirting with Wesley.[11]

After winning the fellowship in March, he began to spend less time in Oxford and devoted more time to helping his father at Epworth parish. Thus, his early adult transition concluded with his having gained a fellowship at Oxford, his ordination as deacon, and some successful preaching in neighboring parishes. It was also evident that he was strongly attracted to young women, and that he had a tendency to create romantic triangles in which he did not seek the young woman's hand in marriage but made life uncomfortable for the young man whose intentions were more serious than his.

Entering the Adult World (1726-1732)

His father did not leave Epworth and the next three years of John Wesley's own life were spent mostly there, assisting his father in his parish duties. In addition to the normal round of duties performed by the curate, he helped his father in his research for a book on Job. His biographers are generally agreed that his father was difficult to work under, and the fact that Wesley was his son made it all the more difficult. But their conflicts during this period centered less on parish matters than on more personal issues. In 1726 Wesley began to take an interest in a young local woman, Kitty Hargreaves, and his father immediately disapproved when he began to suspect that he was courting her. The elder Wesley sent Kitty away, but Wesley, while agreeing that self-denial in these matters is to be commended, continued to see Kitty that summer. In July he vowed to "Never touch Kitty's hand again"[12] and in August made a resolution in his diary never to touch a woman's breasts again.[13]

A more serious conflict with his father developed over his sister Hetty. Apparently, she had allowed herself to be seduced during her courtship with a local lawyer. When her father found out, he was violently angry and forced her into marriage with another man, a local plumber, as punishment. Her marriage to the plumber was to prove an extremely unhappy one for her. John took his sister's side, and preached a sermon on charity toward those whom we consider wicked. His father resented this criticism, and said to Wesley's younger brother Charles, "Every day, you hear how he contradicts me, and takes your sister's part before my face. Nay, he disputes with me, preaches. . . ."[14] Wesley apologized to his father for his lack of filial obedience when he discovered that his father was considering taking official action on the matter because a curate preaching against his rector violated church law. It is significant that Wesley's mother had helped him draft the sermon in question.

In 1728, at the age of twenty-five, he was ordained a priest while serving in his father's parish. The same year he was alerted to the fact that he might be asked to return to Oxford as a tutor at Lincoln College, because the college suddenly found itself short of fellows who could undertake tutorial work. In 1729, the rector of Lincoln College wrote to him, offering him the position, and noting that although his father would not be able to secure another curate as satisfactory as he had been, he hoped the elder Wesley would not hinder his son's return to Oxford. Wesley seems to have welcomed the opportunity to return to Oxford in light of the continuing tension between his father and himself, and the limited social and intellectual stimulation that Epworth offered. He did return to Epworth from time to time, partly to see his family and partly to be with Kitty Hargreaves.

As in the case of Newman, Wesley's decision to return to Oxford as a tutor was the central event in his "Age 25 Shift." As his father's curate, he was in something of a dead-end job in a rather remote location. By returning to Oxford, he would build on his earlier success in receiving the fellowship from Lincoln College. It also meant placing any marital intentions on hold, and this may well have been an important consideration in his father's willingness to relinquish him.

When he arrived at Oxford, Wesley moved into university activities with enthusiasm, working with the eleven students assigned to him and lecturing in the college hall on the Gospels, Acts of the Apostles, and the Pauline Epistles. The illness of the rector of Lincoln College in 1730 and his subsequent death in 1731 placed Wesley in somewhat the same position as Newman, also a young tutor who was in a position to influence the selection of the new rector. He supported Euseby Isham, who was fifteen years his senior, as the new rector. Isham was elected and, as it turned out, was a good choice in light of Wesley's subsequent activities at Oxford. Isham continued to be generally supportive of Wesley even though he was occasionally embarrassed by his religious activities. On the other hand, like Newman, Wesley was later in danger of being stripped of tutorial responsibilities due to his religious work.

The most important feature of his work at Oxford, and the source of subsequent difficulties, was his involvement in a small religious group that his younger brother Charles had initiated six months before John returned to Oxford. Charles had been at Oxford for three years as a student when he decided on a program for self-improvement. V. H. H. Green points out that Charles embarked on this program for self-improvement "partly under pressure from his mother, partly because of his awareness of his own idleness, and partly because he had become alarmed at the spread of deism among members of the university...."[15] The group first consisted of Charles and two or three fellow students who agreed together to observe the methods of study prescribed by the statutes of the university. This gained them the name of "methodists," the name that eventually survived, but as the group grew it was also referred to as the Sacramentarians, Bible Moths, Bible Bigots, and the Holy Club. When John Wesley came up to Oxford, he agreed to help organize the group and, because of the fact that he was a University fellow, he gave the group a visibility it had lacked during its first six months. Under his guidance, the group drew up a list of books they would read, and developed a spiritual formation program that included frequent attendance at Holy Communion and regular periods of prayer and Bible reading.

The group evoked much attention and some derision almost from the very beginning. Undergraduates were especially dubious about it. So also were some senior members of the university, but there was no organized opposition to the activities of the Holy Club. In fact, the Bishop of Oxford took a kindly interest in the project and, before long, the group was attracting fellows of other colleges and even a few townspeople, both husbands and wives. The group also began to go beyond its emphasis on personal piety and initiated a project of visiting the two Oxford prisons. They prayed with the prisoners and administered communion to them, but they also helped with the prisoners' legal and material needs. They supplied fuel, food, and clothing and, because many of the prisoners were debtors, they collected money to pay off their debts and secure their release. They also worked to secure competent legal advice for prisoners at their trials.

Moreover, in addition to their work in the prisons, they started a school for small children in town. Thus, the group's interests began to expand and with this expansion in its program came a substantial growth in membership.

As the Holy Club grew in influence, however, it was subjected to increasing criticism. In the university, the club was criticized for its emphasis on frequent communion and fasting. Both evoked the charge of hypocrisy and self-righteousness. The club was also criticized for its championship of prisoners. One case in particular was disturbing because it involved a young man who had been accused of homosexuality and, in consequence, was unpopular with his fellow prisoners as well as with the townsfolk. A contemporary, Thomas Wilson, was critical of "the Methodists taking the part of Blair who was found guilty of Sodomitical practices and fined 20 marks by the Recorder" because

> Whether the man is innocent or no they were not proper judges, [so] it was better he should suffer than such a scandal given or countenancing a man whom the whole town think guilty of such an enormous crime. Whatever good they pretend it was highly imprudent and has given the occasion of terrible reflections.[16]

The more potentially serious criticism of the club for Wesley personally was the charge made by some fellows of Lincoln College that he was virtually requiring his students to become Holy Club members. As Green puts it:

> Wesley denied that he brought pressure to bear on his pupils to join the Holy Club, but he had so strong a personality and was too convinced of the rightness of his cause to let the challenge go unanswered. His pupils were invited to breakfast, stayed to pray and found themselves going to communion at Christ Church and visiting the prisons; some of them reacted critically, but if they did so they found themselves involved in heart to heart talks, in emotional reconciliations which retarded, if they did not actually prevent, their withdrawal from the society.[17]

Wesley remained on good terms with the rector of Lincoln College, but his colleagues were becoming increasingly critical of his influence on students, and were also concerned that one of the younger college fellows had joined with him.

These criticisms, while mounting, were not enough to dissuade him from continuing his work. In 1732, however, the Holy Club suffered a blow that, although it did not slow the growth of the group, had a sobering effect on its members, including Wesley. This event was the death of one of the club's members, William Morgan, in August 1832. Morgan had been an enthusiastic member of the club, and had contributed to the club's work much of the money sent to him by his father for food and books. He had been very active in their work with prisoners; he was, in fact, responsible for suggesting this initiative. But in May 1732 it was apparent that Morgan was in bad shape, both physically and mentally, and Wesley suspected that his death was not far off. Morgan seemed to want to die. During the early summer months, when he was home in Dublin, he began to have fits and convulsions. He talked wildly and incoherently, contending "that enthusiasm was his madness" and that the Wesleys had hindered him from throwing himself out the window.

When he died, much publicity was given to his death, and it was widely rumored that his illness was the result of physical and religious austerities forced on him by the Holy Club. Wesley wrote to Morgan's father to assure him that the club was not responsible for his son's death, and the elder Morgan was so convinced by Wesley's letter that he also entrusted his younger son to Wesley's care at Lincoln College. Green says that Wesley was right when he pointed out that the club was not directly responsible for young Morgan's physical austerities (that fasting had only recently become a part of his teaching), but he also contends that "Morgan's subsequent madness was in part a result of his excessive concern about religion," and that the club exacerbated an already neurotic reliance on religion.[18]

The death of William Morgan in 1832 marks the end of Wesley's "entering the adult world" period. By this time, the twenty-nine-year-old Wesley had proven his ability to function effectively in a ministerial capacity. The bulk of his parish work had been as curate to his father, however, and during much of the time that he served in this capacity, considerable conflict occurred between the two men. Because he served under his father, this experience in ministry did not enable him to test his abilities as a parish minister adequately. When he returned to Oxford, he considered the possibility of accepting a curacy and, in fact, tried it briefly, but found he did not have the time to devote to it. Thus, his experience in the parish ministry had not given him the kinds of experiences that would have helped him determine his aptitude for parish ministry.

On the other hand, when he returned to Oxford, it became clear to him that a career limited to tutorial and scholarly work was not enough. Thus, he clearly welcomed the opportunity to become involved in organizing the club and directing its activities. Moreover, the club's prison work was indicative of his deep concern for social justice. In this, he was very similar to Phillips Brooks at the same stage in life, and although the Morgan case drew attention to potential dangers of the club's emphasis on personal piety, his support of the defendant in the homosexual case is clear evidence of the club's willingness to champion unpopular causes. In light of these two issues, it is clear that his work was potentially very controversial, and yet to this point he had been able to move into these controversial activities without provoking university or ecclesiastical officials to curtail his work. This is a tribute both to the restraint of these officials, especially the rector of Lincoln College, and to his own skill in maintaining good lines of communication with these officials even when they disagreed.

Age Thirty Transition (1732-1737)

Wesley's account of the Holy Club and its objectives satisfied the elder Morgan, but the incident made people at the university much more aware of the Methodists. Criticism from other quarters of the university was increasing, but Wesley continued to receive at least tacit support from his colleagues at Lincoln College. It is true that in 1733 the rector was assigning him fewer students. In August 1733 he wrote his mother, "If I have no more pupils after these are gone from me, I shall then be glad of a curacy near you; if I have, I shall take it as a signal that I am to remain here."[19] Still, if he was being assigned few students, it was also the case that Lincoln College admitted only eight men in 1732 and eleven in 1733, so his reduced tutorial load may well have been a result of declining enrollments and not, as in Newman's case, a decision to terminate this tutorial relationship. Wesley had a talk with the rector about the fact that his pupils were going to communion at Christ Church and, while opposed at first, the rector relented and allowed the young men to go. Thus potential crises were defused before they could get out of hand.

The Holy Club had been hurt by the death of William Morgan, yet it survived the crisis and continued to grow during the months that followed. In fact, it was during this time that George Whitefield, then a financially poor student working his way through college, joined the group. Wesley, however, was not quite the same. As Green points out, "at the close of 1733 and the beginning of 1734 there were signs of depression and rejection. . . . Once in a moment of despair he had thought of becoming headmaster of Skipton School."[20] If William Morgan had not died, Wesley might not have become depressed and dejected, but the criticism it provoked, including magazine articles, disturbed him. Even though his own letter to Morgan's father and a rebuttal of the criticisms written by William Law, a noted Anglican clergyman and author of *A Serious Call to a Devout and Holy Life,* were successful in laying many criticisms to rest, Wesley recognized that the club was placing him in a difficult position in his college. Another reason for Wesley's despondency during this period is that his old friends, the Kirkham women, were settling down with their families and, while still friendly toward Wesley, were less anxious to have him visit them. On the other hand, Wesley probably felt that his old friends were not suffering enough for the Gospel, that they were living in comfort while he was working in prisons and courts.

In addition to these difficulties at Oxford and his increasing distance from old friends, Wesley's father's health had been failing for some time. In June 1731, the seventy-one-year-old Samuel had fallen off a wagon and suffered a severe concussion. In October 1732, Wesley's mother reported that his father was "in a very bad state of health. He sleeps little and eats less. He seems not to have any apprehension of his approaching exit, but I fear he has but a short time to live."[21] When Wesley returned home in January 1733, his father was so ill that prayers were said, commending him into the hands of God. He rallied unexpectedly, however, and by the end of the month was out of immediate danger. By the end of the year, he was actually well enough to travel to Oxford at Christmastime to be with his son.

During his illness in 1732-1733 Samuel Wesley began to consider the question of the future of Epworth parish. He wanted to have a hand in finding his replacement and, in fact, was anxious to have one of his own sons carry on the Wesley tradition at Epworth. Wesley's older brother Samuel was not in a position to consider the position because he had recently become the headmaster of a school. Charles was not yet ordained. So John, partly by default, became his father's choice to succeed him and his mother was in strong agreement.

He discussed his father's hope in this regard with his mother when he visited his father in January 1733, but he was reluctant to accept the parish from the start. He told his mother that he did not think he was physically strong enough to carry out the work that the parish would demand of him. Months later, in November 1733, his father wrote him and asked him to accept the position because this would preserve the work he had been trying to do for forty years and because of the "dear love and longing which the poor people have for you."[22] It is also likely that his father felt that John's coming to Epworth would provide a home for his mother and two unmarried sisters. He remained resistant to the idea, responding to his father by pointing out that he could not do the good he was doing at Oxford at any other place. At Oxford, he was not subject to the idle conversation that was unavoidable in the outside world. Also, at Oxford he had a few like-minded friends whose commitment to personal holiness was similar to his own, and he had at least as many opportunities for useful service to the poor that he would have at Epworth:

> There is scarce any way of doing good to our fellow creatures for which here is not daily occasion. . . . Here are poor families to be relieved; here are children to be educated; here are work houses wherein both young and old want, and gladly receive, the word of exhortation; here are prisons to be visited, wherein alone is a complication of all human wants. . . .[23]

Even though Epworth parish had 2,000 people for whom he would be responsible, it could not provide the variety of opportunities for service that he already had at Oxford. Moreover, Oxford offered him a freedom from financial worry that he would not have at Epworth; indeed, taking the position at Epworth would mean losing his fellowship and its assurance of a regular salary.

When his older brother Samuel heard that he had turned down Epworth, and learned what his arguments against it were, he wrote Wesley accusing him of insincerity, and telling him that he was avoiding his ordination vows in refusing the cure of souls. Knowing that his brother was in no position to criticize (since he had refused the position also), he responded in an evasive way, but his brother's criticism of him pricked his conscience and he wrote to his bishop in Oxford and asked whether his ordination vows placed him under obligation to accept the post. The bishop assured him that they did not, but his conscience still bothered him and he intimated that he might be willing to take the living after all. By this time, however, it had been offered to another man who had accepted it.

In addition to feeling conscience-stricken after refusing Epworth parish, Wesley also realized that his letter extolling the virtues of his life and work at Oxford had been an exaggeration. As Green puts it,

> It is fair to suggest that he was less satisfied with life at Oxford than he appeared to argue in his letter to his father. He felt the call and challenge of a wider sphere than that presented by a provincial University town. What he and his friends were doing had made little perceptible impact on the majority of the junior and senior members of the University. Yet fundamentally the decision was rooted in more personal considerations. John Wesley was introspective by nature. He did not feel that the work that he was doing gave him the inward peace and spiritual serenity which should be the mark of the true Christian.[24]

A few months later, in April 1735, Wesley's father died. His debts were greater than his assets and his large work on the book of Job was not yet finished. John Wesley finished the work and, according to his father's request, presented the book to Queen Caroline, to whom it was dedicated. Mrs. Wesley left Epworth, staying with a daughter and then with her son Samuel for a time, then took up permanent residence with a daughter whose husband had been a member of the Holy Club at Oxford.

At thirty-two, Wesley's life now took a most unexpected turn. He and Charles went down to London in the summer of 1735 and, while there, he was introduced to Colonel James Oglethorpe, who was looking for a clergyman who could serve as chaplain to the English community at Savannah, Georgia, and preach to the neighboring Indian tribes. Oglethorpe knew of his work at Oxford and was most impressed with his prison work. Many of the Georgia colonists were debtors whose freedom from prison had been gained by Oglethorpe in exchange for their services in Georgia as a military defense against a Spanish advance from the south. Evidently, Oglethorpe impressed on Wesley that he could, in effect, continue the kind of work he had been doing at Oxford but on a much larger scale. After consulting with his mother, older brother, and others, Wesley decided to go, taking his brother Charles, who would serve as Oglethorpe's secretary. Benjamin Ingham, a member of the Holy club, and another acquaintance, Charles Delamotte, would also go. Other members of the Holy Club who at first agreed to go subsequently dropped out.

A major advantage of this particular undertaking was that, in contrast to accepting the living at Epworth, he would not need to relinquish his fellowship, and he undoubtedly expected to return to Oxford on a relatively permanent basis after his return to England. He did not know at the time that he was virtually severing his ties to Oxford when he set sail in October 1735.

Green suggests that Wesley's father had "sowed the seed" for this decision, for the elder Wesley had often talked about becoming a missionary himself.[25] Thus, if Wesley had disappointed his father in refusing Epworth parish, he was, nonetheless, fulfilling his father's own dream. Having completed his father's scholarly work by finishing the book on Job, he was now completing his father's dream of becoming a missionary in a foreign land, having only the previous Sunday to his embarkation personally presented his father's book to the queen.

While enroute to America, he became well acquainted with a group of twenty-six German Moravian Brethren who were going to Georgia to join a group of Brethren already there. This acquaintance with the Moravians was to have a very important influence on his career when he returned from Georgia. He also became acquainted with two women, a Mrs. Hawkins and a Mrs. Welch, who were to make trouble for both Wesleys in Georgia. Shortly after they arrived in Georgia, Mrs. Hawkins and Mrs. Welch, hoping "to get a rise out of the naïve young minister,"[26] told Charles that they both had adulterous relations with Oglethorpe, and Charles, believing them, repeated the story. When Oglethorpe learned that Charles had spread the story, he was furious with the young Wesley and made his work as his personal secretary almost impossible. When John sought to assist his brother, Mrs. Hawkins also attempted to discredit John by inviting him to her home and then threatening him with a pistol and a pair of scissors. When he struggled against her, several men came into the room but did not come to his aid. Before he could escape, he had disarmed her but she had bit him through his coat. Clearly, the two women were bent on causing Charles and John to fail in their mission to Georgia. Since the previous chaplain to Savannah had been replaced because of his attempt to seduce his maid, it was apparent that the two women were worried that the Wesley brothers would attempt to raise the moral level of the colony, something they and many others did not want. Charles returned to England the following summer while John stayed on.

The far more serious threat to Wesley's ministry in Georgia, however, was his involvement with Sophy Hopkey. Only a few days after he preached his first sermon in Savannah, Wesley met Sophy at the home of her uncle, Thomas Causton, who was the director of supplies and chief magistrate of the settlement. She was eighteen years old at the time, fifteen years his junior.

Wesley's first mention of Miss Hopkey occurs in a journal entry written shortly after he assumed ministerial duties in Savannah:

> At my first coming to Savannah, in the beginning of March 1736, I was determined to have no intimacy with any woman in America. Notwithstanding which, by the advice of my friends, and in pursuance of my resolution to speak once a week at least to every communicant apart from the congregation, on March the 13th, I spoke to Miss Sophy Hopkey, who had communicated the Sunday before, and endeavoured to explain to her the nature and necessity of inward holiness. On the same subject I continued to speak to her once a week, but generally in the open air, and never alone.[27]

They were always in the presence of her friend, Miss Fawset. Soon after, however, Wesley was visiting in the Causton home, and when he left the room, he overheard Mrs. Causton say, "There goes a husband for my Phiky," her nickname for Miss Sophy.[28]

Shortly thereafter, Mrs. Causton said to Wesley, "Sir, you want a woman to take care of your house," to which he replied, "But women, madam, are scarce in Georgia. Where shall I get one?" Mrs. Causton answered, "I have two here. Take either of them. Here, take Miss Fawset." But Wesley replied, "Nay, Madam, we shan't agree. She is too merry for me." "Then take Phiky; she is serious enough." Wesley protested, "You are not in earnest, madam," to which Mrs. Causton replied, "Indeed, sir, I am; take her to you, and do what you will with her."[29] He resisted the offer, but this was only the beginning.

For the next several weeks Wesley was in Frederica, Georgia, where his brother Charles had been assigned, but when he returned in early July, Mrs. Causton asked him to speak with Sophy alone because Sophy, she said, "was utterly ruined, being in love with and resolved to marry a notorious villain, one Mellichamp, then in Charleston for forgery." She added, "Sophy minds nobody but you; if you will be so good as to step into the garden, I will send her to you."[30] Miss Sophy came out to the garden. As Wesley tells it, she was

> all in tears, and with all the signs of such a distress as I have ever seen. She seemed to have lost both comfort and hope. I stayed with her about an hour. At the end of which she said she was resolved to seek comfort in God only, and through his help to tear from her heart an inclination which she knew did not tend to his glory.[31]

Wesley's friends felt it was now his duty to see her more frequently, and he began meeting with her once every two or three days, being careful as he did so "to speak only on things pertaining to God."[32] But on July 23, after he had talked with her for some time, he "took her by the hand and, before we parted, kissed her. And from this time I fear there was a mixture in my intention, though I was not soon sensible of it."[33]

Green suggests that Wesley's relations with Sophy Hopkey ran a familiar course:

> She consulted him about her spiritual state. He felt ill and she nursed him. She fell a victim to his charm and learning, dressed in white because it pleased him. . . . He taught her French. She became a regular and devout member of his congregation. Their friendship in the small community inevitably promoted gossip.[34]

As their relationship became more serious, he began to consider the possibility of marriage. Her uncle and aunt seemed to favor the marriage, but she did not encourage Wesley because she had promised Mr. Mellichamp that she would either marry him or not marry at all. When Wesley responded, expressing "a sudden wish, not of any formed design," that he would "think myself happy if I was to spend my life with you," she burst into tears and said, "I am in every way unhappy. I won't have Tommy [Mellichamp]; for he is a bad man. And I can have none else. Sir, you don't know what danger you are in. I beg you would speak no more on this head."[35] She seems to imply that if she chose Wesley over Mellichamp, the latter would do him physical harm. On the other hand, as Green points out, Wesley had in fact proposed marriage, and the Caustons were very much in favor of it, and Sophy's rejection, a "preliminary" one, "really meant nothing at all."[36] Wesley consulted with Mr. Toltschig, the Moravian pastor in Savannah, about the matter, but when the latter said he saw no reason why they should not marry, he became more confused than ever. He then consulted his friends, Benjamin Ingham and Charles Delamotte, who had accompanied him to Georgia, and they recommended that he leave town for a few days so that he could think more rationally about it.

He did leave town briefly, but soon he returned to Savannah to transact some business. While there, he longed to see Sophy but restrained the impulse. As he awaited the boat that was to take him away again, he

> walked to and fro on the edge of the water, heavy laden and pierced through with many sorrows. There One came to me and said, "You are still in doubt what is best to be done. First, then, cry to God, that you may be wholly resigned, whatever shall appear to be His will." I instantly cried to God for resignation. And I found that and peace together. I said, "Sure it is a dream." I was in a new world. The change was as from death to life. I went back to the town of Irene wondering and rejoicing; but withal exceeding fearful, lest my want of thankfulness for this blessing, or of care to improve it, might occasion its being taken away.[37]

When he came back to Savannah three or four days later, he resumed his relationship with her. His friends again warned him against this relationship, that if it continued it could only culminate in marriage. But her uncle became actively involved by taking him on a tour of the plantation he would provide the couple if they were to marry. If this confused him still more, the crowning blow was struck by Sophy herself. While he was away she had dispensed with the man she had pledged to marry, but then began to see another man who proposed marriage to her. Wesley first learned of this development when her aunt asked him to publish the banns of marriage for her and her new suitor. He suspected that he had been informed of her relationship to the other man so that he would act before it was too late. But he refused to be pressured. As he puts it, "I reasoned thus, 'Either she is engaged or not; if she is, I would not have her if I might: if not, there is nothing in this show that ought to alter my preceding resolution.'"[38]

The next time he saw her she was with her new suitor. While this meeting caused him an almost indescribable "complication of passions and tumult of thought,"[39] he sought to treat the occasion as a pastoral visit in which he exhorted her and her suitor to "assist each other in serving God with all their strength."[40] When he returned home he went into his garden and walked up and down, seeking rest but not finding it:

> I did seek after God, but I found him not. I forsook Him before: now he forsook me. I could not pray. Then indeed the snares of death were about me; the pains of hell overtook me. Yet I struggled for life; and though I had neither words nor thoughts, I lifted up my eyes to the Prince that is highly exalted, and suppled the place of them as I could. . . . And about four o'clock He so far took the cup from me that I drank so deeply of it no more.[41]

He immediately wrote her uncle a note indicating his mind was settled; he would not marry her under any conditions. Her uncle came to his home within the hour, informing him that he had not yet consented to her marriage to her new suitor. Wesley did not relent. Later that evening Sophy came to his home for a prayer meeting. After the others had gone, he confronted her, "Miss Sophy, you said yesterday you would take no steps in anything of importance without first consulting me."[42] She replied that she had little choice but to marry her new suitor because she could no longer endure living in the same house with her uncle and aunt. Just then, her suitor entered the house and abruptly took her away.

The following morning Wesley went to see her. He asked her if she was now fully resolved to marry the other man. When she said that she was, he admonished her not to marry for the wrong motives. He pointed out that marrying merely to avoid other problems is not a good motive, because these other problems would continue to plague her in the married state. Having said this, he went home "easy and satisfied."[43] The following day she set out for a neighboring town and was married there by another minister.

After she and her husband settled down to married life in Savannah, Wesley refused her the sacraments because she had not been faithful in her Christian obligations. Her error was in presenting herself for communion without informing him of her intention to commune prior to the service. His refusal to allow her to take communion angered her husband, and on August 8, 1737, he obtained a warrant for Wesley's arrest. The following day, Wesley was brought before the magistrates on the charges that he had defamed her character and had repelled her from communion. He denied the first charge and challenged the competence of the court to deal with the second, because it concerned only a matter of ecclesiastical discipline. Her uncle also demanded that Wesley vindicate himself before the whole congregation, and became indirectly involved in the court case by tampering with the jury that had been chosen to deal with the suit against Wesley. To some extent, his efforts backfired, because a minority of the jury drew up a counter declaration on the charges against Wesley, and this left the legal case up in the air. The charges were not dismissed, but he was not immediately sentenced.

The greater threat to Wesley, however, were the reports of the whole affair that would be heard back in England. At first, he was opposed to returning to England to defend himself against false reports, especially the report that he had acted against her out of revenge. But by October 1737, two years after he had arrived, he had more or less decided to return to England, sensing that he could no longer minister effectively in Georgia. Because he was not paid in money, however, but in board, room, and a clothing allowance, he was forced to go to Sophy's uncle to request money to pay for his return trip. This alerted her uncle to his intentions, and on December 2 the magistrates summoned him and informed him that he must not leave Georgia until cleared of all charges. He countered that the court had not stipulated that he was obliged to remain in Georgia until his case was completed, and reiterated his intention of leaving when he had made up his mind to leave. In the afternoon the magistrates ordered security officers to prevent his leaving the colony and forbidding any person from helping him to do so. This was the signal to him that he had no choice but to leave, and that evening, after prayers, he and Delamotte set off for Charleston. Three weeks later he set sail for England hoping, however, that some day he might return to America.

In leaving America in the manner he did, his return had all the appearances of flight. Yet, he had warned the magistrates of his intentions, and because of his three-week stopover in Charleston, he gave them opportunity to pursue and detain him if they had wanted to. If, therefore, he was not technically fleeing the country, his actions, nonetheless, left a bad impression and he was clearly embarrassed by the whole affair. One of the Moravians wrote in his diary on December 15:

> Received news that Mr. Wesley had gone secretly at night to Charlestown by way of Purrysburg, to go from there in all haste to London. I do not know what moved him to so quick a resolution, so hurtful both to his office and to God's honor.[44]

More important than the circumstances of his departure, however, were the larger implications of the whole affair for his ministry. As Martin Schmidt points out,

> Wesley's spiritual development received a stronger step forward from the affair with Sophy. God Himself drew near in a way such as he had never known before. He experienced the fact that God inclined His ear to him even when he himself was not wholly surrendered to the divine will. This was a starting-point for the understanding of prevenient grace, which is stronger than the human will. . . . The relationship with God is radically withdrawn from the sphere of the rational and moralistic, and becomes a reality painfully experienced. In this way it reached a new depth, the dimension of spiritual conflict.[45]

But if it strengthened his spiritual development, the affair was clearly harmful to his ministry in the immediate sense. Schmidt also notes

> Wesley had gone to America with the highest hopes. One after another they were smashed. His main concern, the mission to the heathen, was forced by the pressure of events more and more into the background. It was the leading men of the colony who

were responsible for this. The careful but pitiful attempts he made to keep it alive can only have revealed the actual situation the more clearly to him and made it more oppressive.[46]

Another more subtle implication of this affair for Wesley's ministry is that it revealed a problematic feature of his ministerial style: When he was personally threatened—both hurt and frustrated—by Sophy's willingness to marry her new suitor, he dealt with this situation not as her former suitor but as her minister. He talked to her as her minister, giving her and her suitor pastoral advice, thereby defending against the pain and hurt she had caused him. In other words, he used the fact that he was her pastor to disguise and fend off his emotional responses to what was happening. Furthermore, after the marriage he used his professional role in a way that gave the appearance of vindictiveness. Being human, he experienced confusion, frustration, and hurt. It would have been preferable, however, to have incorporated this sense of vulnerability into his professional identity rather than using his professional role and prerogatives to hide behind these feelings. Even if it was true that he had the church law on his side in refusing her communion, and even if it was true that she was flaunting the church's procedures, he could have handled the issue in a more judicious manner, recognizing that both he and Sophy were acting out a complex set of emotions toward each other within a larger context of mutual vulnerability. He was far from home, and she was unhappy in her domestic surroundings.

Another indication that he was not above using his pastoral office to reprimand both Sophy and her uncle was the fact that he preached a sermon on 1 Kings 21, the story of the theft of Naboth's vineyard by King Ahab and his Queen Jezebel by trumping up false charges against Naboth which led to his being stoned to death. The congregation would not have missed the implied message that Sophy and her uncle were depriving Wesley of his ministry in Georgia.[47]

His departure from America in December 1737 signaled the end of his "age thirty transition" period. On his trip home, he considered the effect of his two years in America and complained that "I went to America to convert the Indians; but oh, who shall convert me?"[48] He was discouraged and depressed. But when he returned to London in February and began to write an account of his activities in Georgia, he expressed his conviction that, as Martin Schmidt says, God's hand was in all that had happened just because it had turned out so differently from his expectations. Neither the decision to go to America nor his experiences there were anything like his original plans. They had gone contrary to his own wishes, and this led him to recognize as a deeper meaning in his life the fact that God had humbled him. God had proved him; God had shown him what was really in his heart and brought him to despair of himself.[49]

He also considered the effect of his work in Georgia on the people there, and was understandably modest:

> All in Georgia have heard the word of God. Some have believed, and begun to run well. A few steps have been taken toward publishing the glad tidings both to the African and American heathen. Many children have learned "how they ought to serve God," and to be useful to their neighbor.[50]

Although he did not say he did not accomplish very much, he felt that his experiences in Georgia were more important for what they taught him about himself than for what he accomplished there. Even so, at the end of his age thirty transition, the implications of his sojourn in Georgia for his subsequent personal and professional life were still very unclear.

The Tasks of the Novice Phase

How well did Wesley handle the major developmental tasks of the novice phase? How well had he laid the foundations for the next period of his life?

Forming a Dream. Wesley made major progress toward formulating his Dream when he returned to Oxford as a tutor. Through the Holy Club, he began to view the Christian life as one of holiness issuing in witnessing to the Gospel through an exemplary life, social service, and courageous preaching. He found himself struggling the hardest with the matter of personal holiness. He had little difficulty incorporating personal holiness into his own self-image, but he found it exceedingly hard to maintain this personal holiness in his life, especially in his relations with women. He struggled against temptations that threatened this self-image of personal holiness and, from time to time, succumbed to these temptations. Given his emphasis on personal holiness, his Dream was remarkably free of the desire to satisfy personal ambitions; had he sought the fulfillment of personal ambitions, this would have been evidence of his failure to follow the dictates of a life of personal holiness. Thus, at Oxford, his activities were not designed to help him achieve promotions in the university. Moreover, he did not attempt to parlay his Holy Club activities into gaining a more secure or prestigious position in the church. His willingness to go to Georgia was itself an indication that he did not seek advancement through the normal channel of appointment to a rectorship. Thus, while his reluctance to accept his father's rectorship in Epworth might have been viewed at the time as motivated by a desire to wait for a better position, his subsequent decision to go to Georgia should have laid such suspicions to rest.

Of the five ministers in our study, Wesley's Dream is most notable for its emphasis on self-denial. If personal holiness was the central motif in his Dream, this holiness reflected itself in his personal life in a tendency to renounce any personal interests and to focus almost entirely on developing ways and means of communicating the Gospel. What especially disturbed him in Georgia, therefore, was that for so much of his time there he allowed himself to become diverted from living his life in accord with his Dream. The question is whether his Dream was set too high and was too difficult to sustain. In other cases in this study, the Dream provided an impetus for growth and achievement. For him, the Dream tended to remind him of how much he had fallen short of his objectives, even though he had accomplished as much, by the age of thirty, as any other minister in this study.

Forming an occupation. Wesley does not seem to have experienced any difficulty in determining that the ministry would be his chosen profession. He received considerable encouragement from his parents in this regard, and he seemed to find this supportive, at least until his parents began to put pressure on him to begin his ministry in Epworth. But although he chose the ministry as his career, he was not extremely anxious to take over a parish. His older brother had become a headmaster of a school, and his younger brother Charles had not opted for the parish ministry, so it is quite possible that their father's difficulties in the parish as they were growing up turned them away from parish ministry. When he did agree to help his father at Epworth as curate, he experienced enough difficulties to cause him to welcome a return to Oxford. Although many of these difficulties were due to his relationships with his father, he did not find his ministry in Epworth so confirming that he would seek a rectorship when it appeared some years later that he would be leaving Oxford.

In going to Georgia, however, he again undertook regular parish duties, and again encountered serious difficulties. These duties became so time-consuming that he never got around to his missionary work with the Native Americans in western Georgia. His involvement with Sophy Hopkey caused by far the greatest controversy in Georgia, but some of the charges brought against him by her uncle centered on his handling of regular parish duties. When her uncle requested a hearing before the congregation, he added a number of complaints to the original charge that Wesley refused communion to his niece. These included such criticisms as the fact that he divided the Sunday service into two parts, baptized by dipping even when the baby was frail, assumed the title "Ordinary" taken over from the Moravians, and a variety of similar charges. His conduct of the parish had clearly created some difficulties and these, together with his refusal to allow Sophy to take communion, suggested that he was somewhat imperialistic in his pastoral style.

In contrast, he was extremely effective in his direction of the Holy Club. In this work, he could essentially determine what he wanted to devote himself to and, as he pointed out in his letter to his father, at Oxford he had been able to perform his ministry without having to participate in the idle chatter and superficial conviviality that would be required of him in a parish context. Thus, the Holy Club provided an alternative to ministry in the local parish. Significantly, it was not until he later worked out a form of ministry that was also not limited to the local parish—itinerant preaching throughout England—that he experienced an advancement in his chosen profession that entailed major modifications in his life structure. As he told Bishop Butler in 1739, in "being ordained as Fellow of a College, I was not limited to any particular cure, but have an indeterminate commission to preach the word of God in any part of the Church of England."[51] This was said at age thirty-six, when he was "becoming his own man."

In directing the work of the Holy Club, he was also forming his own professional identity. The work of the Holy Club was remarkable for its combination of personal piety and social action. It is therefore noteworthy that his eventual loss of interest in the club was due to criticism of both facets of its program. The Morgan case called into question the club's emphasis on personal holiness, and the Blair case called into question its emphasis on social action. When faced with such criticism, he did not decide to fight for the survival of the Holy Club but disengaged from it by accepting the offer of the chaplaincy in Georgia. Since he also left Georgia when the criticism against him was mounting, we may have here a personality trait of accepting controversy up to a point, but then backing away from it when it becomes highly threatening. Although criticized for leaving Georgia when he did, this was consistent with a pattern (beginning with his curacy in Epworth) of removing himself from difficult situations when they threatened to get out of hand. Unlike Edwards, who stayed with a difficult situation long after it had become hopeless, Wesley had a good sense of timing, and knew when the situation could no longer be rectified. On the other hand, unlike Newman, he did not attempt to make his withdrawals into a major test of his own and the other participants' sincerity and good faith.

This difference may well cut to the heart of the basic difference between his way of handling conflict in his occupation and the life patterns of decline and of breaking out. He did not remain long enough in a difficult situation to suffer the serious decline that Edwards experienced. But neither did he think, as Newman did, that in leaving the situation he was "breaking out" for good. When he left Oxford to go to America, he had every intention of returning. When he left America, he thought it very possible that he would go back. At the conclusion of his age thirty transition, what remains to be seen is how this professional style proved conducive to advancement involving major modifications in life structure.

Mentor relationships. It does not appear that Wesley had any relationship that could qualify as a mentor relationship. Rector Isham at Lincoln College cannot be considered a mentor for, even though his uneasy tolerance of the Holy Club was very helpful to Wesley, he was not a mentor in the sense of an older person who helped Wesley make his way into his profession. In some ways, his entry into his profession was similar to that of Edwards because his family, especially parents (but also his older brother Samuel) co-opted the role of mentor. His father was the minister from whom he gained his earliest training, and no other single individual, whether a teacher or another minister, had this kind of direct influence on his entry into the ministry. His biographers also stress the influence of his mother on his professional development. He consulted his mother, not his father, when faced with a difficult situation or decision in his ministry. One significant difference between his relationship to his mother and Edwards with his mother, however, is that his mother encouraged him to break out of traditional models of ministry—she supported his work at Oxford, including his prison ministry, and supported his decision to go to America. In contrast, Edwards' mother simply wanted him to take his grandfather's church and carry on the family tradition in a rather traditional way. True, Susanna Wesley wanted her son to return to Epworth and become a parish minister there, but when he served his father as a curate, she encouraged him to break church traditions by criticizing the rector, his father, in a sermon. Perhaps, then, her very encouragement of her son's autonomy in his first parish position enabled him to assert his independence even when she herself asked him to return to Epworth and assume his father's duties. In other words, even when he resisted her own verbal requests and suggestions, he knew that he was following her deeper message that she wanted her son to "become his own man." This encouragement of independence was to help him considerably in the years ahead. For, given his lack of a mentor, his advancement in his profession was to require much personal initiative. He did not receive much help from older ministers, nor did he seek it out.

Forming a marriage and family. As we have seen, Wesley was having a most difficult time in regard to marriage. He seemed to be able to begin a relationship with a young woman without much difficulty, but when these relationships threatened to become serious, he would begin to vacillate. In two cases, this led the young woman to marry someone else. But in each of these cases he remained in close contact with the young woman, creating a difficult situation for her in her relationship with her husband. Obviously, he had great difficulty in making the commitment to marry—indeed, he felt that it was God's will that he remain single and thus continue to honor his commitment *not* to marry—but neither could he let the young woman go with equanimity and grace. The Sophy Hopkey affair was the most potentially damaging of these relationships because it threatened his reputation as a minister. Why he had such difficulties in forming a marriage is difficult to answer. In the Kitty Hargreave case, his father was opposed to the relationship. Yet, Wesley did not take the opposition of his father as the final word on the subject, but continued to see Kitty throughout the summer. In the Sophy Hopkey case, his friends were clearly opposed to the relationship and yet, here again, Wesley continued to see her. Thus, he did not feel obligated to terminate these relationships simply because others opposed them. The problem, it seems, was more personal, relating to his view that he could not be a good minister and be married at the same time. As Martin Schmidt points out, when Wesley became involved with Sophy it "became ever more difficult for him to keep to his original and confessed initiative of concentrating on the business in hand and the pastoral oversight."[52] In relinquishing Sophy, he was able to return to his pastoral role, almost with a vengeance, as suggested by his rather legalistic employment of church law in his refusal to allow Sophy to take communion.

A psychodynamic view of his failure to marry during the early adult era might focus on certain unconscious conflicts regarding women. His statement that he began to be "afraid" of Sophy may support such a view. His closeness to his mother might also be a clue to some unconscious conflicts regarding marriage. The important point for our purposes here, however, is that on the conscious level he felt marriage and his career were incompatible. As we have seen, this sense of the incompatibility of his profession and his involvements with women was articulated in his Dream. Personal holiness meant resisting the temptations of a close, physical relationship with a member of the other gender. Thus, we have his Dream and his occupation on one side, the formation of a marriage and family on the other. It was not until his Dream and occupation underwent significant modifications in the settling-down period that he could seriously entertain the possibility of marriage.

Settling-Down Phase

Settling Down and Becoming His Own Man (1738-1744)

Wesley's first task on returning to England in February 1738 was to meet with the trustees of the Society for the Propagation of Christian Knowledge who oversaw the assignment of chaplains to Georgia. He appeared before the trustees in April at the termination of his appointment to Georgia, and they made it clear that they were very dissatisfied with the way he conducted himself and his ministry in Georgia.

What should he do now? During his absence, the Holy Club at Oxford had continued its activities, with Charles Wesley's earlier return from Georgia helping to put it into better shape. Should he return to residence at Oxford and attempt to revitalize the work of the Holy Club? He was tempted to return to Oxford, but was undecided. During the following month he had a great deal of contact with a young Moravian preacher, Peter Bohler, whom he met in London on his return to England. Bohler was planning to go to Georgia in a few weeks, so it was natural that they would meet to talk together about their common interests in Georgia. Bohler accompanied him to Oxford on one occasion and attended meetings of the Holy Club, but Bohler found their meetings not to his liking because they were too stiff and formal. When Wesley went back with Bohler to London, he attended Bohler's services which took place in an atmosphere of tense emotion. Wesley frequently wept during these meetings. Bohler convinced him that he was in need of conversion, that he was not yet in a state of grace. Anxiety over the Sophy Hopkey affair, and news that his brother Charles had taken seriously ill with pleurisy, contributed to his receptivity to Bohler's view of his spiritual condition.

Bohler left England for America on May 4, 1738, but three days before his departure he attended the first meeting of a religious society on Fetter Lane that Wesley had founded through Bohler's encouragement. Wesley's founding of this society suggests that he had decided to remain in London and not return to Oxford. During the following week he also preached at two churches in London, where he was not well received. Then, two weeks later, on May 24, he attended the meeting of the Moravian religious society on Aldersgate Street. He indicated later that he was reluctant to go out that night, but went out of a sense of obligation. However, as he heard Luther's preface to Paul's Epistle to the Romans being read, "I felt my heart strangely warmed. I felt I did trust in Christ, Christ alone for salvation; and assurance was given me that He had taken away *my* sins, even *mine,* and saved *me* from the law of sin and death."[53] This was Wesley's conversion experience—his well-known "Aldersgate experience."

A full discussion of the experience is beyond my present purposes. It should be noted, however, that besides observing its influence on his spiritual state, he felt that it would have a very significant effect on his ministry to others. He was now convinced that what had been missing in his ministry before was a spirit of love. Before meeting Bohler and experiencing conversion, he had taken the opposition of others to his work as a sign that God was on his side. Now, he became persuaded that his ministry ought to manifest itself in respect and love toward his listeners. This change in attitude was an extremely important factor in the success he was to experience in the next few years. In terms of his developmental tasks, this clearly had the effect of modifying his *Dream*. Personal holiness remained the core of his Dream, but it was now to be tempered with love and greater tolerance of human weakness.

He did not, however, immediately expand his ministry beyond the work he was doing with the society on Fetter Lane. He preached in nearby churches, but when he talked on justification, he was told that he was not to preach in these churches again. On June 11, he preached on "Salvation By Faith" in St. Mary's Church at Oxford, and three days later he set out for Rotterdam to visit the Herrnhut, the original Moravian Brethren settlement. He stayed at the Herrnhut for two weeks, and came away in August convinced that its way of life was like that of the early Christians. Although critical of the Moravian Brethren's acceptance of governance by their founder, Count Zinzendorf, he also noted that the Count had been away from the Herrnhut for two years and the community had gotten along well in his absence. In a similar way, his biographers suggest that when he began to develop a number of Methodist societies throughout England, Wesley was conscious of the need for strong lay leadership during his absence from a given society.

When he returned to England he resumed his leadership role in the Fetter Lane society and preached in Church of England parishes in the area. But one by one the churches were closed to him both because his sermons dealt with issues of justification, regeneration, and new birth, and because he was becoming known in London as the leader of a separate religious society. This state of affairs continued until December when George Whitefield returned from his first mission to America. He had been extremely popular in America, including Savannah, Georgia, where he founded an orphanage. He also reported that Wesley had laid an excellent foundation for the work that he was able to do in Georgia, and that Wesley was held in high esteem by the people there. In light of Wesley's problems in Georgia, it would appear that Whitefield was either doing Wesley a kindness or else the Georgians felt they had not been as supportive of him as they ought to have been and perhaps appreciated him more now that he was gone. When he returned to England, however, Whitefield encountered considerable opposition to his preaching and by the end of January 1739, he was barred from every London pulpit. He then went to Bristol, but encountered considerable opposition there as well. Barred from preaching in most of the churches, he took to the open air and in March preached to a crowd of 10,000 people. Realizing the tremendous potential of field preaching, he wanted to extend his work to other cities, but felt the newly awakened people in Bristol needed someone to attend to their spiritual needs in his absence. He asked Wesley to come to Bristol and serve in this capacity.

At first, Wesley was reluctant to come; his work with the Fetter Lane society was going well, and he was skeptical of Whitefield's idea of field preaching. But in March 1739 he went to Bristol and two days after his arrival there he preached to a congregation of about 3,000 people in a brickyard. During the following weeks he continued to preach and to organize religious societies made up of people who came to hear him preach. While not as dynamic or electrifying as Whitefield, his preaching had the strange effect of causing some people to go into convulsions, an effect that greatly puzzled him. He continued to preach, despite warnings from the Bishop of Bristol. Then, in June, he returned to London in response to an appeal from his Fetter Lane society, which was disintegrating in his absence. Whitefield was preaching in London at the time, and Wesley preached at one of Whitefield's field meetings. Throughout the rest of the year, Wesley went back and forth between London and Bristol. But, toward the end of the year, a number of people in London told him they wanted to establish a society of their own, with him as their guide. This was done and, before long, the group was so large that they purchased a building, which became the first headquarters of the Methodist society. Thus, within two years of his return to England from America, the Methodist movement was born.

It is unnecessary to document the growth of Methodist societies throughout England in the following years. By 1742, three years later, there were societies at Bristol, London, Kingswood, Newcastle, and various other cities and towns. My concern here is rather to note that

Wesley had now laid claim to a significantly altered life structure by means of the overwhelming success of the field preaching and the organizing efforts that followed. He had clearly advanced in his profession, from a dejected minister just back from what appeared to be a professional failure in Georgia, to the organizer of a growing number of religious societies all over England. The advancement had not come through the normal channels of promotion in the Church of England, but through his and Whitefield's own initiatives. Indeed, the refusal of Church of England parishes to allow them to preach was the circumstance that led Whitefield to turn to open-air preaching.

Wesley's life structure underwent a marked change in the years following the Bristol revival in 1739. Most of his preaching was done out of doors, and his ministry was thus removed from the parish context. In addition, his society work was greatly expanded, stretching the width and length of England. The change was at least comparable in magnitude to the altered lifestyle of those subjects in Levinson's study who were promoted from junior level positions in their companies, with only limited responsibilities, to high senior-level positions with responsibility for overseeing the work of hundreds of employees.[54] Wesley responded to the challenge well, taking on responsibilities that required extensive travel, considerable attention to organizational problems, and a heavy preaching schedule.

By the end of his settling-down period, which I have set at 1744 (he was forty-one-years old), the modification in life structure was complete. In 1739, his older brother Samuel, who had vigorously opposed his new work, died. In 1740, Wesley severed his ties with the Fetter Lane society because the group, which had originally been conceived as a society within the Church of England, was threatening to become a Moravian society. In leaving the group, he effectively severed his ties with the Moravians and, in terms of his personal theology, became his own man rather than continuing to follow Moravian doctrines. Then, in July 1742 his mother died. The following year, he preached on his father's tombstone at Epworth, and was rebuffed from communion by the curate there, who said, "Pray tell Mr. Wesley, I shall not give *him* the sacrament, for he is not *fit*." Green comments on this refusal of communion to Wesley: "If he recalled now a not wholly dissimilar incident in Georgia he did not mention it."[55] And, finally, on August 24, 1744, he preached a sermon at St. Mary's Chapel, Oxford, which, as Green points out, "constituted the turning-point in his relation with the academic world."[56] His sermon, which asked whether Oxford fellows "know Jesus Christ" and whether Oxford undergraduates are not merely "a generation of triflers,"[57] was met with the silence of disapproval. He was never again asked to preach at Oxford. Ninety-nine years later, Newman preached his last sermon at St. Mary's Chapel, thus ending his sixteen-year tenure as its vicar. Newman, however, subsequently left the Church of England, whereas Wesley chose to remain, but on his own terms. Could Newman, had he chosen to, have done the same?

Thus, by 1744, the modification in Wesley's life structure was virtually complete. His profession had undergone a marked alteration as he was now the acknowledged leader of a strong and growing religious movement. The older members of his family, his parents and older brother, were no longer living; he was therefore free to develop his ministry without the threat of serious family disapproval. Also he had effectively broken his ties with Oxford, as well as with the parish structure of the Church of England. He was, in professional terms, thoroughly on his own. His late thirties and early forties were clearly a period of "becoming his own man," of advancing in such a dramatic way that his whole life structure had become altered. True, the foundation for his current ministry had been laid in the Holy Club in his late twenties and early thirties. But oversight of the network of Methodist societies springing up all around the country involved a far more demanding form of ministerial engagement.

CONCLUSION

Wesley's "midlife transition" involved continuing modification of the life structure formed in his late thirties. Work on all four developmental tasks continued. His continued involvement in the development of lay preachers for his societies meant that his own role as *mentor* was increased. His *occupation* continued to undergo change as he met the new demands of overseeing his societies. As noted earlier, his *Dream* continued to focus on personal holiness, and this matter of holiness was a major thrust of the societies' work, but in various ways he, more so than his brother Charles, tempered this objective of personal holiness with love and tolerance for human weakness. However, the developmental task that underwent the greatest reformulation during the midlife transition period was the task of forming a *marriage*. If major changes in his occupation had taken place in his late thirties, it was his middle forties that saw him begin to give serious thought to the possibility of marriage. In line with Levinson's view that the midlife transition occasions a greater sense of inwardness and increased reflection on the problem of attachment versus separation, his biographers believe that Wesley was lonely. As Green puts it,

> The nature of his position, and the streak of impersonality in his make-up, together with his spiritual authority, made him ultimately somewhat lonely and aloof. In spite of his vast correspondence, the immense number of his acquaintances and friends, the genuine concern that he showed for the poor and the sick, the interest that he took in the spiritual and moral condition of his flock, he had few intimates.[58]

Green adds, "his concern for others won their admiration and love, but he found it less easy to create an affectionate mutual relationship."[59] As Levinson suggests, the advancement that leads to modifications in the life structure are often bought at a heavy personal price. The life of the itinerant preacher and organizer could be lonely and tiring.

Evidence of his need for comfort and solace is the fact that the two women with whom he became romantically involved in subsequent years had nursed him to health when he was ill or infirm. When he was ill of a gastric disorder in 1746 he, then forty-three, became involved with a woman, Grace Murray, who was more or less engaged to one of his lay preachers. Through a variety of complications and misunderstandings, some reminiscent of the Hopkey case, Wesley lost out to the other man. Five years later he slipped on the ice, hurting his ankle, and was carried to the home of Molly Vazielle, the widow of a London merchant. One week later they were married. He had noted some months earlier that

> For many years I remained single, because I believed I could be more useful in a single than in a married state. . . . I now as fully believed that in my present circumstances I might be more useful in a married state.[60]

Unfortunately, the marriage did not work out. Green says, it "was indeed the worst mistake of John's life."[61] Seven years later, in 1758, they were permanently separated. Although the marriage was unsuccessful, the fact that he married at all is a strong indication that the life structure modification that began in his middle to late thirties continued well into the middle adult phase of his life. Still, as in the lives of the ministers studied thus far, the decisive period in his ministry was the settling-down period, when there were major modifications in his professional life.

Chapter 6

Orestes Brownson:
Unstable Life Structure

In the unstable life pattern, the life structure remains insecure and in flux throughout the entire settling-down period (age thirty-three to forty). A man whose life assumes this pattern does not actively seek or welcome this instability, and feels that at this stage in his life it is inappropriate. If stability was acceptable in the middle twenties ("entering the adult world"), it is no longer acceptable either to him or to those who may depend on him for support. Typically, a variety of external circumstances and internal problems prevent him from achieving stability, with the very complexity and variety of these factors making it all the more difficult to overcome the instability. Recognizing their need to settle down by solidifying their life structure, men who fall into this group have great difficulty in carrying through on this need, and generally experience much frustration and unhappiness because of this failure.

A representative of the unstable life structure is Orestes Brownson (1803-1876). Brownson was an American Protestant minister in two different denominations in his late twenties and early thirties, then founded his own church in his late thirties. He also became deeply involved in a social movement during his "age thirty transition." Through most of this period he was involved in the publication of religious periodicals and journals. Eventually despairing of his efforts to keep his own church going, he left the ministry in his early forties and converted to Catholicism, continuing his career as a journal editor and writer. As a married man with a family, he gave no thought whatsoever to becoming a priest. He lived the remaining years of his life as a Catholic layman, addressing his journals and periodicals to his preconversion readership, largely Protestant.

As in the four previous profiles, discussion of Brownson will emphasize the early adult era, focusing on both the novice and settling-down phases. But first, I will begin with a brief discussion of his childhood and adolescence.

CHILDHOOD AND ADOLESCENCE (1803-1822)

Brownson was born in 1803 in Stockbridge, Massachusetts, where Jonathan Edwards worked at the Indian Mission some fifty years earlier. His father died when he was six years old. His mother, left with five children, was forced to put the children in foster homes. Orestes was sent to live with an elderly couple in Royalton, Vermont. They were Congregationalists but they rarely attended Sunday church services because they lived four miles from the Congregational church in the center of town. However, he read the Bible and various theological works that were in his foster parents' farmhouse, and even though he did not attend church, he decided at an early age to become a minister.

When he reached twelve years of age, however, he began to feel the need to belong to a church. Although he could have joined the local Congregational church, he was attracted to the Methodists and the Christians, the latter a recently founded sect. Of the two, the Methodist church appears to have had a stronger psychological influence on him, because it stressed hell and damnation more than the other churches. Still, he was uncertain what he should do, and consulted an old woman whose cabin was situated on a corner of the farm. She warned him against joining the Methodists or any other sects, apparently assuming that by process of elimination he would join the Congregationalists. He did not join any church on the basis of this conversation; however, years later, when he was thinking about joining the Catholic Church, he recalled her argument against joining the Methodists and Christians. She had contended that he should not join a church that was founded by a man, but one that was founded by Christ and his early apostles.

When he turned fourteen, his biological mother moved to Ballston Spa in upstate New York, a health resort where she was able to get work, and reclaimed all of her children. He was now able to attend an academy there, but it is unclear how long his formal education lasted. His biographer, Theodore Maynard, writes,

How long he attended this school is uncertain. About such matters he is vague in his autobiography, which is almost entirely concerned with his spiritual development and ignores ordinary biographical details. . . . [He] seems to indicate that he was still pursuing his academic subjects when he was nineteen, whereas his son tells us that he had left the academy and was working in James Comstock's printing office at the time.[1]

He later described his adolescence as a period of severe religious confusion and perplexity. Much of this confusion was due to the religious climate of the times. The early decades of the nineteenth century in America were years of religious ferment and unrest. Religious traditions sustained through years of Puritan hegemony were undergoing collapse, a collapse that, as we have seen, began to occur in the ministry of Jonathan Edwards. With the breakdown of traditional Puritan authority in matters of doctrine and piety, the religious climate was subject to rather violent crosscurrents. Heated debates, schisms, and the founding of new religious groups claiming that only they had legitimate authority were the consequences of this crisis.

This religious crisis had a profound effect on his adolescence. He was reared on a farm in Vermont and moved later to rural New York. The country districts of both states were characterized by religious instability. These areas produced the founders of Mormonism, Millerism, and spiritualism, as well as such revivalists as Charles G. Finney. The authority crisis in institutional religious life was central to this regional instability.

The instability of the social milieu in which he was reared had the effect of making available to him a broad but confusing range of alternative religious groups and ideologies, all loudly competing on the grounds that they were spokesmen for and embodiments of genuine authority. He spoke especially of the "new and corrupting influences" with which he was confused on moving from Vermont to upstate New York at the age of fourteen. He wrote in his autobiography about this period: "My young head became confused with the contradictory opinions I heard advanced . . . and I half persuaded myself that all religion was a delusion."[2]

This confusion appears to have characterized his life to age nineteen. When his adolescent period ended, he was no closer to clarity about his religious perspective. He had not joined a church and, according to his biographers, he continued to fluctuate between belief and doubt. But in 1822 he joined a church and, with this new religious affiliation, he began to enter the early adult transition.

EARLY ADULT ERA

Novice Phase

Early Adult Transition (1822-1825)

In 1822, at age nineteen, he joined the Presbyterian Church at Ballston Spa. In his autobiography, he described his decision to join the Presbyterian Church as an urgent, almost impulsive concern to find a source of guidance:

> One day, when I was about nineteen years of age, I was passing by a Presbyterian meeting-house. It was Sunday, and the people were gathering for the service. The thought struck me that I would go in and join them. . . . It was a common-place affair. But I went out from that meeting-house much affected, and feeling that I had missed my way. . . .[3]

A day or two later he visited the minister, Reuben Smith, and as a result of this interview, he was baptized the following Sunday and was received into the Presbyterian communion. He noted years later that becoming a Presbyterian was "the act of an intellectual desperado,"[4] that he was not following his reason but his need for some authority and guidance in his life. On the other hand, while his decision to join the Presbyterian Church may have been an impulsive act of personal surrender, it also helped him get a job as a schoolteacher at nearby Stillwater. Thus, his decision to enter the Presbyterian Church and sit through a rather "common-place affair" may not have been the inspiration of the moment but the result of his intuition, which proved correct, that he would have a better chance of getting a teaching job if he were a church member. This would also account for the fact that, within weeks after joining the church, he had become most distrustful of it, and began to doubt that it had any value or purpose.

His criticism of the Presbyterian Church was not directed so much at the congregation to which he belonged, but to the theological views of Presbyterianism, especially what he took to be its views on predestination. On the other hand, his attack on Presbyterianism was not based on a cool assessment of its doctrines. By his own acknowledgment, he was in a highly emotional state at the time; his diary entries for the period reveal high states of elation followed by deep despair. In his autobiography, he expressed his feelings toward the Presbyterian Church at the time in terms of his own family relationships:

> It subjected me to all the disadvantages of authority without any of its advantages. The church demanded that I should treat her as a true mother, while she was free to treat me only as a stepson, or even as a stranger. Be one thing or another, said I; either assume the authority and the responsibility of teaching and directing me, or leave me with the responsibility [of] my freedom.[5]

In viewing the Presbyterian faith in terms of the dynamics of the family life of his childhood, comparing Presbyterianism to a foster mother rather than a true mother, he suggested that the church did not want to exercise real authority over him, yet it did not want to allow him freedom either. Perhaps like his own foster parents, it tried to steer a middle course that left him neither the recipient of clear parental authority and guidance nor responsible for his own life and decisions.

Nothing much is known about his experience as a teacher during the year, but his diary does indicate that he was beginning to think seriously about becoming a minister, perhaps even a missionary. When his troubles with the Presbyterian Church emerged during the year, it became clear that he would not stay on as a schoolteacher in Stillwater beyond the year. In 1824, he accepted another teaching position, this one in Springwells, Michigan, only eleven miles from Detroit.

This year in Springwells was a difficult one because he contracted malaria. He lay ill for several months, and this gave him opportunity to read and reflect on his religious and vocational problems. He had evidently borrowed many books from his Universalist maternal aunt when he left Ballston Spa for Springwells, because he spent much of his time during his illness reading Universalist books. His main theological attraction to Universalism was that it provided a counterposition to the Presbyterian view of predestination. Whereas Presbyterians believed that some persons are predestined to heaven and others to hell, Universalists believed that all persons are predestined to heaven. Presbyterians countered that this was a recipe for moral and spiritual laxity, but Universalists responded that the pain and suffering that persons experience in this life is a natural stimulus to moral and spiritual effort. Brownson was critical of the Universalist theologians he was reading and was convinced that their work was full of sophistry, but Universalism did not demand much by way of new beliefs and it provided a position from which to repudiate Presbyterianism. As he put it in his autobiography,

> The truth is, my mind was unsettled, and in reality had been from the time my well-meaning aunt had undertaken to initiate me into the doctrine of Universalism, and I adhered to any fixed doctrines only by spasmodic efforts.[6]

Nonetheless, in the fall of 1825 he applied to the Universalist Association at the General Convention in Hartland, Vermont, for a license as a preacher. His application was accepted and he began ministerial studies under the direction of a minister for nearly a year. On June 15, 1826, he was ordained a Universalist minister at Jaffrey, New Hampshire. With his ordination at age twenty-three, he moved into the next period in his life, the "entering the adult world" stage.

Brownson's decision to enter the Universalist ministry inaugurated his entrance into the adult world. It meant leaving the life of a schoolteacher behind, a life that does not appear to have been notably successful. His application to become a minister also meant committing himself to a religious organization. While the other ministers in our study were already very familiar with the church in which they were seeking ordination, Brownson's direct contact with Universalism was meager. On the other hand, after his ill-fated affiliation with the Presbyterian Church, his decision to enter the ministry was a noteworthy indication of his determination not to allow his experience in the Presbyterian Church to color his attitude toward institutional Christianity in general. His decision to apply for ministerial status was also made easier by the fact that his maternal aunt was a Universalist. We recall that, when he was twelve years old, he went to a neighboring woman to ask her advice regarding his joining a church, and that it was at this time that he first began to consider the ministry as a career. Now, twelve years later, he was again acting on the advice of an older woman in regard to his church affiliation, with direct implications for a career in ministry.

Entering the Adult World (1825-1831)

During his preparation for the ministry, Brownson taught school briefly in Elbridge, New York. While there, he met Sally Healy, who was a student at the school and the daughter of a farmer in whose home he was boarding. On June 19, 1827, a year after his ordination to the ministry, he and Sally were married.

He remained an active Universalist minister for three years following his ordination. He served a number of different churches in Vermont, New Hampshire, and New York. While serving in Auburn, New York, he edited the denominational magazine, *The Gospel Advocate,* and continued his editorship up to the time that he terminated his activities as a Universalist minister in 1829. His interest in journalism was unquestionably whetted by his experience of working in a printing office during adolescence. Besides his work as editor, not much is known about his ministry during these three years. There is no indication that he moved from one church to another because he was forced out. Rather, it is more likely that frequent moves were the norm in a small, struggling new denomination, and that each move he made was to a slightly larger church.

Leaving the church in which he was ordained was the central event in his "Age 25 Shift." This decision was to have ramifications for the next several years of his life, and was destined to give his life the very appearance of instability. The fact that, externally considered, his career as a Universalist minister was going very well, indicates that he was listening to inner voices that were not in concert with the externalities of his life. Conceivably, these inner voices were connected to the fact that he had decided as a young boy to become a minister on the basis of his reading of the Bible and theological books, indicating that the reality of his work as minister was incongruent with what he had dreamed of becoming when he was a boy. In any event, his decision to leave the church in which he had been ordained set him on a fifteen-year quest in search of a church in which he could feel truly at home, a quest that finally terminated in his conversion to the Catholic Church in 1844 (the same year that Newman also converted).

His reasons for leaving Universalism are somewhat difficult to discern, and seem to have had little if anything to do with his parish work. Some evidence suggests that his writings in *The Gospel Advocate* played a role in causing the break. A paper written in June 1829 was criticized by his readers for its implication that the Christian need not believe in anything distinctively Christian. When he attempted to assure his readers that this was not what he intended to say, he offended them further by setting forth his views on judgment, heaven, and hell. He suggested that, while he shared the Universalist rejection of the Calvinist notion of a miserable hell, he was not convinced by Universalism's own emphasis on God's punishment in the here and now. While he found this a useful attempt to retain the idea of divine judgment in lieu of the orthodox view of judgment in the hereafter, he contended that this doctrine, as Universalism had enunciated it, denied the mercy and compassion of God. In the Universalist view, God's punishment occurs naturally and inexorably when humans violate the general laws of nature. In this view, Brownson contended,

> God leaves the sinner to the mercy of the order he has established. He has made the world, adjusted its parts, impressed on it its laws, given it a jog, and bid it go ahead and take care of itself. Then I lose my Father in heaven, for God is only my creator and is no more my father than he is the father of the reed or the oak.[7]

This particular formulation of his objection to the Universalist view of divine judgment was written years later, in his autobiography, and appears to express a more orthodox view of God's actions in human lives than he actually held at the time. Still, it is interesting to note that his later reconstruction of his objection to Universalism employs, as did his objection to Presbyterianism, an argument derived from the dynamics of his own early family life. This time, however, rather than focusing on the distinction between a "true" and "foster" mother, he draws on his experience of the loss of his father at an early age. In his view, the Universalist doctrine of God, as implied in its view of punishment through natural laws, is dynamically similar to the loss of one's father, for the sinner is left to the mercy of the natural environment and God, the one who created him, has ceased to be a living presence in his life.

Although he defended his June 1829 article, he was privately aware that his views at the time were very near unbelief because he could affirm no more than the views any humanist could affirm. Even though his criticism of the Universalist view of divine punishment actually appears to have paved the way for an even more orthodox view, his confusion or uncertainty on these issues caused him to feel that he really had no business being in a Christian pulpit. He was uncertain whether the Bible could be taken as authoritative, and whether there is any sense in which one can talk about divine revelation. He concluded that he was carrying on a pretense in preaching every Sunday. Although he later felt that in making an honest avowal of some of his doubts in *The Gospel Advocate* he was taking a step closer to genuine Christian belief, he was unaware of this fact at the time.

Still, his departure from Universalism was not the clean break that characterized his leaving the Presbyterian Church nearly ten years earlier. As he was separating himself from the Universalist Church he continued to write for *The Gospel Advocate,* and even wrote glowing accounts of the bright future of Universalism. Thus, there is much reason to doubt that his departure from the Universalist Church was due primarily to his dissatisfaction with the church. It certainly played a role, but other circumstances were more decisive, especially the fact that he was developing a new interest in issues of social reform.

As he found himself at odds with Universalist theology, he began to do some extensive reading in social theory. His readings included the works of Robert Owen and William Godwin, both of whom were developing new social theories. Owen's socialistic views, developed in his book *A New View of Society,* were being put into practice in a number of experimental communities, and Godwin's theories in his book *Political Justice* so impressed him that in his autobiography written nearly forty years later he said that this book "has had more influence on my mind than any other book, except the Scriptures, I have ever read."[8]

He read Owens and Godwin while still making statements in *The Gospel Advocate* concerning the bright future of Universalism. However, on returning from a trip to Boston and Hartford where he met with church officials, he decided to hear Frances Wright, who was lecturing at Utica, rather than proceed immediately home. He had already reprinted some of her articles in *The Gospel Advocate,* but it was apparently not until he heard her in person that he was convinced that she "hit upon a just medium between the individualism of Godwin, and the communism of Owen."[9]

Over the next year or so he participated in the social movement led by Frances Wright, and ceased his work in the parish ministry. While Maynard suggests that she was the catalyst for his leaving the ministry, he adds: "Sooner or later the thing would have happened, even had he not encountered her; her influence over his vastly superior mind could not have been great; but the decision nevertheless was reached as a result of that encounter."[10] No doubt, he would probably have left Universalism anyway, yet he spoke very favorably of the Universalist churches he had visited in Boston and Hartford when he was visiting them, and was certainly not at that time planning to leave the Universalist Church. Also, although Frances Wright was probably no match for him intellectually, there were other aspirations besides intellectual growth to which she appealed, such as his desire to be involved in work that would have a positive value, and his need for personal acceptance. In my judgment, she was his first real mentor, and it was her role as mentor, not her sexual appeal, that drew him to her. Unfortunately, a mentor relationship with a woman is open to greater misunderstanding than one with a man, and this misunderstanding was to have a negative impact on his marriage.

He was immediately impressed with Frances Wright's oratory that evening in Utica. Her "fine, musical voice" and her "deep and glowing enthusiasm" appealed to him.[11] When she came to Auburn later that year to deliver a series of lectures, he was similarly impressed. He reports that she opened her first lecture at Auburn by remarking, "in the sweetest manner imaginable,"[12] that she had never been treated as incourteously as in Auburn, even though it was a town of no less than six churches. She noted, with a strong measure of sarcasm, "Perhaps it will not be inappropriate for us to spend one evening in discussing the subject of morals."[13] This blunt criticism of the churches also appealed to him, and his feelings were reciprocated. While in Auburn, she arranged for him to become a corresponding editor for her periodical, the *Free Enquirer.*

He was especially attracted to her advocacy of better social conditions. She sought modification of the laws that allowed imprisonment for small debts, the abolition of capital punishment, and a ten-hour work day. There were other aspects of her program that he either ignored, such as her advocacy of women's rights, or found bothersome. In the latter category, her views on the raising of children caused special problems for him. In her view, children should be raised by the state after the age of one or two, and ought to be kept in state-supported boarding schools until they were sixteen. They could be visited by their parents at regular intervals, but would be wards of the state. Children of the poor would be treated the same as the children of the rich. Later he described this plan as not only intended "to provide for bringing up all children in a rational manner," but also "to relieve marriage of its burdens, and to remove the principal reasons for making it indissoluble."[14] Although it is probably doubtful that she intended her advocacy of a program for the raising of children by the state to be construed as a program that would also make divorce easier, he was most critical of this aspect of her program for social change. As he wrote in his autobiography years later: "I was a husband and father, and did not altogether relish the idea of breaking up the family and regarding my children as belonging to the state rather than to me."[15] The statement, "I did not altogether relish the idea. . . ." is not a very vigorous rejection of her proposal for state control of children, though perhaps in light of his own disrupted childhood, Brownson could see some positive benefits of her plan for some children. Moreover, there was little reason to expect that this particular feature of the movement's platform had any chance of gaining a serious hearing among the American public. Thus, the whole matter was rather academic and he seems to have treated it as such.

On the other hand, there is reason to believe that joining her movement created a potentially serious domestic problem for him, and that her views on childrearing certainly did not contribute to domestic tranquility in the Brownson household, which was then populated by two small infants. His biographers disagree, however, as to how serious this problem was. Biographer Doran Whalen suggests that his wife was jealous of Wright,[16] and while Maynard points out that no direct evidence supports this claim, he admits, "That Sally did not like her husband's being mixed up with a notorious woman is, of course, likely enough; for that matter she was deeply distressed by his heretical and radical tendencies."[17] Moreover, his involvement in the movement led him to leave his congregation; even if he had not resigned, he would have been forced out for his association with Wright. Thus, what may have troubled his wife more than the threat that Frances Wright may have posed a rival for her husband's affection was the fact that his decision to leave his church left the family without a regular income.

In any event, he left the Wright movement in 1831 and having burned his bridges with the Universalist Church, he began his own independent ministry. Robert Owen, who was also involved in the movement, noted that he did so in order to support his family. Biographer Arthur M. Schlesinger Jr. suggests that he finally "realized how idle it was to hold out against the Lord."[18] His decision to leave the movement and begin his own church, however, was greatly facilitated by Frances Wright's move to Europe and her subsequent marriage there. In light of what he took to be her advocacy of a program that would make it easier for husbands and wives to terminate their marriages, her marriage must have been a shock to him, and a convincing argument in favor of his own return to less risky involvements. His bitter denunciation of her husband, whom he had "never trusted," for destroying "her feminine sweetness and grace,"[19] also suggests a feeling of betrayal with which he could not directly confront her. Thus, in returning to the ministry, he was undoubtedly responding to his wife's appeal for a more stable home life, especially in terms of finances. At the same time, leaving the movement was precipitated by the sudden departure and marriage of its leader. His mentor relationship ended as suddenly as it began, and it ended, as Levinson indicates many such relationships end, with a sense of betrayal and hurt.

In leaving the movement and deciding to return to the ministry, he was faced with a very uncertain future. He had left the Universalist Church and had no personal desire, even if it were possible, to return to it, so he spent the next four months as an independent minister in Ithaca, New York, where he was already known through his Universalist connections. His biographers are agreed that his return to the ministry had virtually nothing to do with a recovery of religious convictions or a renewed sense of dedication to the ministry. As Schlesinger puts it, "He was still very far from having recovered a sense of his personal need of religion."[20] In his first sermon as an independent minister in February of 1831, however, he gave evidence that he might be on the verge of a new affiliation, this time with the Unitarians. As he told the people who had gathered to hear him: "I belong to no party, I disclaim all sectarian names. . . . Should I assume the name of any party, it should be Unitarian, as that denomination approximates nearer, in my estimation, to the spirit of Christianity than any other."[21]

As he stood on the threshold of the age thirty transition, then, he was back in the fold of liberal Christianity, and was still searching. As Maynard points out,

Fanny Wright had served a double purpose in his life: she had sharply dragged him out of the haze of Universalism, and she had brought him to the edge of an abyss. From that abyss he had now turned back, one important lesson learned. He did not delude himself into thinking that religion was true merely because it was socially useful; but he had reached the belief that "the conviction that it is necessary for that purpose, if not rudely treated, may, in an ingenious mind lead to something more."[22]

It was for this "something more" that he began to search during his age thirty transition.

Age Thirty Transition (1831-1835)

Brownson began his independent church in February 1831, when he was twenty-eight years old, and he immediately founded a magazine called the *Philanthropist*. Now that he was back in the ministry, he devoted considerable intellectual and moral energy to determining in what ways he could affirm a Christian point of view. Whereas his approach immediately prior to his involvement in the Wright movement was to challenge Christian concepts in favor of an essentially humanistic perspective, he now saw his task as identifying those Christian views that he could, in conscience, accept. Thus, while his views were not very different from before, his approach was now in the nature of a building process rather than a tearing-down process.

On the other hand, his comment in his inaugural sermon that he was closer to Unitarianism than any other group served notice that his return to the Christian fold was not an act of surrender. The actual shift in his views from where they had been during his involvement in the Wright movement would be exceedingly modest. As he pointed out years later in his autobiography,

I had become a believer in humanity, and put humanity in the place of God. The only God I recognized was the divine in man, the divinity of humanity, one alike with God and with man, which I supposed to be the real meaning of the Christian doctrine of the Incarnation. . . . I regarded Jesus Christ as divine in the sense in which all men are divine, and human in the sense in which all are human.[23]

At first, his return to the ministry went reasonably well because he was able to supplement his earnings as a minister with his profits from the magazine. But by the middle of 1832, roughly a year after his return to the pulpit, he decided to disband the magazine because many of his subscribers had failed to pay their dues. During the time that he published the *Philanthropist,* he reprinted several of the sermons of William Ellery Channing, the "dean" of Unitarianism. As he had earlier printed some of Frances Wright's lectures in *The Gospel Advocate,* he was following a pattern here of printing the work of an individual whom he much admired, and hoped to meet. Channing was twenty-seven years his senior, and was therefore too old to function as a mentor, and, in any case, Brownson was probably beyond the age when he needed or wanted a mentor. On the other hand, he saw Channing as the father he had never had; or perhaps more accurately, as the man who brought home to him the reality of the heavenly Father. In a letter to Channing written several years later, he recalled his emotions when he first read Channing's sermons:

> I could have leaped for joy. I seemed suddenly to have found a Father. . . . I had never known an earthly father, and often had I wept when I had heard, in my boyhood, my playmates, one after another, say "my father." But now, lone and deserted as I had felt myself, I too had become a son, and could look up and say "my father"—around and say, "my brothers."[24]

With the failure of the *Philanthropist* and in need of a better livelihood, he began to look for a Unitarian pulpit. His wife went home with the two boys to Elbridge, where her widowed mother lived, while he set out to find a church. It was at this time that he and his family felt the full force of the price he was paying for leaving the Universalists and joining the Wright movement. On the other hand, the adversity they were now experiencing seems to have drawn him and his wife closer together. In a letter written to her from Brattleboro, Vermont, he wrote: "I think of you often, my little boys come to me in my dreams. I embrace you in my sleep, but I awake alone. A kind Father above will yet smile upon us."[25] The extent of their financial straits at the time is indicated by the fact that he reports in this letter that friends gave him a new coat and hat "so I am decently dressed."[26] He hoped to find a position in the New York State area but September came and went without success. In October 1832, he wrote to tell his wife that he was well received at the Unitarian church in Walpole, Massachusetts, ninety miles from Boston, and had been offered a salary of $500: "Not large, but we can live on it."[27] His wife and the boys rejoined him when he secured the Walpole position.

Walpole proved to be a distinct blessing for Brownson and the family. A third son was born to the Brownsons in January 1834. The move brought Brownson within reach of Boston, where he became personally acquainted with Channing. He began to exchange pulpits with Channing as well as with George Ripley, one of the leading Unitarian ministers of his day. Channing was impressed with Brownson's views on social reform as developed in an article in 1834 for the newly established periodical, the *Unitarian*. In this article, Brownson repudiated Frances Wright's emphasis on the state as the major instrument of social reform, and instead argued that social reform begins with improvement of the individual. Here, he was drawing on William Godwin's position. He wrote,

> To effect any real reform, the individual man must be improved. . . . The reformer's concern is with the individual. That which gives the individual a free mind, a pure heart, and full scope for just and beneficent action, is that which will reform the many. When the majority of any community are fitted for better institutions, for a more advanced state of society, that state will be introduced, and those institutions will be secured.[28]

Channing agreed with this essentially conservative approach to social reform, indicating that it accurately stated his own views. There could be no more important endorsement than this.

In February 1834, a month after the birth of his third son, he was approached by two different churches. He was content to stay in Walpole, but one of the churches, in Canton, Massachusetts, would bring him in closer proximity to Boston. In May, he was formally installed at Canton. George Ripley preached the sermon, and one of the leaders of the Universalist Church was in attendance, an indication that some Universalists were no longer upset over his earlier defection. Before he left his church in Walpole, the congregation passed a resolution in which they mentioned some differences of opinion with their minister but primarily attested to their regard for his ability and high moral character.

At Canton he was extremely busy, involved both in his parish and as a Lyceum lecturer. During the time that he remained at Canton he continued to associate with the Boston Unitarians. The longer he associated with them, however, the more persuaded he became that the "advanced minds among Unitarians" were in need of more vigorous leadership, perhaps even a new organization.[29] At first he entertained the thought that Channing was "the one who was to take the lead in the work of reorganization."[30] Before long, however, he began to feel that Channing was incapable of providing the necessary leadership. Writing in his autobiography years later, he observes that he began to recognize that Channing was not "a leader in the world of thought and action. . . . [He] was not and could not be the man to found the new order. . . ."[31] He considered the possibility that he himself might be that "destined man" who could create a new organization or revitalize the old, but when "the thought passed through my head . . . I did not entertain it."[32] He viewed himself as something of an outsider among Boston Unitarians, lacking in social and cultural decorum. But he felt that his very status as an outsider, which would itself disqualify him for such a leadership role, nonetheless enabled him to recognize the weaknesses of Unitarianism—its negativity, its coldness, its lifeless respectability.

He decided, therefore, that he would take action, such as forming his own religious group, his hope being that if he took some preliminary initiatives, perhaps he would convince others of the necessity of a new organization and "prepare men's minds and hearts to welcome it."[33] Judging from his references to this new organization as a "new church,"[34] it was apparent that he intended that it would not simply be a restructuring of the Unitarian church but a wholly new entity. Thus, as he began to enter the settling-down period(!), he was again considering the possibility of leaving an established church and striking out on his own. When other men would have been taking steps to consolidate their positions in the church they presently served, he was embarking on a new venture of very uncertain prospects—the formation of his own religious group in Boston.

In many respects, Brownson's age thirty transition period was the best period in his life. This contrasts with the other men in this study and in Levinson's own study, for whom the age thirty transition from age twenty-eight to thirty-three is typically a time of instability, of questioning one's earlier commitments, and is often marked by vocational confusion, personal frustration, and emotional anxiety. Could it be that the man whose overall life structure is unstable experiences a developmentally unstable period as smoother and less conflict-ridden than others do? After the difficult period during and immediately following his involvement in the Wright movement, his eighteen months in the Walpole church provided the opportunity to return to the normal life of a minister and to reclaim his wife and children from their temporary living situation in Elbridge. Maynard suggests that, all in all, "he may have known no congregation that he liked better than the one at Walpole."[35] The position at Walpole was also the springboard for his securing the church in Canton, where he was exceedingly busy—preaching four times a week and lecturing in surrounding churches. He was also doing considerable writing during this period, and his views were generally well regarded by Unitarian leaders in Boston. It is true that he remained an outsider among some of the Boston intelligentsia. Although he attended meetings of the Transcendentalist Club, where leading Unitarians met to discuss a wide variety of religious, philosophical, social, and literary issues, he never felt comfortable there. But he was not an outcast. Even if the Unitarian establishment in Boston had wanted to snub him, they could not have done so because he was in much demand as a lecturer and preacher.

On the other hand, as the age thirty transition drew to a close, he was just beginning to strike out on a new venture—his own religious group—whose chances of success were extremely uncertain. Although it would be inaccurate to compare this new venture to his involvement in the Wright movement, for there were significant differences between the two situations, a similar pattern is evident, that of relinquishing a solid situation in an established church in favor of a project whose future was most uncertain.

The fact that he was embarking on this project may tell us something about his own perceptions about his age thirty transition. I have suggested that these were, in many ways, the best years of his life, but this view is based on the fact that he made considerable progress in the developmental tasks of occupation, marriage, and family. He had established himself in his occupation as minister in a highly respected church, especially in the Boston area, and his marriage and family were now on a stable footing precisely because his vocational career was moving in a positive direction. His own perceptions, however, were undoubtedly different because a major aspect of his Dream for his life had been laid aside after his withdrawal from the Wright movement. How much this fact weighed on his mind during the age thirty transition is difficult to determine. However, as the age thirty transition came to a close, he was clearly restless to be doing more in the area of social reform. In his perception, the age thirty transition probably looked less like a period of consolidation than a period of retreat. He now seemed anxious to revitalize his ministry by moving from the suburbs of Boston to the inner city. His church in Canton was no longer much of a challenge to him.

The Tasks of the Novice Phase

As we take stock of Brownson's life at the end of the age thirty transition, he was beginning to negotiate some developmental tasks quite well after a rather rocky beginning, yet others posed major questions.

Forming a marriage and family. With the possible exception of Jonathan Edwards, Brownson had less difficulty in the area of actually finding a marriage partner than the other ministers in our study. Not much is known about Sally Healy, the young woman that he married, but it is fair to say that she supported his decision to enter the ministry since he had applied for ministerial status before he met her. It is not known whether she was a Universalist before he met her, but this does not seem to have been a stumbling block in their marriage. The fact that she was a religious person is indicated by her concern that her husband, in going to work for the Wright movement, might lose his religious faith. Even allowing for the fact that this concern for his religious faith may have been prompted in part by a more fundamental concern for the survival of her marriage, a woman without religious interests would be unlikely to have expressed this concern. On the other hand, undoubtedly his involvement in the movement created difficulties for his marriage. We know that two children were born to the Brownsons during the first two years of marriage whereas none were born during the next five. We can only speculate on the effect of Brownson's involvement in the Wright movement on this aspect of the marriage.

Even if we discount the claim of biographer Whalen that his wife was jealous of Frances Wright, we do know that she was never supportive of her husband's involvement in the movement. Thus, for more than a year he was involved in activities that appear to have meant a great deal to him professionally, but for which his wife had no enthusiasm. We also know that his return to the ministry was less the result of a new level of mutual understanding between them, and due more to financial necessity and Wright's departure to Europe. Thus, we may assume that the months following his return to the ministry were not entirely happy ones. He was back in the fold but not because he really wanted to be. His spirit was more one of resignation to unavoidable circumstances. On the other hand, the fact that the marriage survived this period and lasted until his wife's death in 1872, a marriage of forty-five years, is itself a testimony to their capacity to live through difficulties and find the necessary courage to continue on. His biographers credit Sally Brownson with having uncommon strength and maturity in her handling of her husband's emotional instability and restless spirit.

Forming an occupation. In the early part of the novice phase, he made significant progress in this developmental task. He had made the decision to become a minister and had been licensed to preach by the Universalist Church. By the time he became involved in the Wright movement at age twenty-seven, he had spent three years in the ministry and had become the editor of the church's periodical. We may assume that he would not have been entrusted with the editorship unless he was considered one of the more promising young ministers in the denomination. Also, his involvement in journalistic efforts probably reflected an accurate self-appraisal of his preaching abilities. As Maynard points out,

> He was much more of a journalist than a preacher; in fact his preaching and lecturing were only journalism—of a kind less effective than his written word. His was not the ability, so essential to the public speaker, of getting into immediate contact with his audience. His physical presence and his resonant voice stood him in good stead; and people listened with respect to a man so obviously sincere. But he was always rather aloof in the pulpit or on the platform. Not so when he took his pen in hand; then— only then—was he able to take his audience into his confidence.[36]

The reasons why he was more personally engaged in print than in person are not entirely clear, but one factor was that the aggressiveness and polemical outbursts that his written work exhibited were more controlled and restrained in public settings. He found in religious journalism an excellent medium in which to express his views, and this provided him an area in which he could work relatively conflict-free.

On the other hand, early in the "entering the adult world" period of his mid-twenties, there were already indications that his formation of an occupation would prove more difficult than for most young ministers. Because he had not been associated with a church during his childhood and adolescence, his effort to become established in the ministry was unusually complicated. He not only had to wrestle with the question of whether he wanted to become a minister, but also had to determine in which church he would serve as a minister. His decision to try the Universalists because his aunt was a member indicates that he sought a church in which he could claim some family roots. But in committing himself to a ministerial career in a church to which an aunt belonged, the family connection was not as binding as it would have been if parental support were involved. Perhaps this is why he liked to talk about his first two affiliations as though he were establishing a parent-child relationship. The Presbyterian Church was to be his "true mother" (but proved a "foster mother"), and the Universalist Church deprived him of a true "fatherly" relationship to God. In any event, his decision to become a Universalist minister was based largely on his aunt's affiliation with the group and his private readings in Universalist literature. We may assume that he also had direct familiarity with Universalist churches, but his decision to become a Universalist minister seems to have been arrived at in the privacy of his room rather than as a result of extensive social contacts with Universalists. Thus, when he began to experience some difficulties as editor of *The Gospel Advocate,* it was probably all too easy for him to decide that he could do without the Universalists. The deep family roots and social heritage that may have prompted another young man to ride out the criticism were simply not a strong restraining factor in his case. Also, the fact that he served several churches in the first three years of his ministry meant that he had not experienced the sense of being a real part of a congregation. No evidence indicates that he was forced out of any of these churches, yet such frequent moves meant that he did not develop an enduring relationship with any single congregation. His roots were wide rather than deep.

Another indication of potential difficulty in the formation of his occupation as a minister was the brevity of his education and training for the ministry. A formal theological education does not ensure effective ministry, but there is reason to believe that he would have profited greatly from a seminary education. He had strong theological interests and was deeply concerned about issues of faith and doctrine. However, his reflections on these issues were usually carried out in private, without teachers or fellow students to affirm or challenge his views. Conceivably, he would have revised his pattern of committing himself to a theological system, only to repudiate it later, had he been introduced to a less impulsive model of theological reflection. He considered it to his advantage that, as a self-educated man, he retained the originality that a formal education often destroys. Yet, his son astutely observed that "books did him almost as much injury and tyrannized almost as absolutely over his mind as professors would have done."[37]

All these factors (family roots, high mobility, theological education) were indicators of a potentially troubled ministry, but they are not in themselves a sufficient basis for detecting trouble in his occupation as a minister. The critical change in his formation of an occupation as a minister was his decision to abandon everything that he had worked toward as a young minister and to join the Wright movement. His decision to join the movement on the basis of a single lecture was impulsive, reminiscent of his decision to join the Presbyterian Church on the basis of a single heartwarming service. Still, it did reflect a deeper desire to free himself from commitments to Universalism that he could probably not honor in the future. It also reflected his increasing concern for an ethical perspective that would take social issues with greater seriousness than manifested among the churches and sects of his day. So, even though his attraction to the Wright movement was partly due to the personal attractiveness of Frances Wright, and to his desire to be well thought of by a person of national prominence, it would not be fair to attribute his involvement in the movement solely or even primarily to these personal interests. Moreover, as indicated earlier, it would be appropriate to view his relationship to Frances Wright as a mentor relationship. He looked to her as a person who could introduce him to a more accomplished group of individuals, both intellectually and socially, than he encountered in his church work.

Mentor relationships. Brownson lacked mentors throughout the initial stages of his early adult transition and entering the adult world periods. Although he related to various ministers, including the Presbyterian minister who baptized him, and the Universalist minister who was responsible for overseeing his training for the ministry, these relationships did not develop into a real mentor role of introducing him to the profession and helping him become established in it. Quite possibly, this gave him greater freedom in that when he left the church, there would be no sense of guilt or remorse for having let his mentor down. Also, because he lacked a father for much of his early life, he would probably have expected this mentor to carry the burden of being a father to him, a role that a mentor cannot perform and still function as a mentor. Still, the lack of a mentor meant he had to rely largely on his own efforts in growing into his chosen profession. Without extensive experience with ministers as he was growing up, he lacked a model that he might emulate or adopt, with appropriate modifications, in his own ministry.

As indicated, Frances Wright was his first real mentor. Despite his youthfulness (twenty-six years old) and inexperience, she included him in her work, and gave him important assignments in the movement. As Maynard puts it, they shared a mutual respect: "Each perceived the other's sincerity and courage and ability; neither objected to the other's supreme self-confidence."[38] He gained a great deal from this relationship in terms of his professional growth. It enabled him to work on projects of national importance and become acquainted with other prominent advocates of social reform. Her marriage and decision to live in Europe was a deep personal blow to Brownson, not because he had visions of marrying her, but because at a critical period in his relationship with her, she placed her own personal needs above the cause to which he had become dedicated at some risk to his relationships with wife and children. She did not betray him in any direct or personal way, but neither could she continue to serve as his mentor. This mentor relationship, however, had the duration typical of such relationships, and it continued to inform and inspire his social reform ideals long after their association was abruptly terminated.

In my view, William Ellery Channing played a different role. Once it became clear that Brownson was going to pursue a career in the church rather than remain in the movement, Channing provided a model of a successful, free-thinking clergyman. In this sense, he was more an ideal than a mentor. Nonetheless, Brownson made effective use of Channing; undoubtedly, his acceptance into Unitarian circles in Massachusetts was largely through Channing's influence. While other Unitarians found him somewhat boorish and lacking in social breeding, Channing was quite able to overlook all this. However, Channing did not seem to have the leadership abilities that Brownson believed the church urgently needed. His disappointment in Channing, together with his earlier disappointment in Wright, eventually led him to the view that he should not place his confidence in individuals but in a corporate body, one that claimed to have roots that could be traced to the earliest stages of Christianity.

Forming a Dream. There are definite indications during the entering the adult world phase that Brownson was beginning to integrate his dreams into his life structure. Having experienced a broken family life in childhood, one of his enduring dreams was for acceptance by others. His marriage and his acceptance as a ministerial candidate by the Universalist Church were two very significant ways in which this part of his Dream was integrated into his life structure. On the other hand, he also seemed to have difficulty in handling these expressions of acceptance. Perhaps his childhood experience, especially being a foster child and then reclaimed by his mother, led him to question the sincerity of those who did accept him. Both in his ministry in the Universalist Church and in his marriage, he worked against this acceptance shortly after he had achieved it. The Universalist Church, being an organization, let him go. His wife did not, and his biographers give her great credit for staying with a man whose career was very unstable. Nonetheless, the motivational pattern was essentially the same in both cases—he seemed to mistrust the acceptance of others because beneath a confident demeanor he suffered from low self-esteem and was also reluctant to entrust his life and future to others who may prove to be untrustworthy. As the Frances Wright situation turned out, this mistrust was partially justified; as his mother, through no fault of her own, had abandoned him, Wright, with less justification, had done the same.

Another part of his Dream involved his intellectual skills and interests. Possessing a good and inquisitive mind, he wanted to become recognized as a scholar. Without much formal education, his scholarly achievements were really quite remarkable. They included his ability to read German and French philosophical works in the original, his breadth of learning, and his vigorous writing style. But without a formal education, he lacked a reference point from which to evaluate his scholarship, and he lacked the credentials of a university trained scholar, a fact that later resulted in his being passed over for a Harvard professorship in philosophy. However, in the period with which we are concerned here, his major difficulty in the area of intellectual skills and interests was that he was not very effective in using these abilities in behalf of his desire for acceptance. As Maynard points out, his analyses of the weaknesses of Universalist theology were presented in *The Gospel Advocate* in a rather flippant tone.[39] He had not learned to use his intellectual abilities in a judicious manner. In his defense, it should be noted that the religious climate of the times was characterized by polemical claims and counterclaims. Still, in criticizing Universalist theology, he did not use his intellectual capacities to combat the views of other groups but rather to identify the vulnerabilities of his own group. While some fellow Universalists chalked this up to his impulsive personality, others were less tolerant, considering his editorials an act of infidelity.

He appears to have recognized that his intellectual aggressiveness was harmful to his more basic desire to be accepted by others. Years later, in his autobiography, he observed that the world "may have misconceived my real character. It has allowed me the stronger, the harsher, but denied me the softer and more amiable qualities of our nature. It has supposed me incapable of generous sympathies and firm attachments."[40] He contended that this evaluation of his character, while superficially accurate, failed to take account of his childhood deprivations which caused him to be more aggressive and solitary than nature had destined him to be:

> The unfriendly circumstances of my earlier life . . . forced into notice much which in ordinary cases is concealed, and gave a disproportionate development to qualities, of which nature gave me indeed the germ, but which she never intended should form the prominent traits of my character. My youth was one of hardship, privation and suffering.[41]

Here, he suggests that he tended to overcompensate for childhood deprivations. If so, this overcompensation took the form of intellectual aggressiveness and social distance. His aggressiveness required others to recognize and not ignore him, yet it also worked against his deeper desire to be accepted by others, to be recognized for his capacity for "generous sympathies and firm attachments."[42]

A third and final feature of his Dream was his desire to be involved in enterprises of practical personal and social value. This desire was evident, for example, in his vocational uncertainties in his early twenties. Having considered the possibility of becoming a missionary, he soon rejected the idea because, as Maynard puts it, he wondered "whether it actually does much good."[43] Also, he criticized both Presbyterian and Universalist theology on grounds that they were ineffective in providing individuals with the resources they required to deal with their practical concerns. He criticized the Presbyterian Church, for example, because it failed to provide practical guidance in helping him deal with questions of religious authority. He criticized Universalist theology because it seemed to reject the role of God in human affairs. By emphasizing the inexorable laws of nature, Universalism could challenge the Calvinist view of a punitive and capricious deity, but this also had the effect of deemphasizing God's active role in human affairs, especially at the social level.

As the victim of a broken home, he was unusually sensitive to the role that the church might play in the area of social action, but by the time he had joined the Wright movement, he was not optimistic that the church would prove an effective catalyst for social change. He strongly resonated with Frances Wright's charge that the churches were an obstacle to dealing with social problems. When she announced that he was to become a corresponding editor of her *Free Inquirer,* he was undoubtedly flattered by her observation that he was a minister who had "renounced the chair of dogmatism to pursue inquiry in the field of nature and human life."[44] He was never content to debate theological issues on dogmatic grounds, but always explored them in terms of their social and cultural implications. Unfortunately, his reluctance to engage in dogmatics as such, and his doubts about the role of the church in dealing with social issues, caused him to believe he had nearly lost his faith. In retrospect, he could say that his "honest avowal of unbelief was, under the circumstances, a step that brought me nearer the kingdom of God."[45] But at the time this rejection of dogmatic theology in favor of social action informed by humanistic ideals appeared to be nothing but the loss of his Christian faith.

As we look at the developmental tasks of the novice phase in general, the unsettling feature of Brownson's life profile at the conclusion of the novice phase is his involvement in the Wright movement. It is unsettling not because of his involvement in a movement per se, but because it was bought at the expense of his achievements in the developmental tasks of forming an occupation and developing a family life. Neither of these two developmental tasks was entered in a precipitous manner. Why he was subsequently willing to disrupt this carefully laid foundation of occupational and marital stability is difficult to determine on the basis of available evidence. His biographers suggest that he was not an engaging preacher, and this may have caused occupational discomfort. His wife had given birth to two children during the first three years of their marriage, and this may have caused marital strains of one sort or another. Perhaps because he lost his own father, he was uncertain as to his role in the family.

These very speculations point out one of the unique problems involved in attempting to determine why his life manifested greater instability than the other subjects in our study. This is the fact that, more than with any of the other subjects, we seem to need to return to his childhood to gain some understanding of his adult life and career. His own statement that his "childhood deprivations" had a major effect on his adult life suggest that he engaged in much of the same kind of analysis. The suggestion that he looked to churches for parental care and guidance does not seem odd in his case, whereas the same suggestion in the case of our other subjects might appear to be rather precious psychologizing. My point here is that his very instability is difficult to explain in terms of his current situations and involvements. We cannot quite understand why, after a successful trip to Boston and Hartford in which he saw evidence of the growth of Universalism, he was prompted to stop over in Utica so that he could hear Frances Wright. Because we cannot quite understand it, we search in his childhood for answers. Had he become so accustomed to a disrupted family life in childhood that he unconsciously anticipated the failure of his own family life? Did he choose to hear Frances Wright because he had been deprived of a warm and soothing maternal voice through much of his childhood? Did he resent his wife's attentions to their two young sons as he thought of the years in which he was deprived of his mother's attentions? Some validity may be found in each of these speculations, but the important point is not that they may or may not be valid, but that his behavior at this stage in his life prompts us to search his childhood for explanations.

This review of his handling of the four developmental tasks of the novice period suggests that instability is not so much the result of a failure to handle all four of these tasks, but more the consequence of the fact that the objectives of one or two of these developmental tasks conflict with one or two of the others. Brownson is not the only one of the five ministers in this study who experienced such conflicts, but the others tended to resign themselves to a flawed structure, typically, by placing one developmental task on indefinite hold, whereas he tried to reconcile these tasks and did so in ways that mostly revealed their incompatibilities. The primary conflicts were between his Dream and the occupational form it took, and between the formation of his marriage and family and the formation of a mentor relationship.

The Settling-Down Phase

Settling Down and Becoming His Own Man (1836-1843)

In early 1836, at the age of thirty-three, Brownson moved to Chelsea, across the Mystic River from Boston. He had no definite pastoral duties except some preaching at Charlestown, only a few minutes away by ferry. He now set out to do what he had been giving serious thought to for nearly two years, the formation of his own church "which shall embody the most advanced ideas and sentiments of the Race, and be *The Church of the Future*."[46] In March 1834 George Ripley had written to him, proposing just such a church. What Ripley had proposed to him was that he come to Boston and address himself to people

> who are disgusted with Orthodoxy and insensible to Liberal Christianity in any of the modes, in which it is now presented, but who would gladly hear the Gospel preached in the spirit of Jesus, in a way to meet their intellectual and moral needs.[47]

Ripley went on to point out that, in such a work, he would be able to deal with "larger and different classes of men from those to whom you now have access." Clearly, Ripley meant that he should take his message to the middle and lower classes, thus serving, as Maynard puts it, as a "free lance Unitarian evangelist."[48]

In 1836 he acted on Ripley's idea. Without rejecting the Unitarian Church, he formed his Society for Christian Union and Progress, with meetings in Boston's Lyceum Hall and Masonic Temple. His society was at first very successful. His original intention was to appeal to all classes, with an emphasis on the needs of the poor and working classes, but he was advised by others against focusing on the poor because the poor already have the gospel preached to them while it was the working classes that had drifted away from the church. He was also advised against trying to enlist the wealthy because the working classes would come to the meetings only if the upper classes were not in attendance. He was apparently disposed to respond favorably to this advice because, since his involvement in the Wright movement, his social concern was directed toward the working classes. Maynard expresses it rather simplistically when he says, "Not yet was he completely free from Fanny Wright's apron strings,"[49] but there is truth in the view that his Society for Christian Union and Progress was intended to benefit the same class of people to which the Wright movement had addressed itself.

There was, however, a significant difference in his understanding of what his society was all about. Unlike the Wright movement, his society had a strong Christian basis. In his sermons he stressed the possibility that individuals are capable of "living Christ."[50] In saying this, he was simply affirming his faith in humanity and its capacity to work toward progress and reform, but the way in which he now affirmed this faith was to emphasize the human capacity to live the life of Christ, leading Elizabeth Peabody to write a letter to him in which she related that a woman she knew had exclaimed to her after hearing a sermon of his, "this is preaching Christ."[51] He also wrote his first book during this period, *New Views of Christianity, Society, and the Church*. This book, too, placed considerable emphasis on Jesus and the atonement. He gave the atonement his own formulation, as being the binding together of spirit and matter, but the important fact is that he saw his work at this time as providing a Christian foundation for social change.

His society began to flourish. Channing first had doubts about his views on the plight of the workingman, feeling that he exaggerated the workingman's physical plight and did not say enough about his spiritual condition, but in the end he said that he preferred Brownson's "morbidly sensitive vision to prevalent evils, to the stone-blindness of the multitude who condemn him."[52] Channing also contributed financially to the society. Brownson did have difficulties with prosperous individuals who thought the society was too radical and that he was fanning the flames of social conflict. He also had problems with some of his more liberal followers who felt that he did not go far enough in pressing for social reform. Still others believed that his sermons were un-Christian and blasphemous—especially those sermons that emphasized humanity's capacity to live the life of Christ and to contribute to the ushering in of the kingdom of God. Yet the society survived these clashes and criticisms, and continued to grow.

By the late 1830s or early 1840s, however, the society had begun its decline. He does not report the details of this decline in his autobiography, but says simply that he had resigned himself to the fact that "man is an indifferent church-builder."[53] However, he acknowledges his own responsibility for the failure and points out that the society might have succeeded if he had possessed the requisite personal qualities:

> My society at one time was prosperous, but in general I could not pride myself on my success; yet I saw clearly enough, that with more confidence in myself, a firmer grasp of my own convictions, a stronger attachment to my own opinions because they were mine, and a more dogmatic temper than I possessed, I might easily succeed. . . . I was in fact . . . too distrustful of myself to succeed.[54]

The effects of the decline of his society on Brownson were more subtle than those that followed his involvement in the Wright movement. He had a popular periodical, the *Boston Quarterly Review,* whose readership was very loyal, and this provided a reliable income. He considered giving up the periodical in 1839 but it was still going strong in 1842. The changes in his life this time were more qualitative. He began a gradual withdrawal from his relationships with the Boston Unitarians, and with the exception of his continuing friendship with George Ripley, he began cutting ties with the Transcendentalist movement.

The critical year was 1842, when he was thirty-nine. In June of that year he wrote Channing a long letter which was published later as a pamphlet titled, "The Mediatorial Life of Jesus." The views expressed in this pamphlet were an extension of his views developed in sermons for his society, but they went much further by emphasizing not merely the importance of men "living Christ" but of Jesus' own role as the savior of the world. At the beginning of the letter, he addressed Channing as "my spiritual father" and observed that it was his writings that had brought him to a "living faith in God."[55] Considering that he read Channing's writings in the aftermath of his involvement in the Wright movement, it would be fair to say that he was not simply engaging in pleasantries or flattery. He then proceeded to the substance of his letter, his argument that Jesus' life can be viewed as mediatorial. He acknowledged that, in offering this view, he would again be subjected to the criticism that this was simply a new half-baked idea of his. He could anticipate this charge because in the past when he discovered

> that I was not understood, or rather, that I was misunderstood, I have from time to time changed my point of view and my phraseology, with the hope of being able to communicate my real thought. All in vain. I have only gained a sneer for my versatility and frequent changes of opinion. I have at times wondered at this; but I am satisfied that it was owing to the contrary tendencies at work in my mind, and to the fact that I had not fully mastered what I wished to say, and therefore had only lisped and stammered, instead of articulating clearly and distinctly.[56]

He contends, however, that he is now certain in his mind that what he has to say in this letter will stand the test of time. Acknowledging that his reading of Leroux's *De l'humanité* was instrumental in turning his thoughts toward the idea of Jesus as mediator, he also insists that the application of this idea of mediatorship to theology is his own contribution.

In his view, the idea of Jesus as mediator is the key to all theological issues. From this perspective, he believes he can

> show that the doctrine that human nature became depraved through the sin of Adam, and that it is redeemed only through the obedience of Christ, that the doctrine which teaches us that

the Mediator is truly and indissolubly God-man, and saves the world by giving literally his life to the world, are the great "central truths" of Christianity, and philosophically demonstrable.[57]

He acknowledges that these are "orthodox" ideas, and thus recognizes that they run counter to Channing's views at various points, especially on the matter of human depravity. But he is convinced that he can present these views in such a manner that Channing will not refuse them, despite the fact that Channing had given some support to "that deification and worship of the human soul, which has within a few years past manifested itself among our transcendentalists."[58] He also attempts to temper this criticism of his "spiritual father" by noticing that he, too, would have to renounce views that he had argued for over the year, especially the fact that he had, like Channing, emphasized the natural goodness of humanity and had taught that Christianity does not stand or fall with the historicity of Christ. Now, in stressing the mediatorial role of Jesus, especially in redeeming human nature, he was repudiating these earlier views.

His letter to Channing went on to spell out one important implication of his new understanding of the mediatorial role of Jesus. This is that it implies a new understanding of communion between man and man, and man and God. As he puts it, "The coming of Jesus communicated a new life to the race, which by means of *communion* of man with man shall extend to all individuals."[59] Thus, through his life, Jesus communicated a new life of human communion which secures a "oneness of life" running through the whole human race. This "doctrine of communion," as he called it, was the practical effect of his view of Jesus as mediator.[60]

It was also the feature of his new views that most troubled Channing. Responding to Brownson's letter, Channing said that the notion that Jesus' life effects a communion that extends to all men sounds like Universalism:

> Some passages of your letter would lead an incautious reader to think of you as a thorough-going Universalist and as asserting the actual appropriation of the life of Christ to the whole human race, past or present, will they or nill they."[61]

Then, apparently not wanting Brownson to feel that he was being critical of his new views, he added, "Let us see you at the head of a really earnest and vital society of your own. God made you for something more than to scatter random shot."[62] This expectation of Brownson's leadership of a vital society of his own, coming at a time when his society was declining, seems a little ill-timed. Also, the comment that God made him for more than to "scatter random shot" implies the very criticism that he hoped his letter would not evoke. How he responded to Channing's letter is unclear, except that he proceeded to publish the substance of the letter in a pamphlet. Channing died in October, four months after this exchange of correspondence, and thus their relationship was terminated by an external circumstance at a time when it appeared that it might end of its own accord because Brownson was clearly moving away from Channing's theological perspective.

The doctrine of communion that Channing compared to Universalist views was very important to Brownson. He discusses this doctrine in the chapter of his autobiography titled "Man No Churchbuilder," thus implying a relationship between his doctrine of communion and the failure of his religious society. At the same time that he was writing Channing about his view of the mediatorial life of Jesus, he was writing his article, "Leroux on Humanity," for his *Boston Quarterly Review,* and in this article he related the doctrine of communion to various Catholic ideas, including transubstantiation, purgatory, and the communion of saints. Through his doctrine of communion, each of these traditional Catholic notions could be reinterpreted and, in his view, thereby salvaged. Clearly, the doctrine of communion was beginning to open the door for his eventual conversion to the Catholic Church.

What, precisely, was his doctrine of communion? As developed in his autobiography, perhaps the clearest statement of the doctrine, he points out that it is based on the proposition that man can live only through mutual cooperation with others: "Influence, inflowing, flowing-in—what is this but the very fact I assert, that our life is the joint product of subject and object?"[63] He cautions, however, that this mutual influence among men is inadequate to sustain life. Man also has continual need of communion with God:

> Man lives and can live only by communion with God: "Man lives and can live only by communion with what is not himself. . . . He cannot lift himself, but must be lifted, by placing him in communion with a higher and elevating object."[64]

Here, he argues that an adequate concept or doctrine of communion requires the transcendence of God. Unlike Leroux, who contends that man communes with nature through property, with fellow man through family and state, and with God through humanity, he argues that "the communion of God through Humanity was in effect no communion at all."[65] God must somehow transcend humanity in order for communion to occur between subject and object.

In coming to this view, he recognized that he would have to abandon his "doctrine of no God but the God in man, or the identity of the human and the Divine,"[66] but this was a small price to pay for the conviction that he "was headed, for the first time in my life . . . in the direction of real Christian beliefs."[67] His account in his autobiography of his insight into the true nature of communion conveys great excitement, almost as though it had triggered a religious experience. It is useful to compare his account of the effect that his doctrine of communion had on him personally with his earlier criticism of Universalist theology. In Universalism, he said, "God leaves the sinner to the mercy of the order he has established."[68] In contrast, the doctrine of communion asserts that God freely intervenes in the established order. This realization that God is free to act in relationship with other forms of existence, including, of course, human activities, was a matter of great excitement for Brownson. His description of how this insight affected him personally reads like a religious experience:

> This threw a heavy burden from my shoulders, and in freeing God from his assumed bondage to nature, unshackled my own limbs, and made me feel that in God's freedom I had a sure pledge of my own. . . . He was free to love me as his child, and to do me all the good his infinite love should prompt. I was no longer chained, like Prometheus, to the Caucasian rock, with my vulture passions devouring my heart; I was no longer fatherless, an orphan left to the tender mercies of inexorable general laws, and my heart bounded with joy, and I leaped to embrace the neck of my Father, and to rest my head on his bosom. I shall never forget the ecstasy of that moment, when I first realized to myself that God is free.[69]

It is difficult to determine to what extent Brownson was thinking of the dynamics of his own childhood, especially the loss of his father, in his account of the ecstasy he felt as he understood the implications of his doctrine of communion. But what *is* clear is that he has come to a thoroughly new theological understanding that was quite different from the Unitarian theology of his day, and rooted in a more orthodox Christian understanding of the transcendence and providence of God. Conceivably, he could have chosen to trace the origins of this view to Puritan theology, rather than to its more distant Catholic roots, but one practical effect of this new theological view of communion for his professional life would have been the same in either case—namely, that he could no longer remain affiliated with liberal Christianity. Thus, as he came to the end of the settling-down phase of the early adult era, he again confronted the problem of where to go from there.

If the failure of his Society for Christian Union and Progress and his adoption of the doctrine of communion is viewed as marking the end of the settling-down phase, it is fair to say that he had not established the professional stability one normally desires during this period. His difficulty in keeping his society going suggested to him that he lacked the necessary leadership qualities to "build" and sustain a church. At the same time, his theological views were clearly moving away from the Unitarian Church, so it was quite unlikely that he would simply return to leading a Unitarian congregation. Thus, his future once again had a very open-ended quality about it. Rather than "settling down" to a solid career in the Unitarian ministry—his professional location at the beginning of the settling-down phase—he was no longer employed as a Unitarian minister and had begun to repudiate its liberal theology. He was no clearer about his life pattern now than he was at the beginning of the settling-down period. His professional life was as uncertain as it had ever been, and his age—thirty-nine—was no longer in his favor. After all, he was nearing the end of the "settling-down phase," and was more unsettled than ever.

He recognized, however, that if his doctrine of communion placed him at odds with Unitarian theology, it placed him more in line with either the Episcopal or Catholic Church. For a number of reasons, he began to think most seriously about affiliation with the Catholic Church. He was initially inclined toward the Episcopalians (he advised his friend Isaac Hecker, who eventually became a Catholic, to become an Episcopalian). But one argument he offered against joining the Episcopalians himself is that, although he felt doctrinally closest to them, they would require his reordination and this would be a denial that "the Congregational communion is an integral part of the church Catholic."[70] Although this argument might seem a bit odd, inasmuch as the Catholic Church would be even less inclined than the Episcopal to recognize the validity of the Congregational Church, it does make sense considering that, in joining the Catholic Church, he did not anticipate becoming a priest. His marriage status would preclude that possibility. Thus, if he felt that the failure of his society was due to his lack of leadership capacities, he may well have been prepared at this stage in his life to end his work as a parish minister of a congregation. If he became a Catholic, this would effectively terminate his career as a parish minister.

Another reason that the Catholic Church loomed larger than the Episcopal in the planning of his future was that his articles on Jesus' mediatorial role and his doctrine of communion were being read by the Catholic community. In his letter to Channing, published as a pamphlet, and in his article on Leroux's treatise, he had expressed views that would have more appeal to the Catholics than to the Episcopalians of his day. Thus, in his article on Leroux's treatise for the *Boston Quarterly Review,* he noted that his doctrine of communion makes a case for purgatory because it suggests that those who have passed from us still commune with us: "The secrets of the country lying on the other side of that dark river death, are not so well kept as it is sometimes alleged,"[71] and on this basis he argued that there is a great truth in the doctrine of purgatory as well as the doctrine of the communion of saints. These two concepts, together with the idea of apostolic succession, are based on

> the profound truth of the solidarity of men in humanity, and of humanity, through Jesus, in God. . . . It is only by a living communion of the individual with humanity, through humanity with Jesus, and through Jesus with God, that he can be redeemed and sanctified."[72]

To be sure, he was careful to say that he was not adopting these Catholic doctrines, but was simply recognizing that from the perspective of his doctrine of communion these concepts reflected a "great truth."[73] Still, these comments on Catholic doctrines leave no doubt that he was becoming favorably disposed to the Catholic Church.

The decisive event occurred in 1843 when he wrote a series of articles on the mission of Jesus. First published in his own journal, some of the articles were reprinted in various Catholic periodicals. Buoyed by this unexpected recognition, he began to consider converting to the Catholic Church:

> Till I commenced writing this series of essays, I had no thought of ever becoming a Roman Catholic; and it was not till I saw my articles copied into a Catholic journal, that even the possibility of such a termination of my researches presented itself to my mind."[74]

This recognition appealed to his desire for acceptance, especially since it was acceptance of intellectual efforts which, in focusing on his doctrine of communion, also had practical implications for the improvement of human life in its corporate dimensions. Moreover, we are told by one of Brownson's biographers that Sally Brownson and all the children except Orestes Jr., their firstborn, were prepared to convert without resistance:

> Sally, who had grieved deeply, if silently, during the early years of their marriage, at witnessing his growing unbelief, now encouraged him to become a Catholic, and her own candid heart readily accepted the faith to which he had attained only with so much struggle.[75]

When the time came, Orestes Jr. abandoned his resistance and also converted. Thus, this new move would not threaten Brownson's family relationships. Nor were personal relationships at stake, for Channing had died in October 1842 and Brownson did not convert until 1844. Thus, despite—or perhaps because of—the fact that Brownson's conversion from the Unitarian Church to the Roman Catholic Church was far more radical than Newman's conversion from the Church of England, the effects on his family and even his professional relationships were much less acrimonious.

But what about his professional life? If he was no longer involved in some form of ministry, what could he do and how would he support himself? Evidently, this was not a pressing worry for him. He did think about becoming a lawyer but chose simply to sustain himself with his publishing ventures and lectures. After his conversion he continued to publish his quarterly review, which had nearly a thousand subscribers at the time of his conversion, and he continued to direct it toward his former associates rather than toward the Catholic population.

This is not to say that the conversion was easy, for he had considerable trouble with the bishop who supervised his admission into the Catholic Church. Neither did the conversion provide a new stability in his life. On the contrary, the next two decades of his life were as unstable as the decades traced here. But, in becoming a Catholic, he had found a religious system that was large enough to encompass the major dimensions of his Dream. He found personal acceptance, he found a whole new set of issues to which he could apply his intellectual skills, and he found an institutional structure, already intact, that reflected his emerging social views. The price he paid for this affirmation of his Dream at this stage in his life was that, when other middle-aged men are tending to modify their Dream and to reduce its emotional hold on themselves, Brownson was following his Dream with greater intensity. He was doing so with the knowledge that his conversion to the Catholic Church was more likely to limit than enhance his professional options in the future. With his conversion to the Catholic Church in 1844, his career as a minister was permanently ended.

CONCLUSION

What were the major reasons for Brownson's instability? In my judgment, the basic reason for his instability was personal insecurity. Because of a deprived childhood and lack of formal education, he was insecure in his role as a minister and had doubts about his abilities as a scholar. His insecurity as a minister climaxed when his society failed and he lost confidence in his ability to lead a church. His insecurity as a scholar was perhaps less obvious, but in his letter to Channing he acknowledged that he tended to write impulsively and was then forced to clarify his writings when they were misunderstood. Such impulsivity is a reflection of insecurity.[76] His willingness to revise his views when criticized indicates that he was insecure about them and was therefore inclined to give his critics the benefit of the doubt. Moreover, he published most of his articles in his own journal thus creating his own market rather than seeking publication in established journals. As his own editor, he could ensure the dissemination of his views, but he must have felt that his work might not have been published if left to the judgment of another editor. This insecurity about his own scholarship seems to have been a strong factor in his response to the publication of his views in Catholic journals. Here was an entirely unsolicited acceptance of his views from unexpected quarters. His insecurity made him especially responsive to expressions of acceptance, and he responded to such expressions with greater enthusiasm than they necessarily invited or warranted.

One final comment before concluding my analysis of Brownson: It might occur to some readers to raise questions about my placement of Newman in the "breaking-out" pattern and Brownson in the "unstable" pattern because both became Catholics at the conclusion of the settling-down era. Would it not be more accurate to view Brownson as the "breaking-out" type also? I have pondered this suggestion, but have come to a negative conclusion on the following grounds: Newman fits the "breaking-out" pattern because he had worked very hard within a life structure with very definite characteristics—minister in the Church of England and vicar of the university chapel—but arrived at a point in his life when this was simply not working. For the various reasons discussed in the chapter on Newman, he felt that the life structure in which he was working was seriously flawed and that he needed to formulate a new one.

I doubt that Brownson had the same sense of working for years within a life structure and then deciding to break out of it when it failed to work. It is more accurate to say that he simply did not have a clearly established life structure. This was especially true in the case of his professional life, the area that Levinson's study indicates is the most important factor in determining stability. Newman remained vicar of St. Mary's Church for fifteen years and was associated with Oxford University even longer, but Brownson did not remain with any single parish for more than two years and his career manifested considerable geographical mobility. Furthermore, although Newman was raised in the Church of England and remained in it until his conversion, Brownson was not raised in any particular church and belonged to three different denominations before his conversion. Finally, Newman's theological views underwent change during his twenties and thirties, but during that time they remained within the established theological traditions in the Church of England. In contrast, Brownson's views had manifested a wide range of perspectives from humanism to orthodox Christianity. Thus, particularly in the area of occupation, Newman's life structure was extremely stable— in spite of his involvement in a religious movement—while Brownson's was much more unstable and subject to frequent change.

Another difference between Newman and Brownson was the duration of their struggles over the question of conversion to the Catholic Church. Newman's struggle lasted nearly seven years, and involved considerable soul-searching and much reflection on the pain he was inflicting on others as well as himself; Brownson's conversion occurred within two years of his development of the doctrine of communion, and the major conflicts involved misunderstandings with the bishop who directed his conversion. The prolonged struggle that Newman experienced is more indicative of the "breaking-out" pattern (with its psychological pain), whereas Brownson's relatively brief conversion period is more typical of the unstable pattern.

These differences between the conversions of Newman and Brownson are only the more obvious ones. Others could be noted, but these point to the fact that conversion to another religious institution may occur within more than one of the five sequences, and thus two conversions to the same institution can be quite different. Although externally the same, their emotional tonality and their role in the formation or dissolution of the life structure may be markedly different.

Chapter 7

Five Models of Professional Formation

The foregoing studies indicate that the most decisive years in the lives of these five ministers were in the middle through late thirties—"the periods of settling down" and "becoming one's own man." Although their careers took very different paths, the one common feature in their development as ministers was the fact that these years were extremely important. Success or failure in the middle to late twenties was not nearly as critical to a given minister's future as success or failure in the middle through late thirties.

In addition to supporting the conclusion that the middle through late thirties are extremely important in the career of the minister, the foregoing studies have enabled us to explore the strengths and weaknesses of each of the five life sequences as models of professional formation. In concluding this study, I concentrate on the positive and negative aspects of each of these five models of professional development. The following discussion is offered tentatively because it is based on the life of one individual in each type.

ADVANCEMENT WITHIN A STABLE LIFE STRUCTURE

This professional model in ministry is the pattern that most of us identify as the "successful minister." In this model, the minister moves to increasingly larger and more challenging churches, has numerous opportunities to move from one church to another if desired, and is frequently under consideration for larger leadership roles at the regional or national level.

One important characteristic of this model is that this advancement process may *begin immediately on graduation from seminary.* In Brooks' case, advancement began as soon as he graduated from seminary, when he took a church that other recent graduates may well have felt incapable of handling. As it turned out, this was a good decision, at least in terms of this professional model, because this particular church could provide him with more support and with more resources than could a smaller, struggling church. Thus, while the church placed great demands on him, it also provided him with greater resources for carrying out his objectives. This suggests that one major characteristic of the "advancement within a stable life structure" model is that the minister is likely to begin advancement with certain advantages over other ministers at the same stage of development. These advantages, however, are integral to the advancement process itself. It is not a matter of, for example, being the son or grandson of a minister (as in Edwards' case), but of having advantages directly related to the church structure itself. Brooks realized enormous advantages in beginning his ministry in a medium-sized church in an urban area. By doing a good job in this church, he was in an excellent position to move to a larger urban church next, and this is precisely what happened.

A second characteristic of this professional model is that one's *ministerial style is well-balanced*. Brooks was an excellent preacher, but this was coupled with careful attention to the organizational aspect of the church's life, serious attention to his role as a teacher, involvement in matters of social concern and community enterprises and, as his career developed, increasing attention to pastoral counseling. He developed his skills in three or four major functions of ministry. By beginning his ministry in a relatively complex organizational and social setting, some of the impetus for his development of a well-balanced ministry originated in the setting itself, though it is also the case that, already in seminary, he was developing along a number of lines.

A third characteristic of this professional model is that it takes its toll in terms of *physical and emotional health*. On one occasion, the church granted Brooks a leave of absence for fifteen months due to his physical and emotional fatigue. On another occasion, friends noticed that he was suffering deeply inside. He carried his own personal burdens more or less alone and, especially after his move to Boston, seems to have lacked any close friendships through which he might have been upheld and strengthened. Fortunately, the congregational leaders were sensitive to his need for relief and were generous in their vacation policies. If ministers who fit this particular pattern of professional formation serve in churches whose leaders lack such sensitivity, they will very likely need to change churches, or resort to other means (e.g., personal therapy), to gain relief from the physical and emotional pressures. Brooks appeared to find personal therapy in writing and delivering his sermons.

A fourth characteristic of this professional model is *an independent but nonaggressive attitude toward church authorities and ecclesiastical structures.* In the early years of his ministry, Brooks gave his attention to his parish and had little to do with the larger ecclesiastical structures. By the time he reached the settling-down period, he was already so well established in his own parish and in the community that his bishop could exert relatively little control over him. For example, the bishop in Boston reprimanded him by letter for allowing a non-Episcopalian minister to participate in a wedding he had conducted, yet this was a rather mild, even ineffective sanction against him. More important is the fact that he turned down opportunities to become an assistant bishop. The minister who is advancing within a stable life structure seems to prize his independence of ecclesiastical authorities too much to place himself in a subordinate position to these authorities. The minister of a large urban parish tends to enjoy such independence.

A fifth characteristic is the paradox of success leading to *the sense of lost opportunities.* On numerous occasions, Brooks was offered other parishes and positions on seminary and university faculties. On each occasion, he rejected these offers. One senses that he held no serious regrets for turning down other parish churches, but that he had strong regrets when he did not accept seminary administration or teaching positions. Much of this regret may be attributed to the desire to serve as mentor to younger men training for the ministry. Although he could do some mentoring as the senior pastor in a multiple staff ministry in Boston, seminary teaching or administration would have given him a more concentrated role as a mentor. He rejected such offers partly because he questioned his ability to hold his own in a community of scholars, and also because he would have to relinquish some of the independence he enjoyed as the pastor of a large urban church. Nonetheless, the minister who fits this model of professional formation experiences the very real pain of having to choose between two or more desirable opportunities. Something within him causes him to want to try out these opportunities (the challenge, the need for new types of experience), but he is basically cautious in his orientation to life, and thus stays with what he knows is working well instead of taking a chance on an opportunity that may or may not prove successful. Thus, he differs from the minister whose advancement leads to major modifications in life structure. The latter will take risks, and do so at an early stage in his career (his thirties), that he will not take. As this model of professional formation implies, stability is preferred to the challenge of new and different types of ministry.

DECLINE OR FAILURE WITHIN A STABLE LIFE STRUCTURE

This professional model in ministry is very similar to the first model, in that both reflect stable patterns. But whereas the first results in continuing advancement, the second results in decline or failure. On the basis of what is known about Jonathan Edwards, we are able to determine some of the characteristics of this model of ministry.

First, in this model, the minister is likely to be the victim of some *serious errors in judgment*. Edwards made two such errors. The first error occurred after the Great Awakening. He had already created potential problems with his congregation by leaving his own church to preach at various other churches. These absences may have been acceptable if he had not attempted to prolong the awakening in his own church by continuing to preach on awakening themes long after his congregation had lost interest. A second error in judgment was his handling of the "bad book" dispute. By failing to differentiate between the children who were accused and those who were being called as witnesses, he invited the ire of many of his parishioners. In both cases, he was insensitive to the current needs and feelings of the congregation. All ministers make mistakes and cannot avoid offending some parishioners, but these two examples, especially the latter, are clear indications of Edwards' inability to sense the general mood of the congregation. Moreover, in both cases, he did not try to correct the situation after he encountered resistance, but continued to act as though he had no other options than to keep preaching the sermons and proceed with the investigation of his parishioners' children. Given more flexibility or less defensiveness, he may have been able to turn both situations into occasions of greater mutual understanding and trust.

A second characteristic of this model is that the minister is likely to be the victim of *mistreatment by his congregation*. In Edwards' case, the church handled the payment of his salary in an erratic manner. As a result, the pastor's salary issue was a continuing bone of contention in the church. Some members resented the salary Edwards was being paid, and this resentment surfaced when they complained about his wife's extravagance. The salary dispute was a festering sore in Edwards' ministry at Northampton parish, but this could have been averted if the parish had established strict procedures for paying their minister from the very beginning.

In addition to the pastor's errors in judgment and the congregation's mistreatment of him, a third contributing factor in the decline or failure model is that both minister and congregation encounter *difficulties that extend beyond the local context*. In Edwards' case, there was a long-standing policy in New England churches that the minister would remain as pastor of the congregation for life. It was already apparent to many ministers and congregations that this policy was not working very well, but the apparatus for helping ministers and congregations address this problem had not yet been established. Furthermore, this problem could not be handled solely on the congregational level, for if a congregation established a policy of shorter terms for its ministers but other churches did not follow suit, this congregation would be placing its ministers in an impossible employment situation. As it was, Edwards' dismissal left him with few employment opportunities in America. Had he been able to leave his congregation in Northampton after his first awakening and building program, he would have been acclaimed as a highly successful minister. In contrast, Brooks' ministry occurred at a time when it was expected that a minister could move from one church to another, and he availed himself of this broader policy. Thus, the pattern of decline or failure is due in part to problems that transcend the local parish context, problems that the individual congregation and its minister cannot handle very effectively on their own.

A fourth characteristic of this model is that the minister experiences special *difficulties in one area of his ministry*. Edwards realized success in many areas, including worship, organizing, preaching, and evangelism. He encountered particular difficulties in his work with the youths, even though he had special skills in this area as a result of his work at Yale as a tutor. During the first awakening, the youths were responsive to his efforts to raise their spiritual level. During the second awakening, however, the youths were unresponsive and resisted his efforts to exercise pastoral oversight of their lives. In their resistance they were supported by their parents. Thus, in a field of ministry that meant much to Edwards personally, he experienced great frustration.

Had Edwards been a minister today, he would almost certainly have asked the church council to authorize a new associate minister position with primary responsibility for youth ministry. It is worth noting, however, that Solomon Stoddard had been successful in obtaining an assistant, Edwards himself, who was assigned to working with the youths. Evidently, Edwards was considered too young while in his thirties, or too expensive, or both, to warrant an assistant. In any event, it is quite possible that the congregation's dissatisfaction with Edwards would have been directed toward his associate instead. As Rene Girard points out in his study of scapegoating, two contesting parties will typically avoid destroying each other by finding a third party toward which they both may redirect their aggression.[1] Without such an outlet, Edwards continued to battle with his congregation.

A fifth characteristic of this model is that the minister is likely to *begin his ministry with certain disadvantages;* as I will indicate momentarily, he shares this characteristic with the minister who fits the model of instability. Edwards began his first permanent parish position as an assistant to his grandfather. As a result, his work was inevitably compared with that of his grandfather, and changes in the church's operating procedures established under his grandfather's ministry were especially difficult to achieve. He was always in the shadow of his famous grandfather. Other ministers of this type may have entirely different disadvantages as they embark on a career in ministry, but some of the causes of decline or failure seem to be present very early in a young minister's career, even though the effects of these causes may not become evident for many years. It was not until Edwards had been a minister of Northampton parish for more than a decade that he attempted to replace his grandfather's liberal policy regarding communion with a more stringent policy, and even after all this time had elapsed the congregation still resisted the change.

A sixth characteristic of this model of ministry is that its stability is partly due to the pastor's *fear of instability*. Although Edwards initiated religious awakenings and thus recognized the value of an emotional or affective religion, he was very careful to keep the revival within limits. He instituted songfests to drain off excess emotional energy, and when the awakening resulted in acts of suicide, he was profoundly disturbed that awakenings could get out of control. Edwards seemed fearful of emotional instability, a fear that may be attributed to his father's desire to raise his own children in a stable and calm atmosphere because his own upbringing had been quite different. Thus, Edwards' ministry reflected stability, but this was not primarily due, as it was for Brooks, to a sense of personal security and confidence in his abilities, but rather to a fear of instability. Neither Brooks nor Edwards took major risks during their careers, but for Edwards this reluctance to take risks had a psychological impetus, whereas for Brooks it was more a matter of deciding that he was better off following his established course.

One of the striking similarities between Brooks and Edwards is that both died in their fifties, while the other three ministers in the study lived into their seventies (Brownson) and late eighties (Wesley and Newman). Since the two who lived the longest were those who modified or attempted to break out of their life structure, and the two who lived the shortest lives had stable life structures, one might ask whether the attempt to form an altered or new life structure in midlife gave them the impetus to live longer—as though they now had a second lease on life. I will develop this point in the epilogue.

BREAKING OUT:
FORMING A NEW LIFE STRUCTURE

This professional model has been part of the Christian ministry for centuries, but it is becoming increasingly prominent in our era because leaving the ministry for another profession or leaving the parish ministry for another form of Christian ministry does not carry as much of the social stigma it used to carry. This is paralleled by greater acceptance of entrance *into* ministry in one's thirties or forties.

Some of the major characteristics of this professional model can be identified in the study of John Henry Newman. The first is that the minister whose career follows this pattern is likely to have experienced deep *frustration in his quest for advancement.* One who fits the previous model of decline or failure certainly experiences frustration in his job, but I am pointing here to the direct frustration of efforts to advance in one's profession. In Newman's case, his attempts to secure major professorships at Oxford were thwarted by those who did not want him in these positions. Thus, his was not the experience of decline or failure in his profession, but of outright defeat in his efforts to progress in his chosen field.

A second characteristic is that one allows his career to be shaped by *personal needs that are incongruent with the desire for professional advancement.* Newman, for example, was most responsive to his need for friendships. At times, this need caused him to act in ways that were hurtful to his own professional advancement but meant a great deal to him personally. Although responding to personal needs is undoubtedly an element in the other four models of professional formation, much greater tendency exists in the other models to find a means of reconciling these personal needs and professional aspirations, or to subordinate the personal needs to one's professional goals. It is difficult to imagine, for example, that Brooks would have left his church in Boston for the sake of personal needs—such as marriage or the desire for a quiet life in the country. In contrast, when Newman was faced with the prospect that the younger men in his group at Oxford might turn to other leaders, leaving him with few if any friends to associate with on a daily basis, he decided to cast in his lot with these younger men, and did so at the risk of losing his older friends who were more distant from Oxford and more settled in their own careers and family life. It is noteworthy that Newman's autobiography, *Apologia Pro Vita Sua,* is dedicated to the men who also converted to the Catholic Church and joined him in forming a religious community in Birmingham. In contrast to Brooks and Edwards, Newman had several very close and enduring friendships.

A third characteristic of this model is that one has difficult relationships with those who are *in authority over him.* Of the five ministers in our study, Newman had the most direct conflict with his superiors. These conflicts began with his altercation with Hawkins, escalated to conflicts with university officials during the period of the Oxford Movement, and eventually came to involve the bishops of the Church of England. During his audience with the pope after his conversion, he bumped his head against the pope's knee when he bent to kiss the holy father's foot. This clumsiness turned an act of obesience into an episode that he and his friends found quite comical. Later, Newman vigorously opposed the Ecumenical Council ("Vatican I") decision to proclaim papal infallibility. The frequency and intensity of his conflicts with his superiors suggests that he had strong ambivalences regarding their authority over him. He felt obliged to be deferential toward ecclesiastical authorities but at the same time felt that they were not worthy of deference because they were not serious about the exercise of their office.

A fourth characteristic, related to the third, is that the minister who fits this model sees an *urgent need for change*. He feels very strongly that the church cannot simply operate as it has done in the past. Newman felt that time was running out on the church, that it was losing its power to shape events. This sense of urgency led him and others to develop a reform movement within the Church of England. Thus, the "breaking-out" model is likely at first to express a need for reform of the church (local, regional, or national) to which the minister has dedicated himself, and only later does it eventuate in withdrawal from this organization. This means that the breaking-out pattern is likely to evolve rather gradually and, in its beginning stages, may look like some of the other models of professional development. This study indicates, however, that the signs of breaking out ought to be present by the time the minister has reached his middle to late thirties.

A fifth characteristic of the "breaking-out" model of ministry is that it reflects a complex *interplay of modernity and tradition*. For example, Newman wanted to restore the church to its earlier power and influence, yet he made considerable use in his ministry of available inexpensive printing methods, enabling him to economically disseminate his tracts throughout England. This combination of deep respect for tradition and openness to modern technology may have been puzzling to his fellow ministers, and may have made it difficult for them to "place" him both in theological and ecclesiastical terms. In Newman's case, he was theologically and temperamentally at odds with the world in which he lived, and yet was more open than most of his fellow ministers to the use of modern technological advances, new organizational models, and so on.

ADVANCEMENT LEADING TO MAJOR CHANGES
IN LIFE STRUCTURE

This professional model may appear to be quite similar to the first model, because both involve advancement, but a number of important differences occur in the two patterns.

One major characteristic of this model is that it typically involves taking professional *risks that could have resulted in significant professional losses*. Wesley is an excellent example of the minister who was willing to embark on new professional activities without clear assurances that these activities would work out. His decision to go to America was one instance of this, and his agreement to go to Bristol when George Whitefield invited him there was another. In taking such risks, Wesley jeopardized his accomplishments as leader of the Holy Club and of the Fetter Lane society, but he was the kind of individual who seemed to enjoy responding to a challenge. This is perhaps a requisite personality trait of the minister who fits into this professional model.

A second characteristic is that the major changes effected in the life structure, at least in its professional dimension, are due more to *changes in the social context* in which one ministers than to changes in one's basic style of ministry. For example, in developing his Methodist societies, Wesley continued to focus on the same interests and concerns of his earlier ministry (especially in terms of preaching and organizing), but these same concerns took on new dimensions in his Methodist societies. His preaching in the small rooms in which his societies met took on a new emotional power that it lacked when he had preached in the larger churches. In similar fashion, his method of organizing these societies was not much different from his organization of the Holy Club at Oxford. In organizing working-class people into these groups, however, he was employing his proven organizational principles in a much different social context. Thus, the modification of his professional life was largely the effect of a change in the social context of his ministry.

A third characteristic of this model, and one that differentiates it from the model of decline or failure, is that the minister in this model will *disengage from a frustrating professional commitment* rather than attempt to work with a hopeless situation. This minister seems to make more astute assessments of the continuing value of his current pastoral activities than does the minister who experiences decline or failure. When Wesley found himself in an impossible situation in Georgia, he left the situation before he could become involved in long drawn-out legal and congregational battles. One of the Moravian pastors felt that Wesley's departure dishonored himself and his profession, but this inclination toward disengagement rather than fighting a losing battle is an important characteristic of the minister who fits this professional model. Such disengagements are not thought of as failures but as strategic withdrawals.

A fourth characteristic of this type is that major changes in one's professional development have a direct effect in *changing other aspects of an individual's life*—family relationships, personal lifestyle, and so forth. It is unlikely that major modifications in one's ministerial role will leave the other areas of life unaffected. In Wesley's case, changes in his professional situation as director of the Methodist societies also led him to give serious consideration to marriage. This illustrates that advancement involving major professional changes will affect other areas of one's life. It will probably require significant adjustments for the family and will undoubtedly lead to significant rethinking of one's dreams for one's life.

A fifth characteristic of this model is that the minister is likely to experience extended *periods of emotional deprivation,* such as loss of support, loneliness, and dejection. Although the first model discussed here may involve considerable disappointment and frustration because a variety of valuable opportunities must be rejected, this fourth type experiences deeper and more longer periods of frustration in which he feels the whole world is against him. For example, Wesley had to endure longer periods in which he was not sought out and when, in terms of his standing and visibility in the church, he was virtually unknown. Many of his sermons focus on themes of emotional and spiritual deprivation—when God's will does not seem to be working in one's life. But Wesley cautions against despair in such times and emphasizes the importance of not allowing current deprivations to become overwhelming, but to continue to look for opportunities in which life may flourish once again. If Brooks experienced what we would today call "professional burnout," manifested in fatigue and temporary loss of vitality—a weariness in well-doing—Wesley seems to have gained vitality from the very fact that progress was slow and setbacks were many.

A sixth characteristic of this professional model is the maintenance of *uneasy relations with persons and groups with whom one was associated before the major advancement occurred.* Whereas the breaking-out pattern leads to an irrevocable break with the past, especially in terms of professional commitments, the minister in this model does not make such a total break, but finds his continuing links to the past rather frustrating. For example, when Newman converted to the Catholic Church he had virtually nothing to do with friends who remained in the Church of England, nor did he seek to maintain ties with the Church of England and its various constituent parts (including Oxford University),[2] but when Wesley advanced to his role as director of Methodist societies, he continued to maintain ties with the Church of England. However, as his last sermon preached at Oxford indicates, his relations with the parent organization were uneasy, characterized by much ambivalence.

THE UNSTABLE MODEL
OF PROFESSIONAL FORMATION

It is important to emphasize that instability should not be equated with failure, even though instability and failure sometimes go hand in hand. Orestes Brownson was a minister who had obvious gifts and abilities and who experienced more effectiveness as a minister than many who fall into one of the other categories. This model of ministry, then, includes ministers who reflect varying degrees of effectiveness in their profession. What unites them is not their ineffectiveness, but the instability of their pattern of professional formation.

A first characteristic of the unstable pattern is that one is likely to have entered the ministry with *certain preestablished disadvantages.* Brownson had the disadvantage of not having roots in any particular denomination or religious group. Although roots in a particular denomination can be limiting, they are also a major advantage to a minister in dealing with the tacit dimensions of the life and goals of the congregation he is serving. In addition to disadvantages directly related to his professional development, the minister who fits this type may also enter the ministry with personal burdens. Brownson experienced instability in his early childhood and adolescence due to the loss of his father and separation from his mother. The important issue here is not the existence of such problems, but rather that they resulted in additional problems more directly related to his career as a minister, such as lacking a sense of belonging to any particular religious group.

A second characteristic of the unstable pattern is that the style of *ministry is not well-balanced.* Whereas the first model of professional development usually manifests ability to perform well in a number of areas of ministry, and continuing growth in others, the unstable pattern usually reflects a style centered on one area of ministry. Such a minister may be able to disguise this deficiency for a time by approaching his entire ministry from the perspective of the area which he knows quite well. For example, he may function as the "preacher" not only when engaged in delivering a sermon but also when visiting the sick, conducting a meeting, or teaching a class. Or, he may function as the "administrator" not only when engaged in matters of organization but also when preaching and conducting worship, when visiting the sick, etc. This approach may work for a time, but before long it wears thin, and the congregation begins to complain that "he is a good preacher but he is not able to handle the other important duties of a minister." He then moves to a church that has been longing for good preaching and is therefore willing, at least initially, to sacrifice expertise in other areas of its corporate life for the rejuvenation of this particular area.

Brownson's style of ministry lacked balance. Due to his familiarity with the printing business, he was a capable publisher, especially in the use of media to draw attention to doctrinal and social issues, but his biographers are not positive about his abilities in other areas of congregational ministry. They say that he was not as effective in the pulpit as he was in his journalistic work, and they say nothing favorable about his handling of other areas of his parish work. Moreover, in commenting on the failure of his own church, Brownson volunteers that he was not a very good organizer, and his Walpole congregation (the church where he got along best of all) felt he was capable and of high moral character, but they disagreed with him in many of his views. Thus, his ministry lacked the balance that is necessary over the long run. Although Brooks is largely known today for his preaching, he is well worth studying for his effectiveness as a minister, especially his ability to manifest a balance that did not require compromising his convictions and fundamental values.

A third characteristic of the unstable model of professional development is a tendency to be *impulsive in one's professional decisions.* Brownson's decision to leave the Universalists and join Frances Wright's movement is a case in point. Wesley was able to take risks, but these risks (going to America and responding to Whitefield's request to come to Bristol) were tempered by the fact that he would be working under the auspices of a church society or at the invitation of a trusted friend. Brownson's decision to join the Wright movement had none of these built-in securities and gave the impression of being almost totally capricious.

A fourth characteristic of the unstable professional model is an *incongruity between one's theological views and one's current institutional commitments.* On numerous occasions, Brownson's thinking was inconsistent with his current professional commitments. During the period that he was serving as a Universalist minister, he felt he was without any real Christian beliefs, but during his Unitarian period, his beliefs were closer to Christian orthodoxy than Unitarianism allowed. Thus, there was often a discrepancy between his current theological views and his ministerial role, and this made it difficult for him to enter his role with complete devotion. The other types of professional formation certainly allow for major changes in belief and role (Wesley and Newman are cases in point), but much greater congruity exists between where they are theologically and where they are professionally. Newman, for example, was constantly monitoring his theological changes to ensure that his actions as a minister in the Church of England were not based on deception, either of himself or of others. We might say that, in contrast to Newman, Brownson's theological views and professional activities were continually out of phase with one another.

A fifth characteristic of the unstable pattern is that the minister becomes *preoccupied with a single issue or problem, theological or practical.* Although his tendency to give rather superficial attention to a wide variety of theological and practical issues gave Brownson's work a very undisciplined appearance, he returned again and again in his thinking to the theme of how man can know that God is at work in human affairs. This theological problem, finally solved with his doctrine of communion, was a continuing concern from the time he joined the Presbyterian Church until his conversion to the Catholic Church, and it was a factor in each of his intervening changes in affiliation. This continuing preoccupation with a particular problem or issue, even when the issue is a very important one, is more reflective of this professional pattern than the tendency to talk rather superficially about a variety of issues. The unstable minister works the same theme over and over again, while the more stable minister has greater freedom to move to new theological and practical issues.

CONCLUSION

As indicated earlier, the characteristics of each of the five models of professional formation presented here are offered with considerable tentativeness. They are based on the study of only one minister in each of the five types. On the other hand, in every case the characteristics were derived from the study itself. Moreover, many of these characteristics are also found in the corresponding life sequences of Levinson's subjects. This effort to identify characteristics of the five professional models in ministry should therefore prove useful to ministers who not only seek a better understanding of the professional formation of ministers, but who also want to acquire a deeper appreciation for the similarities between their own professional careers and those of the men and women to whom they are called to minister.

Another way to view this study, however, is to think of the five men considered here as living in the same community and therefore as colleagues of one another. We might, for example, imagine that they have gathered for lunch or to study the lectionary text on which they will be preaching the following Sunday. They are all in their mid-thirties. One of them (Brooks) will become a bishop and will die shortly thereafter. Another (Edwards) will become a missionary and then a college president, but will also die before he has assumed any real presidential responsibilities.

Two others (Newman and Brownson) will change their denominational affiliations in a few years' time, and one of them (Newman) will run a boarding school in an impoverished urban context while another (Brownson) will publish a religious journal and lecture all over the country. Eventually, but not until it is evident that he is too old to exert political power within the church, one (Newman) will be honored with his church's highest title, cardinal; and he, characteristically, will agree to accept this honor if he does not have to travel to the city (Rome) where the honor is normally bestowed on the recipients. The other (Brownson), having suffered the loss of his faithful and long-suffering wife, will succumb to alcohol addiction and live out the last of his seventy-three years in lonely obscurity.

The fifth (Wesley) will continue his efforts to establish and sustain his religious societies until his dying day (age eighty-eight) and will prove to have been the founder of one of the largest and certainly the most evenly distributed, geographically speaking, of all American denominations.

Given these outcomes, it may not seem that these five men were "representative" of their profession, for among them is a future bishop, a future college president, a future cardinal, and future founder of a major denomination. This study, however, is intended to show that these men *were* representative of their profession, for their careers manifested the very same patterns that the careers of others, before and after, have also reflected. More important, if these five young clergy had met together for lunch or for Bible study, all five would have perceived themselves to be working in the vineyard of the master who continues throughout the day to go to the marketplace in search of men and women who are able and willing to work. The very fact that their lives followed different patterns of professional formation testifies to the truth that there is no single or "correct" way to pluck and harvest the grapes, for the master of the vineyard desires in his workers diversity over uniformity, and plurality over singularity.

A further point to be made, however, is that each minister will experience and reflect the pattern to which he belongs in his own idiosyncratic way. In his essay, "The Importance of Individuals," William James quotes "an unlearned carpenter" of his acquaintance who once said in his hearing, "There is very little difference between one man and another; but what little there is, *is very important.*"[3] If other patrons of the restaurant in which our five ministers were having lunch together looked over at their table, they might be inclined to see only a group of young clergymen, five men of the cloth. But if one of these patrons had asked to join their company to break bread with them, he or she would perhaps have discovered that each was following a different pattern of professional formation and each was doing so in his own way. Thus, the five men in this study represent a type of professional formation, but they also represent themselves, each a unique individual. James concluded his essay on the importance of individuals with an appeal in behalf of the study of individuals:

> Heaven forbid us from tabooing the study of these in favor of the average! On the contrary, let us emphasize these, and the importance of these; and in picking out from history our heroes, and communing with their kindred spirits,—in imagining as strongly as possible what differences their individualities brought about in this world, while its surface was still plastic in their hands—each one of us may best fortify and inspire what creative energy may lie in his own soul.[4]

Epilogue

As I acknowledged in the introduction, this study has several limitations. One is that it does not take into account the second-career male minister. Another is that it focuses exclusively on the male minister and may be less applicable to women ministers. I indicated, however, that second-career male ministers and women ministers may have reason to read this book, and I suggested what these reasons might be. In this epilogue I will expand on these suggestions and propose a more fundamental reason why they might take this study seriously despite somewhat limited relevance to themselves.

This more fundamental reason concerns the central feature of Levinson's theory, which is the idea that the life structure involves an alternating pattern of stability and transition. I believe that a case can be made for the universality of this feature of the theory, but only if the biological foundations of this alternating pattern are considered. If a convincing case can be made for its universality, we may then conclude that, although his theory was derived initially from interviews with twentieth-century Western males, this does not mean that it has no relevance for others.

A standard critique of late twentieth-century developmental theories is that any claims their creators make for the theory's universality are quite mistaken. These critiques state that the theories are a reflection of their creators' own sociocultural perspective (which is, by definition, a limited one). Moreover, they assert that developmental theories fashioned by men betray a distinctly male orientation, and are therefore inapplicable to women, or require considerable modification to make them applicable to women. The best-known text that seeks to expose the male bias of developmental theories is Carol Gilligan's *In a Different Voice*.[1] Her criticisms are especially directed toward the developmental theories of Erik H. Erikson and Levinson.[2]

Interestingly enough, both men made claims for the universality of their developmental models, but whereas Erikson's claim for the universality of his life cycle theory, and the precise nature of this claim, has been the subject of considerable debate,[3] Levinson's claims have received little attention. He argued for the universality of his theory, though he was not altogether clear whether this claim applies to all of its aspects or simply to key features of the theory. I believe, however, that the most fundamental feature of his theory—its emphasis on the life structure—*is* universal, and is so both across time (historical) and space (wherever humans inhabit the earth). Because Levinson shared his critics' own grounds for assessing the universality of a developmental theory (i.e., sociocultural grounds), he failed to make the persuasive case for his theory's universality that he could have made had he appealed instead to biological considerations.

Because he did not explicitly address the universality issue in his two major texts, *The Seasons of a Man's Life* and *The Seasons of a Woman's Life,* I will rely on notes that I took when I attended a week-long course taught by Daniel Levinson and his wife, Judy D. Levinson, under the auspices of the New England Educational Association. During this course he explicitly addressed the universality question. Several class members raised the question at various times during the week. One questioner wanted to know whether the model he had constructed from his study of forty American men between the ages of thirty-five to forty-five could also apply to persons in other societies. Another questioner wanted to know whether the model applied equally to women.

In response to the first question, he replied that the model does not apply in every particular to individuals in earlier historical periods, but he noted that his reading of biographies of individuals from earlier historical eras generally supports the model. As for other cultures, he indicated that he did not know of any culture in which the life structure on which his theory is based does not match the one found in his study of American men. He acknowledged that of course the "quality of life" in the various phases of life may differ significantly, and that significant differences may occur in longevity. The basic structure, however, is the same across cultures. He specifically noted that very little variation exists among individuals (one year at most) as to when a developmental era or phase begins and ends.

In response to the second question, he noted that his studies of women (not yet published at the time) provided conclusive evidence that their basic life structure is identical to that of men. There were no differences in this regard. If true, this claim supported his argument for universality in the sense that, while the women lived in the same society as the men studied, they had very different cultural experiences due to the marked differences in the ways the genders were enculturated.

I have noted that Levinson claimed universality for the basic *life structure* that underlies his developmental theory. By "life structure" he meant a regular, predictable pattern of several years of stability (usually about seven) followed by several years of transition (usually about five). Roughly five years of transition occur between eras (childhood/adolescence, young adulthood, middle adulthood, and late adulthood), and a similar number of transitional years at the midpoint of an era. These transitional periods are followed by roughly seven years of stability. Thus, each era is about twenty-two years' duration, and contains two periods of stability and two periods of transition. He added other dimensions to the life structure idea, including "how the various aspects of the self and world influence the formation of a life structure and shape its change over time," but this stability/transition pattern is the key structural element. In my view, the best case for his theory's universality concerns this structural element of stability/transition.[4]

The various challenges to Levinson's developmental theory on cultural and gender grounds have concerned other features of the theory. Gilligan, for example, criticized his emphasis on the man's "Dream" and his suggestion that a man needs a "Special Woman" to help him bring it to fruition. She also noted that Levinson emphasized the achievement orientation of men and minimized their relationships.[5] In other words, even if Levinson had accurately depicted men's experience, this would hardly carry over to women's experience, which is, after all, highly relational. While Levinson has not to my knowledge been challenged on racial grounds, it may be noted that the black males in his sample of forty men are either hourly wage earners or novelists, and there are no black males in the other occupational categories of executives and biologists. Thus, the study also seems to perpetuate stereotypes of black males. His argument for an underlying life structure (with alternating periods of stability and transition) has not been challenged, either on cultural or gender grounds. Is it universal? In my view, he did not offer a persuasive argument for why he considered it so.

The reasons for this are twofold. The first concerns his tendency to have thought about universality in primarily cultural terms. This was especially evident in the role played by Ray C. Walker, the single Jungian in Levinson's original research group, who encouraged the others—"chiefly Freudian"—to assimilate Jung's ideas into their interpretation of the empirical findings. What is noteworthy in this regard is that Jung's archetypal theory posits that there are transcultural archetypes (e.g., The Great Mother) that assume unique forms in specific cultural contexts (e.g., the Madonna in Western Christianity). Levinson was somewhat influenced by this transcultural view, so that when he claimed universality for his theory of the life structure, he seemed to be thinking primarily in transcultural terms. The question then, is how convincing is a transcultural argument based on archetypal theory? For Jung, its claim rested on an additional supposition that a universal collective unconscious exists, which underlies each individual's personal unconscious. Although this supposition provided Jung with a theory of universal human experience, it involved a rather ahistorical view of societies, and of their cultural changes over time, the very factors that led Erikson to suggest that any theory of human life—his own included—is relative to the exigencies of its own time and place. To appeal for the universality of one's developmental theory on transcultural grounds is to open oneself to the charge that one's way of theorizing itself derives from a particular cultural milieu.

The second reason Levinson did not offer a persuasive argument for the universality of the life structure is that he made little effort to relate his developmental theory to biological development. Although he mentioned biological development in passing in his review of previous efforts to delineate the life cycle, he paid only cursory attention to it in presenting his own theory.[6] (It is perhaps ironic that one of the four occupational groups in his study of males were academic biologists.) Unlike Erikson, who emphasized that the life stages evolve out of a predetermined epigenetic ground plan, Levinson did not link his developmental theory to the biological (or physiological) development of the human organism. In a discussion during the course I attended of the problem of gender-splitting, he noted that Erikson thought of intimacy as a lifelong task, and he observed that we do better at short-term tasks than long-term tasks. He attributed this to the fact that, as a species, the basic issue for humans was at first simple survival. How to make life meaningful is a relatively new issue. Thus, in our concern with the question of a meaningful life, we are "trying to get beyond a relatively primitive biological development," though, unfortunately, "we are not much better than preliterate or early literate societies in this regard."

I do not wish to challenge Levinson's view that making life meaningful is a vitally important issue, however, his comments revealed his desire to get beyond basic issues of biological development. This relative lack of interest in "primitive biological development" in favor of more advanced forms of human interaction caused him to neglect a more obvious basis for claiming universality for his theory rather than the transcultural one. In order to make this argument, two studies, one by Erikson, the other by Freud, are especially useful.

In "Womanhood and the Inner Space," a chapter in *Identity: Youth and Crisis,* Erikson suggested that "an integrated history" of an individual or social group requires consideration of anatomical, historical, and psychological facts, and of their vital interconnections. To avoid identifying these three "orders" with established academic fields, he proposes to call them Soma, Psyche, and Polis, and notes that they can "serve attempts to designate new fields of inquiry such as the psychosomatic field already existing and the psychopolitical one sure to appear." These three "orders" comprise one's "physical, cultural, and individual identity."[7] In *The Life Cycle Completed,* he returned to this issue of the "threefold reality" of human life, and indicated that "Soma" has to do with one's "instinctuality."[8] This threefold model is relevant because it indicates that Levinson has defended his theory—and made claims for its universality—largely in terms of the individual/cultural (or Psyche/Polis) relationship, and therefore neglected the individual/physical (or Psyche/Soma) connection. This is consistent with the tendency in academic settings today to focus on cultural matters, and to critique—and defend—theories and assertions on cultural grounds. Although I have no fundamental quarrel with this way of challenging and defending theories about the individual, such arguments do tend to bracket the biological, the physiological, or the somatic. Also, when they address the biological, they tend to subsume it under cultural thematics on the grounds that our bodies are culturally inscribed, i.e., cultural views inform how bodies are valued or denigrated.[9]

If we consider the human body at its most primitive level—what Levinson calls the need for survival—we may be able to make a different case for the universality of his life structure model. For this,

Freud's rather enigmatic text *Beyond the Pleasure Principle* is especially useful.[10] In this book Freud set forth his theory of the *death instinct*. He posited that we have both death and life instincts in our biological makeup, and that the death instinct is the most primitive, or original, because all matter seeks to return to its original inert state. This was a view widely held in his day by materialists such as Herbert Spencer and F. H. Bradley. The death instinct is reflected in the human organism's desire to die of internal causes—self-inflicted, if you will—instead of by externally inflicted wounds (e.g., accidents, gunshots, freezing temperatures, invasive viruses). In effect, the body wants to arrange for its own demise in order to end its existence on its own terms.

In contrast, the life instincts intend to keep the organism going, to keep it alive and flourishing. These life instincts defend the organism against external threats. Furthermore, because the death instinct is a form of aggression against the organism itself, the life instincts work to turn such aggression outward, against external targets, thereby preserving the organism and seeing to its continued survival. In noting that the life and death instincts are locked in a battle over the very survival of the organism, we might say that Freud put his finger on a "warring within" that may be even deeper and more fundamental than Saint Paul's moral conflicts. It is an ontological state of being, a faultline that runs through each individual existence.

In his discussion of Freud's idea of the death instinct, David Bakan noted that Freud was afflicted with cancer (the eventual cause of death) at the time he was writing *Beyond the Pleasure Principle*. He surmised that Freud was aware that his cancer was an expression of the death instinct, which constitutes a paradox because cancer is actually a form of growth. It is, however, cell growth that is occurring in isolation from other cells. Thus, Freud noted that a major role of the death instinct is "defusion," or separation. It quite literally tears the body apart, separating organ from organ, cell from cell. Following Hans Selye's *The Stress of Life,* Bakan calls this "telic decentralization," and cites a study of cancer cells in which the authors note that "Cancer cells are . . . unable to engage in the kind of communication possible in their normal counterparts."[11]

How does Freud's theory of the death and life instincts relate to Levinson's developmental theory of the life structure? The answer lies in a statement that Freud makes in *Beyond the Pleasure Principle* regarding the vacillating rhythm between the two instincts as follows:

> It is as though the life of the organism moved with a vacillating rhythm. One group of instincts rushes forward so as to reach the final aim of life [which is death] as swiftly as possible; but when a particular stage in the advance has been reached, the other group jerks back to a certain point to make a fresh start and so prolong the journey.[12]

When this notion of a "vacillating rhythm" is applied to Levinson's life structure, we can see that the alternation between stability and transition that Levinson identified is rooted in the struggle between the death and life instincts. If the death instinct seeks to return the organism to its original inertness, then it is mostly aligned with stability, whereas the life instincts are mostly aligned with transition. The life instincts destabilize the organism so that it will be required "to make a fresh start and so prolong the journey." In effect, the life instincts "perceive" that stability leads to premature death.

In considering the five clergymen presented in this study in light of the claim that the life instincts destabilize the organism so as to prolong the journey, it may not be pure coincidence that the two men who experienced "stable life structures" in their late thirties did not live nearly as long as the three men whose lives manifested much greater "transitional" characteristics or even considerable "instability" during the same time period. Consider the longevity of the five clergymen:

John H. Newman	1801-1890	89 Years
John Wesley	1703-1791	88 Years
Orestes Brownson	1803-1876	73 Years
Phillips Brooks	1835-1893	58 Years
Jonathan Edwards	1703-1758	55 Years

Thus, the two who lived the longest were those who broke out of or radically changed the life structure that had been established previously. Could it be that stability in their mid to late thirties in the cases of Brooks and Edwards inhibited the "fresh start" that the other men were required to make in this period, and which led to the prolongation of their life's journey? Of course, external factors were surely also at work here. Still, longevity is one major indicator of an individual's capacity for survival. This capacity was inaccessible to Levinson in his study of men precisely because he focused on living subjects. Biographies enable us to track the vacillating rhythm of death and life instincts from birth to death.

My primary concern here has been to make the case that Levinson's idea of the life structure, with its alternating periods of stability and transition, has a claim to universality, one based not on cultural but on the most primitive biological grounds of personal survival. For an individual primarily concerned with a meaningful life, universality based on survival instincts may not seem to count for much. Yet the aging process itself teaches us that survival has its own meaningfulness, for length and quality of life are interconnected in various and complex ways.

Interestingly enough, Levinson seems to support this argument in his discussion of the young/old polarity, one of the four polarities that arises in the midlife transition. He identifies two major themes in the young/old polarity, the sense of mortality and wish for immortality, and the desire to leave a legacy. In his discussion of the sense of mortality, he notes that

> A man at 40 may have been so beaten down by an oppressive environment, or so consumed in the struggle for survival, that he cannot make the developmental effort to give his life new meaning. The inner flame is extinguished and no further potential can be brought into being. He exists without hope or sense of value. *Such men often die in their forties or fifties. The immediate cause of death may be illness, accident or alcoholism. The basic cause is that neither he nor society can make a space for him to live, and he just withers away* (my emphasis).[13]

This is not to say that Brooks and Edwards died earlier than the others because they lost their zest for living. Nevertheless, Levinson's distinction between "immediate" and "basic" causes of death indirectly supports the argument that there *is* such a thing as too much stability.

Thus, perhaps the most important insight to be drawn from this claim that we are biologically imbued with an alternating pattern of stability and transition is that we should not despair when we perceive that people in similar life phases appear to be more stable than we are. The value of stability should not be casually dismissed, nor should instability be romanticized, but much may be said for those internal processes that jerk us back to a certain point to make a fresh start and so prolong the journey. Returning, then, to the biblical text with which this study began: For a man such as Paul who seems always to have been on the move, an unexpectedly prolonged stay in Ephesus may have been a welcome change from his customary life. Paul justified this decision to remain in Ephesus until Pentecost on the grounds that "a wide door for effective work has opened to me, *and there are many adversaries*" (I Cor. 16:8, my emphasis). I believe that biological rhythm is a better guide for deciding when to remain and when to move on than the presence of external adversaries. For, as Jesus observed in his explanation of the origins of sin (Mark 7:14-23), the threats that originate from within are far more noteworthy than those that originate from without.

Notes

Introduction

1. Daniel J. Levinson with Charlotte N. Darrow, Edward B. Klein, Maria H. Levinson, and Braton McKee, *The Seasons of a Man's Life* (New York: Alfred A. Knopf, 1978).
2. Erik H. Erikson, *Identity and the Life Cycle* (New York: W. W. Norton & Company, 1959).
3. William Stafford, *The Way It Is: New & Selected Poems* (Saint Paul, MN: Graywolf Press, 1998), p. 72.
4. Daniel J. Levinson, *The Seasons of a Woman's Life* (New York: Alfred A. Knopf, 1996).
5. Quoted in William James, *The Principles of Psychology,* vol. 1 (New York: Dover Publications, 1950), p. 372.
6. Erik H. Erikson, *Young Man Luther: A Study in Psychoanalysis and History* (New York: W. W. Norton, 1958), p. 220.

Chapter 1

1. Erik H. Erikson, *Childhood and Society* (New York, W. W. Norton, 1950), Chapter 7.
2. Daniel J. Levinson with Charlotte N. Darrow, Edward B. Klein, Maria H. Levinson, and Braton McKee, *The Seasons of a Man's Life* (New York: Alfred A. Knopf, 1978), p. 80.
3. Daniel J. Levinson, *The Seasons of a Woman's Life* (New York: Alfred A. Knopf, 1996), pp. 97-99.
4. Levinson et al., *The Seasons of a Man's Life,* p. 84.
5. Ibid., p. 86.
6. Ibid., p. 91.
7. Ibid., p. 92.
8. Ibid., p. 155.
9. Ibid., p. 157.
10. Ibid., p. 193.

Chapter 2

1. Daniel J. Levinson with Charlotte N. Darrow, Edward B. Klein, Maria H. Levinson, and Braton McKee, *The Seasons of a Man's Life* (New York: Alfred A. Knopf, 1978), p. 153.

2. Ibid.

3. Raymond W. Albright, *Focus on Infinity: A Life of Phillips Brooks* (New York: The Macmillan Company, 1961), p. 17.

4. Ibid., pp. 18-19.

5. Levinson et al., *The Seasons of a Man's Life,* pp. 56-60.

6. Albright, *Focus on Infinity,* p. 29.

7. Ibid., p. 33.

8. Ibid., p. 34.

9. Ibid.

10. Ibid., p. 40.

11. Ibid., p. 41.

12. Ibid., p. 42.

13. Ibid., p. 45.

14. Ibid.

15. Ibid.

16. Ibid., p. 52.

17. Ibid.

18. Ibid., pp. 50-51.

19. Ibid., p. 46.

20. Ibid.

21. Ibid.

22. Ibid., p. 47.

23. Ibid.

24. Ibid., p. 53.

25. Ibid., p. 54.

26. Ibid., p. 33.

27. Ibid., p. 54.

28. Ibid., p. 61.

29. Ibid., p. 141.

30. Ibid., p. 77.

31. Ibid., p. 79.

32. Ibid., p. 86.

33. Ibid., p. 97.

34. Ibid., pp. 127-128.

35. Ibid., p. 128.

36. Ibid.

37. Ibid., p. 133.

38. Ibid., p. 127.

39. Catherine Clinton, *Fanny Kemble's Civil Wars* (Oxford: Oxford University Press, 2000), p. 214.

40. Ibid., pp. 201-202.

41. Albright, *Focus on Infinity,* p. 129.

42. Ibid., p. 137.

43. Ibid.

44. Ibid., p. 138.

45. Ibid.

46. Levinson et al., *The Seasons of a Man's Life,* p. 99.

47. Albright, *Focus on Infinity,* pp. 127-128.

48. Ibid., pp. 136-137.
49. Erik H. Erikson, *Young Man Luther: A Study in Psychoanalysis and History* (New York: W. W. Norton, 1958), p. 220.
50. Albright, *Focus on Infinity*, p. 187.
51. Ibid., p. 206.
52. Ibid., p. 210.
53. Ibid.
54. Ibid., p. 222.
55. Ibid., p. 263.
56. Ibid., p. 392.

Chapter 3

1. Daniel J. Levinson with Charlotte N. Darrow, Edward B. Klein, Maria H. Levinson, and Braton McKee, *The Seasons of a Man's Life* (New York: Alfred A. Knopf, 1978), p. 154.
2. Ola Elizabeth Winslow, *Jonathan Edwards 1703-1758: A Biography* (New York: The Macmillan Company, 1940), p. 88.
3. Ibid.
4. Ibid., p. 117.
5. David Levin, ed., *Jonathan Edwards: A Profile* (New York: Hill and Wang, 1969), p. 33.
6. Winslow, *Jonathan Edwards 1703-1758*, p. 109.
7. Ibid., p. 115.
8. Ibid., p. 134.
9. Ibid., p. 162.
10. Ibid., p. 164.
11. Richard L. Bushman, "Jonathan Edwards as Great Man: Identity, Conversion, and Leadership in the Great Awakening." *Soundings* 52 (1969), pp. 15-46.
12. Ibid., p. 35.
13. Ibid.
14. Ibid.
15. Ibid., p. 39.
16. Ibid.
17. Ibid.
18. Ibid., p. 40.
19. Winslow, *Jonathan Edwards 1703-1758*, p. 165.
20. Ibid., pp. 162-163.
21. Ibid., p. 117.
22. Ibid., pp. 173-174.
23. Ibid., p. 170.
24. Ibid., p. 266.
25. Ibid., p. 186.
26. Ibid., p. 187.
27. Ibid., p. 186.
28. Ibid., p. 192.
29. Ibid.

30. Henry Bamford Parkes, *Jonathan Edwards: The Fiery Puritan* (New York: Minton, Balch & Company, 1930), p. 164.

31. Winslow, *Jonathan Edwards 1703-1758,* p. 216.

32. Ibid., p. 217.

33. Ibid.

34. Ibid., p. 219.

35. Ibid., p. 221.

36. Ibid., p. 229.

37. Ibid., p. 232.

38. Ibid., p. 235.

39. Ibid., p. 237.

40. Parkes, *Jonathan Edwards,* p. 249.

41. Winslow, *Jonathan Edwards 1703-1758,* p. 227.

42. Ibid., p. 186.

Chapter 4

1. Daniel J. Levinson with Charlotte N. Darrow, Edward B. Klein, Maria H. Levinson, and Braton McKee, *The Seasons of a Man's Life* (New York: Alfred A. Knopf, 1978), p. 157.

2. Ibid.

3. Maisie Ward, *Young Mr. Newman* (New York: Sheed and Ward, 1948), p. 2.

4. Sean O'Faolain, *Newman's Way: The Odyssey of John Henry Newman* (New York: The Devin-Adair Company, 1952), p. 309.

5. John Henry Newman, *Autobiographical Writings,* ed. Henry Tristram (New York: Sheed and Ward, 1957), p. 268.

6. John Henry Cardinal Newman, *Apologia Pro Vita Sua,* ed. Charles Frederick Harrold (New York: Longmans, Green and Company, 1947), p. 4.

7. William Robbins, *The Newman Brothers: An Essay in Comparative Intellectual Biography* (Cambridge: Harvard University Press, 1966), p. 10.

8. John Henry Newman, *Letters and Correspondence of John Henry Newman,* 2 vols., ed. Anne Mozley (New York: Longmans, Green and Company, 1890), vol. 1, pp. 22-23.

9. Ibid., p. 23.

10. Ward, *Young Mr. Newman,* p. 61.

11. Ibid.

12. A. Dwight Culler, *The Imperialist Intellect* (New Haven: Yale University Press, 1965), p. 15.

13. Robbins, *The Newman Brothers,* p. 15.

14. Louis Bouyer, *Newman: His Life and Spirituality* (London: Burn and Oates, 1958), p. 41.

15. Newman, *Letters and Correspondence of John Henry Newman,* vol. 1, p. 38.

16. Ward, *Young Mr. Newman,* p. 53.

17. Culler, *The Imperial Intellect,* p. 20.

18. Newman, *Letters and Correspondence of John Henry Newman,* vol. 1, p. 41.

19. Bouyer, *Newman,* p. 49.

20. Ward, *Young Mr. Newman,* p. 60.

21. Francis William Newman, *Phases of Faith* (New York: Humanities Press, 1970), p. 2.

22. Ibid.

23. Newman, *Letters and Correspondence of John Henry Newman*, vol. 1, p. 67.

24. Newman, *Apologia Pro Vita Sua*, p. 10.

25. John Henry Newman, *The Letters and Diaries of John Henry Newman*, vol. 1, eds. Ian Ker and Thomas Gornall, S. J. (Oxford: Clarendon Press, 1978), p. 308.

26. Ibid., p. 367.

27. Edwin A. Abbott, *The Anglican Career of Cardinal Newman* (London: The Macmillan Company, 1892), p. 305.

28. Newman, *Autobiographical Writings*, p. 200.

29. Ibid.

30. Ibid., p. 201.

31. Ibid., p. 200.

32. Bouyer, *Newman*, p. 76.

33. Newman, *Letters and Correspondence of John Henry Newman*, vol. 1, p. 119.

34. Newman, *Letters and Correspondence of John Henry Newman*, vol. 1, p. 105.

35. Newman, *Autobiographical Writings*, p. 201.

36. Ibid., p. 78.

37. Newman, *Letters and Correspondence of John Henry Newman*, vol. 1, p. 90.

38. Ibid.

39. Newman, *Autographical Writings*, p. 78.

40. Newman, *Letters and Correspondence of John Henry Newman*, vol. 1, p. 91.

41. Newman, *Autobiographical Writings*, p. 205.

42. John Henry Newman, *Verses on Various Occasions* (London: Longmans, Green and Company, 1893), pp. 12-15.

43. Newman, *Autobiographical Writings*, p. 209.

44. O'Faolain, *Newman's Way*, p. 151.

45. Newman, *Autobiographical Writings*, p. 210.

46. Newman, *Letters and Correspondence of John Henry Newman*, vol. 1, p. 169.

47. Newman, *Autobiographical Writings*, p. 212.

48. Ibid.

49. Culler, *The Imperial Intellect*, p. 59.

50. Meriol Trevor, *Newman: The Pillar of the Cloud* (London: Macmillan and Company, 1962), p. 71.

51. Levinson et al., *The Seasons of a Man's Life*, pp. 58-59.

52. Newman, *Letters and Correspondence of John Henry Newman*, vol. 1, p. 201.

53. Levinson et al., *The Seasons of a Man's Life*, pp. 100-101.

54. Abbott, *The Anglican Career of Cardinal Newman*, p. 250.

55. Thomas Mozley, *Reminiscences Chiefly of Oriel College and the Oxford Movement*, vol. 1 (Boston: Houghton, Mifflin and Company, 1882), p. 293.

56. Ibid.

57. John Henry Newman, *The Letters and Diaries of John Henry Newman*, vol. 5, ed. Thomas Gornall, S. J. (Oxford: Clarendon Press, 1981), pp. 313-314.

58. Ibid., p. 313.

59. Newman, *Verses on Various Occasions*, p. 75.

60. Ibid., p. 108.

61. Newman, *Letters and Correspondence of John Henry Newman*, vol. 1, p. 341.

62. Newman, *Autobiographical Writings,* p. 268.

63. Newman, *Letters and Correspondence of John Henry Newman,* vol. 1, p. 416.

64. Newman, *Verses on Various Occasions,* pp. 156-157.

65. Newman, *Apologia Pro Vita Sua,* p. 28.

66. Newman, *Verses on Various Occasions,* pp. 159-160.

67. Ward, *Young Mr. Newman,* p. 238.

68. Newman, *Apologia Pro Vita Sua,* pp. 6-7.

69. O'Faolain, *Newman's Way,* p. 105.

70. Ibid., p. 70.

71. Trevor, *Newman: The Pillar of the Cloud,* p. 166.

72. John Henry Newman, *The Letters and Diaries of John Henry Newman,* vol. 4, ed. Ian Ker and Thomas Gornall, S. J. (Oxford: Clarendon Press, 1980), p. 188.

73. Ibid., p. 205.

74. John Henry Newman, *The Letters and Diaries of John Henry Newman,* vol. 5, ed. Thomas Gornall, S. J. (Oxford: Clarendon Press, 1981), p. 220.

75. Ibid., pp. 240-241.

76. Lawrence F. Barmann, S. J., ed., *Newman at St. Mary's: A Selection of the Parochial and Plain Sermons* (Westminster, MD: The Newman Press, 1962), p. 18.

77. C. Brad Fraught, *The Oxford Movement: A Thematic History of the Tractarians and Their Times* (University Park: The Pennsylvania State University Press, 2003), pp. 89-90.

78. Trevor, *Newman: The Pillar of the Cloud,* p. 192.

79. Newman, *Apologia Pro Vita Sua,* p. 56.

80. R. W. Church, *The Oxford Movement* (London: Macmillan and Company, 1891), p. 119.

81. Newman, *Apologia Pro Vita Sua,* p. 147.

82. Ibid., p. 149.

83. Ibid., p. 151.

84. Trevor, *Newman: The Pillar of the Cloud,* p. 205.

85. Ibid.

86. John Henry Newman, *The Letters and Diaries of John Henry Newman,* vol. 7, ed. Gerard Tracey (Oxford: Clarendon Press, 1995), p. 183.

87. Newman, *Apologia Pro Vita Sua,* p. 156.

88. See Geoffrey Faber, *Oxford Apostles: A Character Study of the Oxford Movement* (New York: Scribners, 1934). Faber was the first to write about the homosexual orientation of various members of the Oxford Movement.

89. John Henry Newman, *The Letters and Diaries of John Henry Newman,* vol. 27, eds. Charles Stephen Dessain and Thomas Gornall, S. J. (Oxford: Clarendon Press, 1975), p. 306.

90. Ibid.

91. Ibid., p. 420.

92. Ibid., p. 306.

93. Ibid., p. 317.

94. Wilfrid Ward, *The Life of John Henry Cardinal Newman: Based on His Private Journals and Correspondence,* vol. 2 (New York: Longmans, Green and Company, 1912), p. 537.

95. Levinson et al., *The Seasons of a Man's Life,* p. 335.

Chapter 5

1. Daniel J. Levinson with Charlotte N. Darrow, Edward B. Klein, Maria H. Levinson, and Braton McKee, *The Seasons of a Man's Life* (New York: Alfred A. Knopf, 1978), pp. 160-161.
2. Kathryn Petras and Ross Petras, eds., *Very Bad Poetry* (New York: Vintage Books, 1997), pp. 107-108; Nick Page, *In Search of the World's Worst Writers* (London: Harper-Collins, 2000), pp. 27-32; and Stephen Robins, *The World's Worst Poetry: An Anthology* (London: Prion Press, 2002), pp. 172-181.
3. Thorvald Källstad, *John Wesley and the Bible: A Psychological Study* (Stockholm: NYA Bokforlags Aktiebolaget, 1974), p. 52.
4. Ibid.
5. Roy Hattersley, *A Brand from the Burning: The Life of John Wesley* (London: Little, Brown and Company, 2002), p. 26.
6. Ibid., pp. 23-24.
7. V. H. H. Green, *The Young Mr. Wesley: A Study of John Wesley and Oxford* (New York: St. Martin's Press, 1961), p. 80.
8. Ibid.
9. V. H. H. Green, *John Wesley* (London: Thomas Nelson, 1964), p. 17.
10. Ibid.
11. Ibid., p. 18.
12. Ibid., p. 19.
13. Green, *The Young Mr. Wesley,* p. 106.
14. Ibid., p. 110.
15. Green, *John Wesley,* pp. 27-28.
16. Ibid., p. 32.
17. Ibid.
18. Green, *The Young Mr. Wesley,* p. 171.
19. John Wesley, *The Letters of the Rev. John Wesley, A. M.,* vol. 1, ed. John Telford (London: The Epworth Press, 1931), p. 139.
20. Green, *The Young Mr. Wesley,* p. 249.
21. Ibid., p. 241.
22. Ibid., p. 242.
23. Ibid., p. 244.
24. Green, *John Wesley,* p. 34.
25. Ibid., p. 39.
26. Ibid., p. 45.
27. John Wesley, *The Works of John Wesley,* vol. 18, eds. Reginald Ward and Richard R. Heitzenrater (Nashville: Abingdon Press, 1988), p. 365.
28. Ibid., p. 366.
29. Ibid.
30. Ibid.
31. Ibid.
32. Ibid., p. 367.
33. Ibid.
34. Green, *John Wesley,* pp. 45-46.
35. Ibid., pp. 46-47.

36. Ibid., p. 47.
37. Ibid., p. 471.
38. Ibid., p. 484.
39. Ibid., p. 485.
40. Ibid.
41. Ibid., p. 486.
42. Ibid.
43. Ibid., p. 487.
44. Green, *John Wesley,* p. 50.
45. Martin Schmidt, *John Wesley: A Theological Biography,* vol. 1, trans. Norman P. Goldhawk (London: The Epworth Press, 1962), p. 208.
46. Ibid., p. 209.
47. Källstad, *John Wesley and the Bible,* pp. 198-199.
48. Green, *John Wesley,* p. 51.
49. Schmidt, *John Wesley,* p. 209.
50. Ibid., p. 210.
51. Green, *The Young Mr. Wesley,* p. 302.
52. Schmidt, *John Wesley,* p. 198.
53. Wesley, *The Works of John Wesley,* p. 250.
54. Levinson et al., *The Seasons of a Man's Life,* pp. 161-162.
55. Green, *John Wesley,* p. 81.
56. Green, *The Young Mr. Wesley,* p. 298.
57. Ibid.
58. Green, *John Wesley,* p. 125.
59. Ibid., p. 127.
60. Ibid., p. 103.
61. Ibid., p. 104.

Chapter 6

1. Theodore Maynard, *Orestes Brownson: Yankee, Radical, Catholic* (New York: The Macmillan Company, 1943), p. 6.
2. Orestes A. Brownson, "The Convert: Or, Leaves from My Experience." In *The Works of Orestes A. Brownson,* vol. 5, ed. Henry F. Brownson (Detroit: Thorndike Nourse, 1882-1887), p. 9. Brownson was fifty-four years old when he wrote his autobiography.
3. Ibid., pp. 9-10.
4. Maynard, *Orestes Brownson,* p. 8.
5. Brownson, *The Convert,* p. 13.
6. Ibid., pp. 26-27.
7. Ibid., p. 37.
8. Maynard, *Orestes Brownson,* p. 29.
9. Ibid.
10. Ibid., p. 33.
11. Ibid., p. 32.
12. Ibid.
13. Ibid.

14. Ibid., p. 37.

15. Brownson, *The Convert*, p. 65.

16. Doran Whalen, *Granite for God's House* (New York: Sheed and Ward, 1941), pp. 58, 64.

17. Maynard, *Orestes Brownson*, p. 33.

18. Arthur M. Schlesinger Jr., *Orestes A. Brownson: A Pilgrim's Progress* (Boston: Little, Brown and Company, 1939), p. 24.

19. Whalen, *Granite for God's House*, p. 70.

20. Schlesinger, *Orestes A. Brownson*, p. 27.

21. Ibid.

22. Maynard, *Orestes Brownson*, p. 43.

23. Ibid., p. 45.

24. Orestes A. Brownson, "The Mediatorial Life of Jesus." In *The Works of Orestes A. Brownson*, vol. 4, ed. Henry F. Brownson (Detroit: Thorndike Nourse, 1883), p. 191.

25. Maynard, *Orestes Brownson*, p. 45.

26. Ibid.

27. Ibid., p. 46.

28. Ibid., p. 51.

29. Ibid., p. 62.

30. Ibid.

31. Brownson, *The Convert*, pp. 78-79.

32. Ibid., p. 79.

33. Maynard, *Orestes Brownson*, p. 72.

34. Ibid., p. 63.

35. Ibid., p. 53.

36. Ibid., p. 45.

37. Ibid., p. 124.

38. Ibid., p. 32.

39. Ibid., p. 20.

40. Brownson, *The Convert*, p. 196.

41. Ibid.

42. Ibid.

43. Maynard, *Orestes Brownson*, pp. 32-33.

44. Ibid.

45. Brownson, *The Convert*, p. 47.

46. Ibid., p. 50.

47. Ibid., p. 52.

48. Ibid.

49. Ibid., p. 63.

50. Ibid., p. 65.

51. Ibid.

52. Schlesinger, *Orestes A. Brownson*, pp. 62-63.

53. Brownson, *The Convert*, p. 82.

54. Ibid., pp. 82-83.

55. Maynard, *Orestes Brownson*, p. 125.

56. Ibid.

57. Ibid., p. 126.

58. Ibid.
59. Ibid., p. 127.
60. Ibid.
61. Ibid.
62. Ibid.
63. Brownson, *The Convert,* p. 129.
64. Ibid.
65. Maynard, *Orestes Brownson,* p. 130.
66. Ibid.
67. Ibid.
68. Brownson, *The Convert,* p. 37.
69. Ibid., p. 140.
70. Maynard, *Orestes Brownson,* p. 135.
71. Ibid., pp. 128-129.
72. Ibid., p. 129.
73. Ibid.
74. Brownson, *The Convert,* p. 156.
75. Maynard, *Orestes Brownson,* pp. 146-147.
76. James E. Dittes, "Impulsive Closure as Reaction to Failure-Induced Threat." *Journal of Anormal and Social Psychology* 63 (1961), pp. 562-569.

Chapter 7

1. Rene Girard, *Scapegoating,* trans. Yvonne Freccero (Baltimore: The Johns Hopkins University Press, 1986).
2. See John Henry Cardinal Newman, *Apologia Pro Vita Sua,* ed. Charles Frederick Harrold (New York: Longmans, Green and Company, 1947), pp. 214-215. Many years later, however, Newman drew up plans for a new college at Oxford for Catholic students. He purchased the land and secured the agreement of the university officials, but his plans were thwarted by an English cardinal who had the pope's ear. This was perhaps the greatest disappointment in Newman's career, as he retained a great love for his alma mater throughout his life, and, in his autobiography, describes the sense of desolation he experienced when leaving Oxford shortly after his conversion.
3. William James, "The Importance of Individuals." In *The Will to Believe and Other Essays in Popular Philosophy* (New York: Dover Publications, Inc., 1956), pp. 256-257.
4. Ibid., pp. 260-261.

Epilogue

1. Carol Gilligan, *In a Different Voice* (Cambridge, MA: Harvard University Press, 1982).
2. Erik H. Erikson, *Childhood and Society* (New York: W. W. Norton and Company, 1950), Chapter 7; Daniel J. Levinson with Charlotte N. Darrow, Edward B. Klein, Maria H. Levinson, and Braton McKee, *The Seasons of a Man's Life* (New York: Alfred A. Knopf, 1978).

3. Lawrence J. Friedman, *Identity's Architect: A Biography of Erik H. Erikson* (New York: Scribner), pp. 420-421.

4. Levinson et al., *The Seasons of a Man's Life,* p. 42.

5. Gilligan, *In a Different Voice,* pp. 151-153.

6. Levinson et al., *The Seasons of a Man's Life,* p. 5.

7. Erik H. Erikson, *Identity: Youth and Crisis* (New York: W. W. Norton, 1968), p. 289.

8. Erik H. Erikson, *The Life Cycle Completed* (New York: W. W. Norton, 1982), p. 90.

9. See, for example, Elisabeth Bronfen, *Over Her Dead Body: Death, Femininity, and the Aesthetic* (New York: Routledge Press, 1992), p. 192.

10. Sigmund Freud, *Beyond the Pleasure Principle,* trans. James Strachey (New York: Bantam Books, 1959).

11. David Bakan, *Disease, Pain and Sacrifice: Toward a Psychology of Suffering* (Chicago: The University of Chicago Press, 1968), p. 37.

12. Freud, *Beyond the Pleasure Principle,* pp. 74-75.

13. Levinson et al., *The Seasons of a Man's Life,* p. 216.

Index

Order a copy of this book with this form or online at:
http://www.haworthpress.com/store/product.asp?sku=5391

YOUNG CLERGY
A Biographical-Developmental Study

_____ in hardbound at $44.95 (ISBN-13: 978-0-7890-2669-9; ISBN-10: 0-7890-2669-4)

_____ in softbound at $24.95 (ISBN-13: 978-0-7890-2670-5; ISBN-10: 0-7890-2670-8)

Or order online and use special offer code HEC25 in the shopping cart.

COST OF BOOKS_____

POSTAGE & HANDLING_____
(US: $4.00 for first book & $1.50
for each additional book)
(Outside US: $5.00 for first book
& $2.00 for each additional book)

SUBTOTAL_____

IN CANADA: ADD 7% GST_____

STATE TAX_____
(NJ, NY, OH, MN, CA, IL, IN, PA, & SD
residents, add appropriate local sales tax)

FINAL TOTAL_____
(If paying in Canadian funds,
convert using the current
exchange rate, UNESCO
coupons welcome)

☐ **BILL ME LATER:** (Bill-me option is good on
US/Canada/Mexico orders only; not good to
jobbers, wholesalers, or subscription agencies.)

☐ Check here if billing address is different from
shipping address and attach purchase order and
billing address information.

Signature_____

☐ **PAYMENT ENCLOSED: $**_____

☐ **PLEASE CHARGE TO MY CREDIT CARD.**

☐ Visa ☐ MasterCard ☐ AmEx ☐ Discover
☐ Diner's Club ☐ Eurocard ☐ JCB

Account # _____

Exp. Date_____

Signature_____

Prices in US dollars and subject to change without notice.

NAME_____

INSTITUTION_____

ADDRESS_____

CITY_____

STATE/ZIP_____

COUNTRY_____ COUNTY (NY residents only)_____

TEL_____ FAX_____

E-MAIL_____

May we use your e-mail address for confirmations and other types of information? ☐ Yes ☐ No
We appreciate receiving your e-mail address and fax number. Haworth would like to e-mail or fax special
discount offers to you, as a preferred customer. **We will never share, rent, or exchange your e-mail address
or fax number.** We regard such actions as an invasion of your privacy.

Order From Your Local Bookstore or Directly From
The Haworth Press, Inc.
10 Alice Street, Binghamton, New York 13904-1580 • USA
TELEPHONE: 1-800-HAWORTH (1-800-429-6784) / Outside US/Canada: (607) 722-5857
FAX: 1-800-895-0582 / Outside US/Canada: (607) 771-0012
E-mail to: orders@haworthpress.com

For orders outside US and Canada, you may wish to order through your local
sales representative, distributor, or bookseller.
For information, see http://haworthpress.com/distributors

(Discounts are available for individual orders in US and Canada only, not booksellers/distributors.)

PLEASE PHOTOCOPY THIS FORM FOR YOUR PERSONAL USE.
http://www.HaworthPress.com   BOF04